Strategies of ethics

Strategies of ethics

Bernard Rosen
The Ohio State University

Houghton Mifflin Company   Boston
Dallas   Geneva, Illinois   Hopewell, New Jersey
Palo Alto   London

87-515

Printed in the U.S.A.

Library of Congress Catalog Card Number: 77-77431

ISBN: 0-395-25077-3

To my children, Elizabeth Samiha and Paul Erich

Contents

Chapter six: Value 180

Chapter seven: Meta-ethics 230

Index 261

Preface

This is a book for those who have wondered about the moral life of human beings. You may think morality is an illusion, you may think it reflects a higher nature of humanity, or you may think it is as much a part of being human as reason itself. Whatever your view, this book is intended to help you to clarify what you believe and to become aware of alternative views that have interested others. A number of different approaches to explaining morality are examined, but, more importantly, the tools for evaluating such approaches are provided. The tools are primarily those of the philosopher, but at times I have borrowed from the psychologist, the anthropologist, and even the physicist. I have a strategy concerning morality that I think is correct, but that is not what should be of primary importance to readers. In writing this book, I have intended chiefly to give you a chance to understand different theories concerning morality and then to choose from among them the one *you* think is best.

In the first chapter you will find two questionnaires designed to help you to locate where you are now—to determine what kinds of theories you are now inclined to hold. Determining your present position does not "lock" you into that position but allows you to place yourself in a tradition. It is the rare person who holds a completely consistent view concerning the moral phenomena, and you will probably discover one or more inconsistencies in your responses to the questionnaires. No matter: it is better to discover that your present views are inconsistent and choose to work at resolving those inconsistencies than to adopt a consistent view that does not really reflect your own views. In addition, the first chapter lays out the basic philosophical tools you will need in your work as an ethical strategist and tells you something about the theories that will be considered in the book.

One view of this book is that almost everyone holds a normative ethical theory—a theory about how we arrive at justified moral judgments concerning things, actions, and people. The problems of normative ethics are as old as the human race, and the record of theories is almost as old as the oldest writings we have. There are those who think that what philosophers are concerned with, even in normative ethics, has very little to do with the moral life of each of us. I do not share that view. The view presented here is that the theories designed by philosophers arise from the problems of individual human beings and are constructed to help solve those problems. The primary emphasis in the book is on normative ethics, although the last chapter, on meta-ethics, outlines problems that have bothered mostly philosophers. The most esoteric concerns of meta-ethics are importantly, though perhaps only distantly, related to everyday moral concerns.

If you already know something about moral philosophy, you will want to know what is new and different about this book, but you will also want to be reassured that the views that have been most important in the history of thought are not left out. The view of normative ethical theories as explanations of a set of phenomena and as tools for deriving singular moral judgments is new in this work. The use of a general scheme to allow direct comparisons of theories in their "bare bones" state is, as far as I know, not to be found elsewhere. The use of questionnaires to enable readers to discover what kinds of views they hold on the topics and theories examined is unique. The method chosen to divide theories concerned with the evaluation of actions from theories concerned with the evaluation of things and persons is different from what is currently being used. The view of value and the method of setting up and evaluating the rival theories of value differ from anything now in print. These are some of the things that are new.

But the theories presented are not so new. The book includes theories that people who are just beginning to think about morality are inclined to hold, and includes them in the forms in which beginners tend to hold them. This means that sometimes a certain argument is presented because it is taken seriously by students although not by professional philosophers. The book also presents theories that are thought to be finalists in the competition in the marketplace of ideas—a competition that quite frequently is judged by philosophers. There will be disagreement about which views belong in the final selection and disagreement about which versions of those views are best. Yet if you think there is a better version of ethical egoism, say, than the one presented in chapter 2, the method of presenting theories advocated in the book should enable you to state this view without any difficulty. You should be able to see which of the criticisms, if any, considered in the book apply to your new version. (If you think you have a version of a view I examine that escapes all the criticisms I present, you might just send it along to me. I would certainly be interested in seeing it.)

Of course, I do not expect all readers of this book to become ethical philosophers; ethics is not an easy subject. Yet many students who read the book in manuscript form found that, once they had mastered the elementary material, especially the material in the first two chapters, they did not have a great deal of difficulty with the rest of the material in chapters 3 through 6. The material in the last chapter appears always to be more difficult. Still, since most people who read this book will be using it in a course, they will have access to a teacher who can explain material that they do not understand. If questions and explanations lead to further discussion, the book will in many ways have fulfilled its purpose. *Strategies of Ethics* is not designed to

bring about a consensus, but rather is meant to stimulate thought and discussion.

I would like to thank S. Boër for help in finding a suitable title for the book. Many graduate students at Ohio State University and the University of Western Ontario assisted with criticisms and helpful suggestions about teaching. Both my publisher and I are grateful for the assistance of those who made professional reviews of the manuscript. These reviewers were John Dreher of the University of Southern California, Fred Hombach of the College of DuPage, Andrew Oldenquist of Ohio State University, and Mary Sirridge of the University of Wisconsin at Madison. Most of the thanks, though, must go to the hundreds of students who have brought this book into existence as a result of a desire to learn, coupled with a resistance to accept something unless they could really understand how it "went." This book represents a philosopher's attempt to say what he thinks is true in such a way that it will be helpful to everyone, not just to other professional philosophers.

One

Chapter one
The strategist's tools

Everyone is familiar with moral phenomena. People must constantly choose among competing ends on the basis of the supposed greater value of one, or they have to weigh duty to other people against their own right to happiness. We say of the actions of criminals or some politicians that they are wrong or that the person involved should have known better. We say of ourselves that we ought to have written a paper or studied for an examination, but that instead a movie lured us away. Usually we notice such behavior and make the corresponding judgments without consciously formulating a theory, for it is easy to make judgments about the pain or joy of other people, about the shape of certain objects, or about the distance of one object from another without consciously formulating theories about those matters. We could, however, consciously formulate a theory concerning one of those judgments in order to make those judgments more easily and accurately. This is one of the aims of morality.

By the time they read a book such as this, most people have been exposed to some kind of theorizing about moral phenomena. Sometimes children are taught to accept apparently simple moral theories, consisting, for example, of a rule like "Always do unto others as you would have them do unto you." Most parents teach their children to act from rules, such as "Do not lie," "You aren't allowed to take what doesn't belong to you," "It is wrong to promise to do something and then not do it," and "Potato chips aren't good for you." Such rules are usually accompanied by instructions on how to use them, and it isn't too long before a child supposes that morality consists of a set of rules to be followed or broken, as the case may be. This impression, whether consciously formulated or not, can be said to be a theory in moral philosophy. It is a theory about the phenomena the child is aware of. As a child grows older, theories about moral phenomena change; they become more complex, taking into account such observations as parents lying; persons they admire stealing; and almost everyone, including themselves, breaking promises or eating forbidden foods such as potato chips.

Most students of physics are aware of the phenomena of physics long before they formally study the subject matter in school. Parents explain that all things fall (except the ones that don't, of course) and that stones thrown in a certain way will break windows and perhaps even heads. The child therefore grows up with a theory of physics that is usually not too inaccurate, because many parents have studied physics and education in this area starts relatively early in the schools. Nonetheless, most people do not have a truly adequate theory of physics when they take their first course in physics. From the beginning, though, students of physics are willing to suppose that there are correct theories in physics, that their own theories are probably incorrect in a variety of ways, and that their teacher will lead them to the correct views. This is not the case in moral philosophy.

An explanation for the different attitude toward moral philosophy might be that many students are convinced that there are no correct theories in moral philosophy as there are in physics. Some people may believe that there is really no such field as moral philosophy at all—that morality is all a "matter of taste." To many people, there are no moral "absolutes." Some people suppose that although we can acquire knowledge in physics, we cannot acquire moral knowledge.[1] Most physicists don't really care if anyone is skeptical about their subject matter. If someone claims that gravity, for example, is really "action at a distance" and that such a thing is impossible, your friendly neighborhood physicist, on being questioned, is likely to suggest that you not bother him with metaphysical speculation. He knows how his equations work, he's aware of what the standards of evidence are, and he knows what results have been achieved in the field. Physicists, in short, only rarely respond to skeptical questions about the foundations of physics.

Philosophers, by contrast, attempt to respond to all questions about the foundations of their subject matter and take most seriously all versions of skeptical arguments. If your local physicist gets into trouble and can't answer a question about his field, he may simply say, "Well, after all, that is the job of the philosopher. Why not go to the philosophy department?" Philosophers have no one to send their critics and skeptics to; philosophy is, traditionally, where the buck stops. Accordingly, in this book a number of skeptical arguments will be considered and a large number of competing theories will be examined. Some of you will be impatient to get on to the questions or theories that interest you, and you can do that simply by using the table of contents or the index. I hope you will curb your impatience, though. A systematic approach will result in a more secure background from which to pursue your interests and a better understanding of the subject matter in general. It is up to each of you to choose the course best suited to your ends.

As author I take positions on the various issues in this book, and it would be intellectually dishonest of me not to point out that one or more of the positions seem better supported by evidence and that others are inadequate. (Such honesty is also an obligation of anyone writing a basic book in

---

[1] There are, to give them credit, some people who suppose that we don't have any knowledge at all. Credit has to be given for taking a consistent stand, for this is often difficult when the views have little to recommend them.

physics.) In addition, however, competing positions will be outlined, and the supporting evidence for those positions will be presented. Competing theories are usually not part of physics books. Some people think the explanation for this is that we have discovered what is true in physics but have made no such discoveries in moral philosophy. Again, though, we shall have to see about that.

The main purpose of this book is to provide readers with the tools and information they will need in order to select the normative and meta-ethical theory in moral philosophy that works best for them. The tools are a theory placement test plus standards of what good arguments and good theories are. The information consists of an outline of the most important theories, the philosophical information needed for an understanding of those theories, and various strategies for evaluating each theory as it is presented.

As an apprentice ethical strategist, you need to know about certain tools that will enable you eventually to construct your own theory of ethics. These strategist's tools are the subject of this chapter. After finishing this chapter you should be more aware than before of the ethical theory you have been holding up until now. You should also have acquired the means whereby you can begin consciously to adopt a theory. It may turn out to be the very same theory you held before studying moral philosophy, or it may turn out to be one that is radically different. My main intention is not to lead you to the "truth" (although I must obviously fulfill my intellectual obligation and tell you where I think it is), but to give you the means to find it yourself. This is so even if it should turn out that the only truth is that there is no truth at all in moral philosophy.

A. Asking ethical questions: A descriptive ethics questionnaire

The first step in finding your own way is to find out where you are now. For that purpose you will find below a questionnaire designed to show you the position you now hold. The questionnaire consists of a number of statements—some specific, some general. Try to respond to as many of the statements as you can. You may be tempted to give what you think to be "correct" responses in terms of your friends, your church, your parents, or someone else. Resist that temptation, and put down only what *you* believe to be correct at this time. Do not worry about what you may later decide is correct, and for now, do not worry about inconsistency. The vast majority of people who fill this out will be swayed first one way, then another. This is to be expected. It is far better to respond according to your real beliefs than to make something up in an attempt to be "philosophical."

Do not look ahead to find the answers; the answers lie with you. If you are not honest with yourself, you will benefit significantly less than you would otherwise.

After you have completed the questionnaire, you will want to know the results. Following the questionnaire, there is a "key" that will interpret what you have done. The key is not a key in the usual sense—namely, something that tells you the right answer—but it will enable you to interpret what you have done. Unfortunately, a complete understanding of your position will await your understanding of most of this book. The bright side, however, is that you should feel no obligation to make up your mind definitively until you have at least finished the book. It is not until you have examined the main theories in moral philosophy that you should make up your mind about which is best (or at least the best as far as you can tell at that time).

In responding to the questionnaire use the code SA for strongly agree; A for agree; D for disagree; SD for strongly disagree; and CA for can't answer (either because you don't sufficiently understand the statement or because you just can't make up your mind). Try to keep CAs to a very few.

1. The only motive anyone has in doing anything is to get something for himself. Even when you help others, it's only because it makes you feel good.

2. Only if you would agree to allow everyone to do what you are doing is your action morally allowable or right.

3. What makes an action obligatory is that it leads to the greatest good for the greatest number. Motives are irrelevant.

4. The only thing that counts in determing whether someone did the right thing or not is the motive. The results of the action are irrelevant.

5. Since we can always turn out to be wrong about a factual claim (for example, we think there are nine planets in the solar system, but perhaps there are ten), we don't really know anything about such matters.

6. The only thing that is *worth* pursuing is pleasure.

7. A good will can't be used for any bad end, but everything else can. So a good will is the only thing that is good in itself.

8. No one knows what is right or wrong, or good or bad.

9. Whenever you justify a specific moral judgment, such as "Slavery in the United States was wrong," you have to make reference to a general rule or principle, such as "All slavery is wrong."

10. Things of value in our society should be distributed to those who can afford them as a result of their success in competing in our economic system.

11. Moral judgments are an expression of personal taste. Just as "Hot

fudge goes well with banana ice cream" is a question of your own taste, so is "Slavery in the United States was a morally bad institution."

12. Those and only those actions commanded by God are our moral obligations; those actions forbidden by God are wrong.

13. Sometimes when you claim that a person did something wrong, you do so on the basis of the person's motives.

14. Hitler's motives, let us suppose, were to improve European civilization, to eliminate crime, to reduce unemployment, and to restore a sense of pride in Germans. In spite of these good motives, his actions with respect to the Jews and Slavs were wrong.

15. When we claim to know something (for example, that the earth is roughly a sphere), we are justified when we have good enough evidence.

16. The things that have value are the things that a society's members believe to have value.

17. Pleasure is a short-lived experience that comes and goes, but happiness is a fairly stable and long-run condition. The only thing that is worth having for itself and not just for what it leads to is happiness, not pleasure.

18. When you come right down to it, you can't ever really tell whether you are doing the right thing in a given instance.

19. Things of value should be distributed to each individual according to need (and we should receive from each individual according to that person's abilities).

20. There are some statements that we suppose are clearly and objectively true, although not necessarily true. "There are nine planets in the solar system" is an example of such a statement, even though, of course, we must allow the possibility that we are mistaken in making this statement and might have to take it back. Moral judgments are like that; we suppose they are objectively true, although we have to allow the possibility that we are mistaken.

21. Lots of factors enter into our moral rules, such as amount of good produced and such special relations as friendship and the repayment of debts. To determine the rightness of an action you have to weigh all the positive and negative applications of these rules.

22. If you want to see whether or not you have a moral obligation to do something, find out what would happen if you did it and what would result if you didn't. The only things that matter are the likely consequences of your action. Motives are irrelevant.

23. When I say that an action is right or obligatory, I say so only because I perceive that the action will be good for me in some way.

24. Although consequences count in determining that someone did the right or the wrong thing, motives also count. It isn't a matter of just one or the other: Motives and consequences are both relevant.

25. There are some specific moral judgments, such as "Slavery in the United States in the eighteenth century was wrong," that we are more certain of than any general rule or principle, such as "All slavery is wrong."

26. Many things are produced in our society that are desired by most people. These things should be distributed equally, numerically when possible, and on the basis of each waiting a turn if a numerical equality is not possible.

27. If you follow the Ten Commandments, you are acting in a morally proper way; if you do not, then you are not. That's all there is to morality.

28. When anyone voluntarily does something, the motive is always to give pleasure to others.

29. If someone sees a person drowning and is motivated to try to save the person, then, whether the effort is successful or not, the action is equally as praiseworthy.

30. If a naked human being is placed on the moon with no oxygen, then, without a doubt, that person will be dead in a very short time.

31. When anyone voluntarily does something, the motive always is to get pleasure for himself or herself.

32. The institution of slavery in the United States was morally bad.

33. It is very difficult, and often impossible, to know what we ought to do in specific circumstances, but we can at least know the moral principles that apply.

34. Things of value in our society should be distributed on the basis of merit.

35. Our moral obligations are solely a function of what the majority of people living in our society suppose are our moral obligations.

36. Sometimes the consequences of an action have to be taken into account when you judge that someone performed a morally right action.

37. Even though no one can know any factual matter with certainty, we still have knowledge of many factual matters.

38. Some people think that love has value by itself, but its value is just the pleasure one derives from being in love and loving.

39. Things of value in a society should be distributed fairly—that is, in a way that each person would agree to before knowing what his or her place will be in that society.

40. To determine whether or not you did the right thing in a situation, you must find out if you performed the action out of love. If you did, then the action is right; if you did not, then it isn't.

41. Some actions have no appreciable effect on me. For example, a soldier's killing a small South Vietnamese child just for sport does not affect me. Such actions may nevertheless be wrong.

42. No one can really have evidence for anything. It's all a matter of personal preference.

43. Pleasure has a value that is independent of the things it may lead to, but so do other things, such as friendship, freedom, and peace.

44. It is very difficult to know the right thing to do, but sometimes, at least, we do.

45. The only reason it is wrong for a drunken parent to beat a small child to death is that when I hear about it, I feel bad.

46. It may have been that slavery in the United States led to more good than bad overall, but it was still wrong to keep slaves.

47. To say that something is true is just to say that the majority of persons living in your society believe that it is true.

48. We all have our own moral opinions, and only about those can we be certain of correctness or acceptability.

49. Some of our motives are to help others.

50. Sometimes actions are right or wrong because of their effect on me, and sometimes they are right or wrong independent of their effect on me.

51. It has happened, on occasion, that a stranger asked directions, and I gave them. In some of these instances, the stranger received valuable information, and my motive in giving that information was to help the stranger and not to help myself or to provide myself with anything of value.

B. Taking an ethical stand

Now that you have filled out the questionnaire, you are understandably eager to know what you did, to have revealed to you what your responses commit you to in the way of positions and theories. In order to make such a commitment intelligible, even in a most casual way, I must say something about the subject matter we shall be studying and the gross divisions within it. The section following the interpretation of the questionnaire is intended to do that, and then the classification of responses to the questions will make some sense. However, one of the purposes of this book is to explain in greater detail the various ethical theories, so do not be surprised if complete understanding is not reached immediately.

1. Key to descriptive ethics questionnaire   The following will be based on the assumption that you agreed (A) or strongly agreed (SA) with the statements. If you disagreed (D) or strongly disagreed (SD), then you can say that you hold the denial of the view stated.

1. Psychological egoism (chapter 2)
2. The "universalizability" principle (If you agree to this, then you are inclined to hold to some kind of rule theory. See chapter 5.)
3. Utilitarianism (chapter 3)
4. A formalistic deontological theory of obligation (chapter 4)
5. General skepticism and an endorsement of the argument from possibility (chapter 1)
6. Hedonism (chapter 6)
7. Kantian theory of value, inconsistent with statement 6 (chapter 6)
8. Moral skepticism (chapter 7)
9. Basic rule theory claim (chapters 4 and 5)
10. A theory of distributive justice—competition as the test of merit (chapter 3)
11. Noncognitivism—emotivism (chapter 7)
12. Theological voluntarism (chapter 4)
13. A denial of teleological theories of obligation, inconsistent with statement 3 (chapter 4)
14. A denial of formalistic deontological theory of obligation (This instance is inconsistent with statement 4. See chapter 4.)
15. A denial of general skepticism (Agreement with this is inconsistent with statement 5. See chapter 1.)
16. Value relativism (chapter 6)
17. Aristotelian theory of value, happiness as the only thing of intrinsic value (chapter 6)
18. Moral skepticism, specifically with regard to obligation (chapter 7)
19. A theory of distributive justice—communism (chapter 3)
20. A form of cognitivism, moral judgments as contingent truths (chapter 7)
21. A prima facie theory of obligation (chapter 4)
22. A teleological theory of obligation (This is inconsistent with statements 4, 13, and 18. See chapters 2 and 3.)
23. Ethical egoism (chapter 2)
24. A nonformalist deontological theory of obligation, inconsistent with statement 4 especially, but also with statements 3 and 22 (See chapter 4.)
25. An act theory of obligation (chapter 5)
26. A theory of distributive justice—equalitarianism (chapter 3)
27. Ten Commandments theory of obligation (chapter 4)
28. Psychological altruism (chapter 2)
29. Denial of a teleological theory of obligation, inconsistent with statement 22 (chapter 4)

30. Denial of general skepticism, inconsistent with statement 5 (chapter 1)

31. Psychological hedonism, a form of psychological egoism (chapter 6)

32. An instance of moral knowledge or justified judgment, inconsistent with statement 8

33. A rule theory of obligation, inconsistent with statement 25 (chapter 4)

34. A theory of distributive justice—meritarianism (chapter 3)

35. Obligation relativism, inconsistent with almost every other theory of obligation (chapter 4)

36. Denial of a formalistic deontological theory of obligation, inconsistent with statement 4 (chapter 4)

37. Denial of general skepticism, with a denial of certainty, inconsistent with statement 5 (chapter 1)

38. An instance that supports hedonism (see statement 6), inconsistent with statement 43 (chapter 6)

39. A theory of distributive justice—rawlsianism (chapter 3)

40. Agapism as a theory of obligation (chapter 3)

41. Denial of ethical egoism, inconsistent with statement 23 (chapter 2)

42. Evidence skepticism, inconsistent with statements 30 and 37 (chapter 1)

43. Denial of hedonism, inconsistent with statement 6 (chapter 6)

44. Denial of obligation skepticism, inconsistent with statement 18 (chapter 7)

45. An instance of ethical egoism (The denial of this is inconsistent with some versions of statement 23. See chapter 2.)

46. A denial of utilitarianism, inconsistent with statement 3 (chapter 3)

47. Truth relativism (chapter 1)

48. Subjectivism (chapter 7)

49. Denial of psychological egoism, inconsistent with statement 1 (chapter 2)

50. Denial of ethical egoism, inconsistent with statement 23 (chapter 2)

51. Denial of psychological egoism, inconsistent with statement 1 (chapter 2)

It is important to understand that many of you will have chosen positions that are inconsistent; this is not just a quirk of a few. Inconsistency is quite natural at this stage, for many theories appeal to different people for different reasons. What is important, however, is to understand exactly why the theories are inconsistent; then you will also understand that no matter how tempting a set of inconsistent views might be, they must not be subscribed to. At this stage in the investigation, though, you should only note that you tend to hold the inconsistent views and not try to determine which view to give up. You may finally want to give up both views and adopt some third position, or you may wish to attempt some method of reconciling the two views that now appear inconsistent.

This questionnaire describes the position or positions you are inclined to hold now. It does not dictate what position you must hold at the end of the investigation. When you have finished with this book, you may wish to return to the questionnaire and see what changes have been wrought.

2. A theory of value   Part of the description of everyone's ethical theory is a theory of value, a theory about the kinds of things that are valuable. In addition to this general claim, people sometimes want to identify specific ends, things, and relations they think are valuable. The following exercise will give you an opportunity to do just that, although by the end you may very well claim that some of the general things you chose in the descriptive ethics questionnaire are valuable.

At any given time, every person has a number of goals or ends. A *goal* or *end* is something you seek to achieve, whether material, spiritual, political, personal, public, or private. Goals need not be long run or final, although some of your goals may be of this type. On a sheet of paper you are to list any three goals you now have. For example, you may wish to lose 10 pounds, to get to class on time, to play touch football on Sunday, or to start a revolution. Simply list any three goals that come to mind across the top of a sheet of paper. A list of three such goals might look as follows:

1. Lose 10 pounds   2. Get to class on time   3. Play touch football
on Sunday

Some of the goals we attempt to achieve we seek primarily, or perhaps even solely, because of what they lead to. For example, the woman who cuts a crisscross in her leg after being bitten by a rattlesnake does so in order to draw out some of the poison. The poison is drawn out, usually, in order to prevent death; the woman may or may not seek to draw out the poison for any other reason. Furthermore, the prevention of death, whether sought for some other reason or not, obviously leads to the attainment of, or makes possible the attainment of, other ends. At any rate, we can all usually recognize the end of a chain of goals, and we can say, "This is a goal I seek for itself, and not only for the things it might lead to."

Beginning with the three goals you listed at the top of the sheet, construct a chain of goals. It does not matter if the same goal appears in more than one chain; you should feel free to draw as many branches as seem necessary. At the beginning, one chain might appear as in Figure 1-1. You might expect the other goals in the figure to have chains leading from them, and the items listed in the first chain to go beyond what is presented; they could. Figure 1-1 is presented only to give you an idea of how to go on.

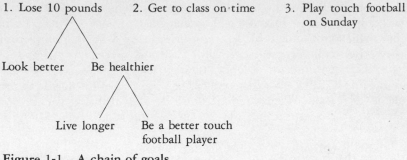

Figure 1-1   **A chain of goals**

After finishing your chains, construct a list of two kinds of items. First, list all the ends of the chains. Second, list any goals on the chain that you suppose are valuable no matter where they lead. (If some such goals occur to you now that you did not put in any chains, you can list them also.) For example, considering only chain 1, we might add:

a. live longer
b. look better
c. be a better touch football player
d. be healthier

Try now, with a separate list, to rank the preceding goals—the most important first, the second most important second, and so on. For example, considering the list presented earlier, we might have:

1. b
2. a
3. c
4. d

There is no key to this kind of questionnaire, as there was to the first one. There is, however, some clarification that can be effected by the application of material in chapter 6, the chapter on value theory. At the end of that chapter you will be asked to examine your values questionnaire to determine which theory of value best explains what you have written down. You should not attempt such an explanation without reading chapter 6.

C. A survey of normative ethics

As you build your own theory of ethics, you will want to have a means to compare and contrast pre-existing ethical theories and to compare your own developing view with the views of others. This section introduces a tool that not only will facilitate presentation and comparison of theories but also will help to explain what the main concerns of ethical strategists are. This tool, which we'll call *Scheme R,* will thus provide an approach to the field of normative ethics as a whole.

1. The general scheme of arguments in ethics   A standard format will be used throughout this book to present the steps in ethical reasoning and the thinking that underlies moral theories. As mentioned above, this format is called Scheme R. The letter 'R' stands for the word 'rule'—namely, the rule that constitutes the first statement in the scheme. Consider the following:

> 1. If any x is F, then x is M.
> 2. This specific x is F.
> _____
> Therefore,
> 3. This specific x is M.

The x is a variable that is replaced by the name of any kind of individual: a person, an action, a specific institution, and so on. For example, one instance of x is 'Socrates', and another is 'drinks hemlock'. F and M are property variables, but F will be used for nonmoral predicates and M for moral or normative predicates—at least usually. For example,

> 1. If anyone (x) dies rather than give up his most firm beliefs (F), then that person (x) is a good person (M).
> 2. Socrates is a person who died rather than give up his most firm beliefs.
> _____
> Therefore,
> 3. Socrates is a good person.

> 1. If anyone (x) holds another person as a slave (F), then he is doing what is morally wrong (M).
> 2. Simon Legree held another person as a slave.
> _____
> Therefore,
> 3. Simon Legree did what was morally wrong.

The first premise of each of the above arguments is a *general moral judgment,* and the third statement is a *singular moral judgment.* The primary concern of normative ethical theories is to provide a means for arriving at *justified* singular moral judgments. A normative theory, when complete, should address other concerns, too. It should discuss and explain topics such as justice, punishment, freedom and responsibility, and rights (moral, legal, and political).

2. Scheme R and the ethical theories   Normative ethics has two main divisions: theory of obligation and theory of value. In terms of Scheme R, we can see the concerns of each of these areas in Figure 1-2.

Nonmoral uses of moral terms or predicates are just as common as their corresponding moral use or sense. 'It is best to enter the Post Office from the front' would not in most instances contain 'best' in a moral sense. Similarly, the 'ought' is not a moral term in 'You ought to put your car in neutral when pushing it'. These uses are not difficult to distinguish in practice from such uses as 'You ought to help those who are in need'. We can distinguish the moral from the nonmoral senses in almost every context without difficulty. In any particular instance in which there is some difficulty, we can clear it up by examining more of the context or by asking a few questions.

Normative ethics is concerned primarily with the justification of the third statement of the general scheme—singular moral judgments. How do we find justified singular moral judgments? Do they exist at all? What if there is disagreement about such judgments? These are some of the questions that arise concerning singular moral judgments. We shall examine some of the theories that purport to explain how we arrive at *justified* instances of statement 3 of the general scheme.

According to *teleological* theories of obligation, all relevant substitution instances of F are consequences (or likely consequences) of x. According to *deontological* theories of obligation, not all relevant substitution instances are consequences.[2] *Formalists* maintain that none of the values of F are consequences; and *nonformalists* contend that some of the values of F may be consequences, but other instances replace F as well.

A simple teleological theory would specify F as 'brings about good consequences for me', and M as 'I have a right to do'. This results in an instance of statement 1 of Scheme R that claims "If any action brings about good consequences for me, then I have a right to do it." Similarly, in a deontological theory, F would be specified as 'is an instance of keeping a promise', and M as 'is obligatory'. This would result in a quite different instance of statement 1 of Scheme R: "If any action is an instance of keeping a promise, then it is obligatory." The second statement, part of a formalist deontological theory, does not mention consequences; the first statement, part of a teleological theory, mentions only consequences. Much more will be said later when these two kinds of theories and how they differ are explained.

We can construct a tree of the views distinguished thus far that may help you keep the relations straight (Figure 1-3).

So far we've been examining Scheme R for its ability to help us generate singular judgments from general rules, but we haven't taken note of the fact that there are different types of rules. Some rules are rules of thumb

---

[2] 'Teleological' comes from the Greek *telos,* meaning 'end' or 'purpose'. Thus, the purpose or consequence of x is F. 'Deontological' comes from the Greek *deon,* meaning 'that which is obligatory'.

	Instances of x	Instances of F	Instances of M
Theory of obligation	a. People's actions (act plus intention) b. Kinds of actions (for example, pain-producing or pleasurable. This is to contrast with instances of type a.)	a. Nonmoral, nonvalue predicates (for example, "If x is an instance of pleasure production, then x is M") b. Value predicates and sometimes degrees of them ("If x maximizes good, then x is M")	Obligatory Not obligatory Right Wrong Obligatory not to Right to Better Worse Morally preferable
Theory of value	a. Things (in a broad sense: people, states of people—cold, angry, and so on—character traits, situations, institutions, etc.) b. Kinds of things	a. Nonmoral, nonvalue predicates b. Obligation predicates ("If the bringing of x into existence is obligatory, then x is M")	Good Better Best Bad Worse Worst Intrinsically valuable Extrinsically valuable Intrinsically disvaluable

Figure 1-2 The divisions of normative ethics

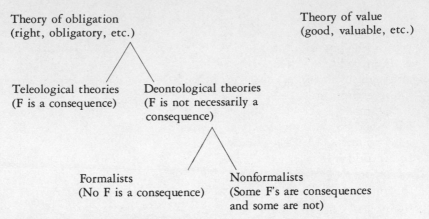

Figure 1-3   Normative ethics

that are useful but, as we all recognize, dispensable. For example, the rule "If there is a certain characteristic sound present, then there is an automobile close by" is a pretty good way of determining whether or not there is a car nearby. If you use this rule, you will be right most of the time, although sometimes—as when a recording of a car is played, or when the car has an electric motor, or when you have impaired hearing—the rule will lead you astray. The rule is not *required* in order to determine that a car is present, for there are other ways of finding this out. Using the rule doesn't always lead to success in determining that a car is present.

In contrast with this kind of rule, consider the rule "If the black king is in check and there is no chess move that will change this situation, then black is checkmated." There is never an occasion when the first part of the rule, the *antecedent,* is fulfilled and the *consequent,* the last part, is not. This rule is one of the defining characteristics of the game of chess, or, to use the terminology we shall be using from now on, this rule is a *constitutive rule* of chess. Such rules are required to justify the judgments falling under them. You can use the rule directly, as was done above, or you can use it indirectly. For example, suppose someone tells you that black has been checkmated. If the person knows something about the game, you can take that as very good evidence that the game is over. However, someone, either the person who told you, or whoever told that person, or whoever told *that* person, at some point must have recourse to the rule that justifies the judgment.

Some philosophers have claimed that rules are always required to justify singular moral judgments, and some have denied this. Those who make the former claim will be called *rule theorists,* and those who deny it will be called *act theorists.* Rule theorists are those who claim that rules, instances of statement 1 of Scheme R, are always required to justify singular moral judgments, instances of statement 3. Act theorists, in contrast, are those who claim that we derive the moral rules from nongeneral moral judgments and the corresponding facts, as represented in statement 2 of

Scheme R. This distinction will be explained in greater detail when it is used in a substantive way in chapter 4. The purpose now is only to allow you to see the position you adopted in the questionnaire. This distinction is, in my view, one of the most basic and important in moral philosophy, although, to be honest, not very many philosophers would agree with my interpretation.

Among those who hold rule theories, some think that individual rules hold good no matter what else is true, and some don't. A rule that holds good no matter what else is true is a *categorical rule,* whereas a rule that can be overridden by another rule of the same type is a *prima facie rule.* There is a lot more to this distinction, but for now, let's look at a few examples just to help us along. On the one hand, the rule concerning checkmate is one that is true regardless of what else is true, either on or off the chess board. Someone may wish you to waive the rules, to stop playing chess, but then we recognize this by saying that we aren't really playing chess anymore. On the other hand, the rule "If a batter swings and misses the ball three times, then he is out" can be overridden by the rule "If the pitcher touches his mouth before delivering the ball, then the batter will be awarded first base." As you can imagine, the situation in moral philosophy is much more complicated, but this gives you some idea of what a prima facie rule as contrasted with a categorical rule is.

One final distinction—between indirect moral rules (or meta-moral rules) on the one hand and direct (or primary) moral rules on the other—will allow us to point out all the main divisions in normative ethics. *Meta-moral rules* are rules that pick out the primary moral rules we apply directly to situations. For example, one meta-moral rule might be "Choose those primary moral rules which, when acted on by all or most, will lead to the greatest good for the greatest number." This rule, by itself, does not tell you whether it is right to tell the clerk at the small grocery store that she has given you too much change. However, it should enable you, so some claim, to pick out a rule such as "Honesty is the best policy" or "Always be honest in word and deed."

To see how this is supposed to work, let's go through the various steps a theory containing meta-moral rules suggests when we are in doubt. Suppose you are in a neighborhood grocery store and the clerk gives you too much change. A *direct rule* theory might suggest some rule such as "Always do what will maximize the greatest good for the greatest number." In this instance you could calculate roughly that the greatest good would result from keeping the money, for the loss is small to the store but the gain means a lot to you—relatively speaking. You could conclude that you don't have a moral obligation to return the money. The meta-moral rule theorist, however, would say that you didn't calculate correctly, for you must consider what might happen if everyone acted in terms of the rule about keeping change when it would benefit them and not hurt others too much. This could lead to a decrease in the overall good instead of an increase.

Put in the general scheme, the two positions look something like this.

Direct (or primary) moral rule theory
1. If any action leads to the greatest good for the greatest number, then it is morally obligatory to do it. (direct moral rule)
2. The action of keeping the store's money leads to the greatest good for the greatest number.

Therefore,
3. It is morally obligatory to keep the store's money. (singular moral judgment)

Indirect moral rule (or meta-moral rule) theory
1. If all or most people acting always from a rule R leads to the greatest good for the greatest number, then that rule is a direct moral rule. (indirect moral rule)
2. "If any action is one of being honest in word or deed, then that action is obligatory" is a rule that, if all or most people act from it, leads to the greatest good for the greatest number.

Therefore,
3. "If any action is one of being honest in word or deed, then that action is obligatory" is a direct moral rule.

4. If any action is one of being honest in word or deed, then that action is obligatory (from statement 3). (direct moral rule)
5. Returning the money to the store clerk is being honest in deed.[3]

Therefore,
6. Returning the money to the store clerk is obligatory. (singular moral judgment)

The preceding, considerably simplified example should show how direct and indirect moral rule theory differ, on occasion, with respect to singular moral judgments. More important, it should show you *why* the two kinds of theories differ. When we examine specific theories, we will develop a fuller explanation of the two kinds of theories and we will see how some of them actually work. For now, the purpose is to show the main kinds of theories so that you can have a preliminary understanding of the positions you took on the descriptive ethics questionnaire.

Exercises: Identifying moral judgments and the evidence that supports them
1. Identify the singular moral judgments in the following list, and construct arguments of the sort represented by the examples of Scheme R.

[3] This might be somewhat confusing because the rule, in statement 4, talks about honesty in word *or* deed, and statement 5 talks only about honesty in deed. If one is *either* honest in word *or* honest in deed, then one has fulfilled the moral rule. You can, of course, fulfill both. If you ask whether Jones had cream or sugar in his coffee, I can say yes if he had either one or if he had both.

a. When the light is red, you can make right turns if the traffic is clear.
b. All instances of telling the truth are right.
c. Jimmy Carter's telling the truth about lusting after women was wrong.
d. Richard Nixon has an obligation to attempt a political comeback.
e. The United States would be immoral if it started a war.
f. Moral obligations are determined by societal pressure.
g. The right way to go is to take I-73.

2. Read some current newspapers or periodicals, and choose what appears to be a moral judgment. Identify it as a singular moral judgment or a general claim, and then reconstruct, as best you can, the evidence presented in support of that claim.
3. Think of a moral disagreement you had with someone in the recent past. Describe, as best you can remember, the singular moral judgments each of you proposed and the evidence each presented. If the disagreement was about a general principle, say if it was a direct or an indirect rule. If it was a direct rule, try to give reasons for claiming that it was supported by an indirect rule or that no such support was intended.

Much of the material that follows is not the primary subject matter of this book, but it is essential nevertheless. These are the most general tools we will use in explaining and assessing the theories we will examine in the rest of the book. If, later on, you forget about a procedure or begin to lose the direction a discussion is taking, you should return to this chapter to get your bearings. To avoid losing your bearings, though, it would be wise now to become familiar with the material in this chapter—including the sections that follow.

You will see a great many arguments and theories in this book, and, naturally, you may need some help in evaluating them. Therefore, we should begin by examining arguments in general.

D. Arguments

An *argument* consists of two sets of statements in a relation. One set, the premise(s), is presumed to support the other, the conclusion(s). There are two main types of argument and, perhaps, a third type: deductive arguments, inductive arguments, and, perhaps, immediate inferences. Good deductive arguments are called *valid*. A *valid deductive argument* is one whose premises provide conclusive evidence for the truth of its conclusion. If the premises of a valid deductive argument are true, then its conclusion must be true. Here are two commonly used forms of valid deductive argument (the form of an argument is what is revealed when the content is abstracted):

Affirming the antecedent
If p, then q.
p.

Therefore,
q.

Denying the consequent
If p, then q.
Not-q.

Therefore,
Not-p.

Two invalid argument forms exist that look very much like the valid argument forms but cannot be used to justify their conclusions:

Affirming-the-consequent fallacy
If p, then q.
q.

Therefore,
p.

Denying-the-antecedent fallacy
If p, then q.
Not-p.

Therefore,
Not-q.

You can show that an argument form is invalid by showing that there is at least one clear case (substitution instance) in which the premises are true and the conclusion is false. This is easily done. For example:

T.   If Paul Newman is a woman, then Paul Newman is a mammal.
T.   Paul Newman is a mammal.

Therefore,
F.   Paul Newman is a woman.

You can see that some arguments of the "affirming-the-consequent fallacy" form have true premises and a false conclusion. Therefore, they do not meet the requirements of valid deductive arguments. This is also true of denying-the-antecedent fallacy. For example:

T.   If Paul Newman is a woman, then Paul Newman is a mammal.
T.   Paul Newman is not a woman.

Therefore,
F.   Paul Newman is not a mammal.

More argument forms will be introduced as they are needed, and they will be explained as they are introduced. No one will become a logician as a result of working with just a few argument forms, but familiarity with them will enable you to organize your arguments more effectively. Since the only way to become familiar with argument forms is to use them, you should try putting some arguments into the forms described above.

We have called good deductive arguments *valid* arguments. Good inductive arguments will be called *acceptable* arguments. An *inductive argument* is acceptable when its premises make its conclusion probable to some degree. The higher the degree of probability, obviously, the more confidence we can have in the conclusion. This suggests one important difference between valid deductive arguments and acceptable inductive arguments: the conclusions of acceptable inductive arguments can be false. This liability, though, is more than offset by the fact that *only* inductive arguments can extend our knowledge. The primary way we come to justify new claims is via induction.

There are acceptable inductive argument forms, but they cannot be relied on in the mechanical way that valid deductive argument forms can, nor do they allow fallacies to be described and detected as readily as the deductive forms do. The forms laid out below should give you a good start in coming to an understanding of what inductive arguments are.

Enumeration
Z percent of the observed members of F are G.

Therefore,
Z percent of F are G.

Statistical syllogism
Z percent of F are G.
x is F.

Therefore,
x is G.

When an inductive argument is of an acceptable *form,* it may not yet be acceptable, for it may have been "misused." For example, suppose one runs an enumeration of the sexes of the people in a large department store, and the observation point is the men's room. On other grounds we know there are very few women to be found in a men's room, so the sample is not well chosen. Such statistics can be called *biased.* In addition to using biased statistics, one can go wrong by having insufficient numbers included in the observation group. If we wish to draw a conclusion about the entire student body at Ohio State University, it would be foolish to choose just the students in the front row of one class.

When we use a statistical syllogism we must be careful that the percentage is higher than 50 percent; the higher it is over that, the stronger the argument. If we find that 80 percent of the students in a class wear or carry watches, then we can justifiably conclude that the first person on the aisle in the second row has a watch.

Notice that we do not include the statement of probability in the conclusion of inductive arguments any more than we include any statement of certainty in the conclusion of deductive arguments. If you have a tendency to forget what kind of argument you are using, it might be a good idea to include some kind of marker, but this is *not required* in either case.

Immediate inferences will have to be discussed when they become relevant. Some philosophers believe that 'I think, therefore I am' is a clear instance of such an inference.

Exercises: Arguments

1. Separate the premises from the conclusions in each of the following valid deductive arguments, and then lay out the arguments as shown in section D. Identify each argument.

    a. If Joanne Woodward is a woman, then Joanne Woodward is a human being. So she is a human being, since she is a woman.

    b. Today is Wednesday, since yesterday was Tuesday; and if yesterday was Tuesday, then today is Wednesday.

    c. Since there is snow on the ground that is not melting, the temperature is below 0° Celsius.

    d. While it is true that if you can't put this argument into standard form you do not fully understand how to do such things, you do understand fully how to do such things and so you can put this argument into standard form.

2. Separate the premises from the conclusion in each of the following invalid deductive arguments, and then lay out the arguments as shown in section D. Identify each argument.

    a. If Jones is dead, then his heart is not beating. So Jones is dead, because his heart is not beating.

    b. If rain is falling and not freezing, then the temperature is above freezing. Since rain is not falling (and freezing), the temperature is not above freezing.

    c. If Anna is a man, then Anna is mortal. Since Anna is not a man, she is not mortal.

3. For each of the invalid arguments in exercise 2, construct a counter-example of the same form that is a clear instance of true premises and a false conclusion.

E.   Theories and phenomena

1. Theories   In the most general sense, *theories* are explanations of phenomena. Since there are many different kinds of phenomena, there are many different kinds of theories to explain them. The same action, for example, can have many different kinds of explanations. Consider the action of someone throwing a fellow student off the balcony. We can give a physical, psychological, teleological, or moral explanation. No doubt many other types of explanation could be given as well.

The physical explanation would enable us to explain why the chair the student fell on broke, why it took only a few seconds for the descent, and other matters such as that. We would provide the appropriate covering laws, and we would relate those laws to other laws if asked to do so. We might also give an explanation of the state of mind of the fellow student who threw him off the balcony. We might point out that this student had an extremely hostile attitude toward those who fall asleep in classes, and that the student who was thrown off the balcony had indeed fallen asleep. This hostile attitude might in turn be explained by other psychological laws that apply to such behavior. A teleological explanation would be made in terms of an end achieved by the action—for example, the person was prevented from continuing to snore in class, or this was a dramatic lesson to others who might think of falling asleep in class. If we gave a moral explanation, we might say that the person who fell asleep was not morally guilty of anything that deserved the kind of punishment he received. We might add that the person who threw him off the balcony was not morally justified and, in fact, is morally blameworthy for having done the action.

The preceding are all different *kinds* of explanations of an event that occurred. They are all apparently consistent, and they complement each other. If someone wanted the fullest possible explanation of an event, then all the explanations listed above, plus many others, would be required. Usually, of course, what we want is some particular kind of explanation, and the longer kind of multiple-theory explanation would not be to the point of the request. If I ask the newspaper carrier why the paper did not arrive, I am not interested in the ancestors of the printers. So different types of explanations are appropriate depending on the interest of those who want the explanation.

The claim here is that ethical theories offer an explanation of moral phenomena. Ethical theories are best understood by being seen in operation. Later in this book we will examine several such theories at work. For now, let's just say that ethical theories are not teleological, and they are not to be identified with some existing scientific theory, such as a sociological theory. Ethical theories attempt to explain sets of phenomena in certain ways. Let us say generally what phenomena are, and then see what kinds of things ethical theories do with them.

2. Phenomena   One fairly neutral way of describing *phenomena* is as those elements accepted at the beginning of an investigation. We perceive them, and then we try, via a theory or a group of theories, to explain them in some way. Phenomena, according to this view, are not unassailable beliefs; they are not necessary truths; and they may not even be truths at all.

Included among phenomena are purported facts and theories. If the theory that explains the purported fact is correct, then the fact is not only a purported fact, but it *is* a fact—a truth, if you want to speak that way. If the germ theory of disease is correct, then it is a fact that measles is caused by the presence of certain microorganisms in the body. (We shall take up questions of how we know which theory is correct and how we can be said to know anything later.)

One phenomenon we may wish to explain is the seeming flatness of the earth that we observe when we climb to a high place and look out. One theory that explains this phenomenon is that the earth is flat, that it is shaped like a pancake. If this theory were correct, then it would be a fact that the earth is flat, and the earth would look the way it does from a high place because it is that way. However, there is another theory that explains the same phenomenon—namely, that the earth, although actually spherical, looks flat both because it is very large in relation to the projections above its surface and because observers are relatively small. These two additional phenomena, which may of course be questioned, allow us to explain why the earth looks flat even though it is a sphere (with only slight irregularities).

The lesson to be learned here is that accepting something as a phenomenon is not the same thing as accepting it as a fact, for what we start with is not always what we hold, or are justified in holding, at the end of an investigation. All theories begin with the phenomena in the area in which the investigation occurs, so to say this is not to say anything exciting or revolutionary; nor is it to say anything specific about the *nature* of phenomena or facts either, for that would not be appropriate in a work of this nature. What phenomena are chosen at the beginning of an investigation might, of course, prejudice the investigation. In a few pages, a list of the important moral phenomena will be presented. Although I do not believe that this list prejudices your choice of the best theory, you should be on guard.

3. Evaluating theories   If we are going to evaluate theories, we need some tools of evaluation. These are the criteria for the acceptability of theories:

1. The theory explains the phenomena adequately and without use of ad hoc devices.
2. In comparison with rival theories, the theory is simpler, is more fruitfully related to theories in other areas, and does a better job of explaining the phenomena.
3. There are positive reasons in favor of the theory.
4. Serious objections can be adequately answered.

The criteria are stated in a general way, for they are intended to be just the criteria that everyone does in fact use in every area. If you think other criteria should be added, then chances are they would be welcome.

To show what the criteria are all about, let's consider an example. Suppose someone claims that the theory that best explains the apparent fact that the room spins after a person turns thirty-three times on one heel is that turning thirty-three times on one's heel causes the room to spin. When we point out that the room is attached to the rest of the house, our friend claims that the whole house is caused to spin. Notice that this is not a consequence mentioned within the theory itself, nor is it a natural consequence of anything in the theory. It is just something that is added on when the original theory gets in trouble. Thus, it is called an *ad hoc addition,* something added on after the fact.

Our next step is to point out that the house is attached to its foundation, which is attached to the lot, and so on. Finally, our friend will (or could) claim that the whole universe spins as a result of a person's turning. This has to be done to keep the theory in contention with its rivals, for example, a theory having to do with the fluid in the ear. All of us are familiar with this rival theory. This theory doesn't require any ad hoc devices to explain the phenomenon of the room's turning, for it explains this seeming fact as just that, and not as something that actually occurs. If we assume that the universe spins, we shall have to suppose that parts of it (for example, those parts not in our solar system) move faster than the speed of light, and we shall have to suppose that there are physical forces, as yet undiscovered, that can move the whole universe around a single place. These consequences of the theory show that it does not fit in with already-established theories in other areas; it certainly does not relate fruitfully to theories in other areas. If we compare the two theories, the World Spinning theory and the Standard Physiological theory (as we can call them), it is clear that the latter does a much better job of explaining the phenomena at hand.

All of us can think of reasons to support the Standard Physiological theory, but there do not appear to be any reasons in favor of the World Spinning theory. Furthermore, the kinds of serious objections raised earlier against the World Spinning theory seem not to be answerable in any adequate way. It is true, of course, that the theorist can find an answer, but this is possible only through ad hoc devices and other troublemaking moves.

The conclusion is that theories are to be rejected because they don't do a good job, not because they don't do the job at all. Anyone can make a theory consistent with the phenomena; all that has to be done is to add enough ad hoc devices. In this way, one can "prove" anything. One can prove that the correct theory concerning Lincoln's becoming President is that he was the illegitimate son of Andrew Jackson. One could maintain, with consistency, that the *Wall Street Journal* is a branch of the *Communist Daily Worker.* However, what one has done when one "proves" a theory in this minimal sense is just to get it on the board with other theories. Of course, the theories picked for the purpose of example are clearly bad ones. The trick is to be able to distinguish the better of two theories when both are pretty good. This kind of skill can be obtained only with practice, and so you are urged to practice. In addition, the rest of this book will be concerned with the evaluation of rival theories in moral philosophy and related areas. You will have ample opportunity to follow evaluations, and you will be urged to join in on a number of occasions.

Finally, we must understand that the criteria are stated generally, that the application in a specific area requires the expertise of practitioners in that area.

Exercises: Evaluating reasons and theories

1. Construct an absurd but consistent theory about the phenomenon of rain. Briefly compare it with the presently accepted theory.

2. Evaluate the following theory of motivation: "Human beings have two motives, to be comfortably warm and to have enough food. All other ends are sought only as means to these two goals." After you have criticized the theory, fix it up so that objections are "met"—even if you have to use ad hoc devices. Now, re-evaluate the theory.

3. Suppose someone offers a theory of motivation that suggests that the sole motive human beings have is to consume petroleum products. A criticism is offered to the effect that actions of individuals to turn thermostats down and to drive at lower speeds are evidence against this theory. The response is made that people know the supply of petroleum is limited, and that if we want to increase the consumption of petroleum overall, we must decrease the consumption now. In the meantime we will discover other supplies of petroleum and more people will be able to afford petroleum products. Evaluate this response to the criticism.

4. Thirty days after Gerald Ford became President of the United States, he pardoned Richard Nixon "for all offenses against the United States which he, Richard Nixon, has committed or may have committed or taken part in during the period from January 20, 1969, through August 9, 1974." Various reasons were given by President Ford for his action.

   a. It would be difficult if not impossible for Richard Nixon to have a fair trial, and certainly a speedy trial would be out of the question. Ford claimed, "a former President of the United States, instead of enjoying equal treatment with any other citizen accused of violating the law, would be cruelly and excessively penalized."

   b. Without a speedy trial and during the period of delay, "ugly passions would again be aroused, our people would again be polarized in their opinions, and the credibility of our free institutions of Government would again be challenged at home and abroad."

   c. "I feel that Richard Nixon and his loved ones have suffered enough, and will continue to suffer no matter what I do. . . ."

The reasons President Ford gave are not meant to offer a legal justification for what he did, for no one really challenged his legal right to pardon former President Nixon. The reasons appear to offer a moral justification for his action. Do the reasons adequately support the claim that he was morally right to pardon the ex-President? What kind of argument is being presented? If you have better arguments, present them and your reasons for claiming that they are better.

F. Moral phenomena

Since we say we are going to examine ethical theories, and since theories explain phenomena, we must have some phenomena before us to explain. Below is a list of some of the more important moral phenomena that ethical theories attempt to explain. After presenting the list and saying what it is and is not, I shall say something more about how the explaining is done and about the nature of ethical theories.

1. Some moral judgments (of value, obligation, and such) are justified, and some are not. (A list of such judgments, even the very clear instances, would be far too long to present.)

2. Reasons support moral judgments. Reasons are given; some of them are taken to be effective, and some are not. Often, when the reasons are thought to be effective, the judgment is held to be justified.

3. General statements, often called *moral principles,* are used to support or justify moral judgments about specific actions or things. For short we can call moral judgments about specific actions or things *singular moral judgments.*

4. There is moral disagreement. This kind of disagreement most often is between persons, but it can also be between groups of people, cultures, and nations. The disagreement is sometimes about moral principles, and sometimes involves only singular moral judgments. A special case of this phenomenon is the conflict of two principles held by a person in a given situation.

5. Circumstances and particular characteristics of people are relevant to the justification of singular moral judgments. No one can be obliged to save a person who is drowning in the Pacific Ocean when he or she is in central Ohio. The mother of a child is obliged to feed her infant, but not the child of someone about whom she knows nothing in a city hundreds of miles away.

6. None of us is morally responsible for what is beyond our control or power to bring about or prevent. This is one part of the "ought implies can" principle.

7. There is a close relation between the acceptance of moral judgments and what is often called *emotive force.* Human beings are not indifferent to moral judgments in the way in which some people can be indifferent to nonmoral judgments. One can be indifferent to "Jupiter has ten moons" but not to "It is wrong for me to betray my friend."

8. People are inclined to act from what they accept as their obligations and feel guilty if they do not so act.

9. People are inclined to pursue what they suppose is valuable and be disappointed if they cannot secure it.

The above is a partial list of the moral phenomena to which any ethical theory will address itself. It should be emphasized that the list is not complete, nor are the items on it undeniable truths. There is no doubt that the list is incomplete, and I shall claim (and many of you will want to claim) that some of the purported facts are not facts at all. However, the present claim is that a list of these kinds of items is the starting place for ethical theories.

Some people have stated that all moral phenomena are linguistic, or at least judgmental. On this view, not only would the list of moral phenomena contain "Jones judges that x is good," but it would contain *only* statements within quotation marks. However, I see no more reason to restrict the phenomena of ethical theories to the language of morals (what is in quotation marks) than to restrict the phenomena of physics to the language of physics (what is in quotation marks). The language of morals is as important as the language of physics; in each case, we are allowed to talk about the subject matter. On some occasions the subject matter is the language itself—perhaps more often in ethical theory than in physical theory—but this difference in quantity does not appear to justify a claim of a difference in quality.

Jones's saying "This action is morally wrong" is a moral phenomenon, but it is difficult to understand why, outside some particular theory, people thought it was the only kind of phenomenon. One can understand, within the context of a particular theory of meaning, for example, why moral statements would be the only subject matter of ethics. However, the kind of theory of meaning that would support such a view is no longer current. Until someone comes up with some persuasive argument to the contrary, we shall suppose that moral phenomena are the kinds of things listed.

The phenomena, as the starting point of any investigation, are not described by incorrigible propositions in relation to which any theory must be tested. This is just the kind of position which the general account of phenomena is meant to rule out. Phenomena are not facts, nor are they accounts of the way things or perceptions appear to us; they are not sense-data-like reports, or any other of the group of very secure, or perhaps even certain, statements that many have suggested are the foundation of our knowledge. A phenomenal report is always corrigible. Theories about phenomena are always corrigible.

G. Knowledge, truth, and justified belief

1. Knowledge   It is generally agreed that there are at least three conditions for knowledge. If person *a* knows h:

1. Person *a* accepts h.
2. h is true.
3. Person *a* has the proper evidence for h.

Evidence (item 3 in the list) can be understood as the result of arguments or a theory that is better than its competitors. For example, we have evidence that the shortest distance between two points on the surface of the earth is part of a great circle. This is directly supported by the theory that the earth is a sphere, plus some knowledge of the properties of spheres. We hold, on most occasions, to a view that vision is a reliable means of gaining information and knowledge about the world. This kind of view is not usually thought of as a theory; but without any distortion, we can say that it is ("seeing is believing") and understand how this theory provides us with a great deal of evidence. We say the ball is red because we see it; its shape is circular because we are looking right at it; and so on.

In addition to such theories as the above, there are, of course, all the theories we are most inclined to think of when we use the term 'theory'. Theories such as the germ theory of disease and the gas laws are clear instances. Insofar as these kinds of theories are justified and we make use of them, they provide us with evidence for the claims we make. It is not an exaggeration to say that most of our schooling consists of coming to understand and apply various theories in different areas of human concern.

Straightforward deductive and inductive arguments also give us evidence. The previous discussion of these types of arguments will help you in understanding their nature. In addition, the use of many such arguments in the course of this book will help to make their use more clear.

2. Truth   *Truth* will be understood as involving a relation between whatever h is about and h. If h is 'The earth is a sphere', then h is true just in that instance in which the earth is a sphere.

It can be established without difficulty that truth and acceptance are different. If truth and acceptance were the same, we would have no effective way of explaining many errors of acceptance. But, as a few examples will show, there is an effective way of explaining many errors. For example, Columbus accepted that he had reached the Orient, but he accepted what was false. Hegel accepted that there were exactly seven planets in the solar system, but he was mistaken. Everyone reading this has made mistakes that are explained by saying that you accepted something that was false.

It should be pointed out that on some matters it is always possible that we are mistaken. Some h's are *necessary* truths ($2 + 2 = 4$, affirming the antecedent); some, the ones about which we can always be mistaken, are *contingent* (the earth is a sphere, Columbus is the capital of Ohio). One way to distinguish the two kinds of h's is to point out that the denial of a contingent truth is not a contradiction, whereas the denial of a necessary truth (or at least of most necessary truths) always results in a contradiction. It is always (logically) possible that a contingent truth is not true—even when it is true.

If someone points out that we may be mistaken about a contingent h, this is only to say that it is a contingent h; it does not show that we do not know h. For one thing, the same possibility of being correct holds. Since the possibilities exist on both sides, the mere possibility can't show anything. An h can be known when it is true; it is not true because it is known.

None of us can "have" truth in the way in which we can have evidence. A person can show us evidence but not the truth of the matter. For a person to know an h, that h has to be true. The person does not have to *know* that the h is true; it need only be true.

3. **Justified assertion**   Since people are bothered considerably by truth, let's talk about being justified in asserting that we know when the first and third conditions (those that deal with acceptance and proper evidence) are fulfilled. If we are justified in asserting that we have this knowledge, we can then be said to know when the second condition also is fulfilled.

Unless someone can come up with some new sense, we shall suppose that the expression 'It is true for' is usually the same thing as acceptance. So when we say that it was true for the man who jumped off the cliff with homemade wings that he would fly, it is the same as saying that he believed he would fly. But he didn't fly. The man who accepts that cancer is cured by burning incense believes it, but he is mistaken. (See section 2 above on truth before you make any moves, for some of them are made for you there.) "Who is to say?" Those who have proper evidence. Those who have the better theory. (Yes, we might be wrong; see section 2 above.)

H. Definitions

There are many equally good theories of definition that can be adopted and used with success. The following way of handling definitions has been found to work well with the rest of the material presented. As far as can be determined, however, no relevant philosophical issues are decided merely by adopting this theory of definition. According to this view, there are two main kinds of definition, *stipulative* and *reportive*.

1. **Stipulative definitions**   There are two kinds of stipulative definition, strange and familiar. A constructed term whose meaning is given independent of existing use is a *strange term stipulation*. For example, I now stipulate that 'donk' means 'a very stubborn human being'. Since no disputes revolve around this term and its meaning, we may accept it readily. However, the claim that 'bird' means 'animal that flies' is objectionable because bats are not birds and ostriches are. A proposed change of a familiar term requires justification, for there is no sense in rejecting, without justification, an established meaning. 'Fish' used to mean, roughly, 'animal that lives in the water'. But as a result of a biological theory, we now find a new meaning superseding the old. This is reflected in the dictionary definition, "Any of various cold-blooded, completely aquatic vertebrates having gills, commonly fins, and typically an elongated body usually covered with scales." [4] The old meaning has become less frequent and will no doubt die out within a relatively short time. A new definition is replacing the old one—a definition based on theory.

[4] *The American College Dictionary,* ed. Clarence L. Barnhart, Harper, New York, 1951, p. 456.

Sometimes both the old and the new meanings continue to fulfill needs of language users. Since Newton, 'force' has had at least two noncompeting uses that are usually distinguished by context. The reason for accepting Newton's definition of 'force' was his theory—his set of acceptable hypotheses. Sometimes nontheoretical arguments are presented for accepting a new definition of a familiar term; for example, the new definition is precise and the old one imprecise, or the new meaning will allow us to capture something (the notion of "emotive force," say) correctly and yet allow us to describe a familiar phenomenon (moral action).

2. Reportive definitions

There are two types of reportive definitions, unmodified and modified. *Unmodified usage reports,* as found in most dictionaries, are almost sheer reports of how a term is used in a given language. Some tidying up of such reports is necessary because usage varies according to person, place, and time. Thus, 'modified' and 'unmodified' are terms of degree and do not represent a hard and fast distinction.

An unmodified report, by itself, cannot solve significant problems about the application of a term. For example, 'justice' in the *American College Dictionary* is defined as "1. the quality of being just. . . ." If we wondered whether 'just' was correctly applied in a situation, or wanted to know the nature of justice, we would not be helped by such a definition.

When a usage report is interpreted, the result is a *modified usage report.* F. C. Sharp gives a good example of this kind of modification.

The subject matter of our studies is still the man on the street. It is what he means by 'right' that interests us. And the difficulty we face is that he cannot tell us. Ask him to define the term, and he will not even understand what you are driving at. The difficulty, however, is not one peculiar to the vocabulary of ethics. Since John Smith cannot tell you what he means by 'cause', 'probably', or 'now', he cannot give a really satisfactory answer to so apparently simple a question as "what is 'money'?"

When we had been told that this milk was very hot, this tool very heavy, this glass very easily broken, and that we had been very naughty, the meaning of 'very' dawned upon our minds, not in the sense that we could define it but that we could use it intelligently. It is in precisely this same way that we can discover what the layman means by the fundamental terms in the moral vocabulary. We watch his use of them. Thereupon, proceeding one step farther than the child, we generalize our observations and in doing so form a definition.

It is indeed a curious fact that men can go through life using words with a fair degree of definiteness and consistency with no formulated definition before the mind. But it is a fact. "I cannot define poetry," says A. E. Housman, in effect, "but I know it when I see it. In the same way a terrier cannot define a rat, but he knows one when he sees it."[5]

Sharp proposes a theory to explain what he finds in unmodified usage reports. The acceptability of his definitions is not a function of the unmodified reports alone, but also of the ability of his theory to account for and explain those reports. Explaining the reports is not the same thing as accepting the reports as truths, for some claims that are part of unmodified reports are false. The claim, for example, that money is always tangible can be reported as part of what people say, but it is false that money is always tangible.

Important definitions are supported by acceptable theories, though some of them begin with reports of usage and others do not. The origin of a theory and its corresponding definition is, of course, less important than its acceptability.

I.   A look back; a look ahead

This first chapter laid the foundation for an examination of the major theories of normative ethics. In this chapter the basic tools of the ethical strategist were laid out, and you were given an overview of the area of normative ethics, as well as some aid in discovering what your own tentative or initial position is. No one should feel irreversibly committed to any position, for the whole point now of reading the rest of this book is to compare all the theories to see which one seems to do the best job. You will have a difficult time in doing this if you have determined that you will stick by a theory for all time and as a consequence won't examine seriously the evidence in favor of the theories to be examined. The best advice I can give is to suspend judgment about which theory is correct until you have at least carefully considered the main rivals. It may be that even after you have done that, you won't want to make up your mind. Your unwillingness would be understandable. However, at some time you *will* want to make up your mind. This book is designed to be an aid to accomplishing that.

There are some who disagree with me about the nature of moral philosophy, as well as disagreeing about which normative ethical theory is the best one. However, the framework provided appears to me, and also to many who don't hold the same normative theory that I do, to be neutral with respect to normative ethics. You can accept the framework and still consistently disagree with the normative ethical theory defended in this book. In short, there are no major meta-ethical or normative ethical questions begged simply by accepting this way of setting up theories for discussion. For example, to agree that there are moral phenomena is not to say

[5] F. C. Sharp, *Good Will and Ill Will,* Univ. of Chicago Press, Chicago, 1950, p. 156.

that they represent facts, and to say that there are moral rules is not to say what kind. These are the kinds of tasks to be performed in the rest of the book.

In chapters 2 and 3 we shall consider the two main orders of teleological views, egoism and utilitarianism. In chapter 3 there will also be a discussion of theories of justice. In chapter 4 the survey of deontological theories will begin with the rule deonotologists. The survey will be completed in chapter 5 with an examination of act deonotology, the view I think is the best.

Chapters 2 through 5 cover theories of obligation, and the only mention of value is general, and neutral with respect to theories of value. In chapter 6 theory of value is covered. This vast area can be covered in one chapter because we shall have prepared ourselves by the chapters on theory of obligation. The kinds of "moves," that is, variations on theories, and the kinds of criticisms found in theory of obligation are found also in theory of value, and so we shall borrow freely from the earlier chapters.

In the last chapter we shall take a look at the main issues in the area of meta-ethics. The emphasis in terms of pages devoted to these issues is not as great as is given to normative ethics. However, those who want to find an acceptable theory for themselves in normative ethics will finally have to confront the issues of cognitivism-noncognitivism, definism-non-definism, and such. Enough material is presented, though, so that the student of moral philosophy can see what the problems and main arguments are.

But we've gotten ahead of our story. One of the views most widely held in ethical circles is *egoism*—in a variety of different forms. It is to this cluster of views we turn next, in chapter 2.

Exercises: Sharpening your critical skills

1. Below you will find a theory of obligation and its supporting evidence. This is not a theory you or anyone else will be tempted to hold, for it is absurd almost on its face value. The purpose of the evaluation is to sharpen your critical skills so that when you evaluate theories you are inclined to take more seriously, you can do so. Please follow the directions in the evaluation, for they are designed to separate out different kinds of issues.

> *Statement of the theory of epistemism:* There is only one rule of obligation, and it is the following direct moral rule: "If any action results in a net gain of knowledge, then that action is right."

> **a. Evaluation of reasons in favor**   Critically evaluate the two following proposed reasons in favor of the theory, but do not evaluate the theory directly yet.
> *Reason 1:* No action of a person can be said to be morally right or obligatory unless that person knows what he or she is doing. The more one knows what one is doing, the better the chance of doing what is right and fulfilling one's obligations. This shows the relation between right and obligatory actions on the one hand and knowledge on the other.

Reason 2: Knowledge leads to control over misery and suffering and makes it likely that we shall be able to eliminate hunger. Since we know it would be right to eliminate such evil things, that is evidence that the gaining of knowledge is right.

b. **Response to criticisms**   Below are two proposed criticisms of epistemism, each followed by a proposed response to the criticism on the part of a defender of epistemism. For now, address yourself not to the criticism itself (it may or may not be any good) but only to the quality of the *response* proposed by the defender of epistemism.

Criticism 1: There are many instances of increasing knowledge that are apparently not right. The Nazis' human experiments are one kind of counter-example, and the knowledge of the total number of underpants owned by persons in the front row of a class is another.

Response 1: The Nazi experiments did increase knowledge, but they also inflicted pain. Since the amount of knowledge gained did not justify the pain and suffering inflicted, the action was not right. The knowledge concerning underwear, similarly, does not represent enough good of other kinds, such as the elimination of suffering, to justify the claim that the action is right.

Criticism 2: There are kinds of actions that are apparently right and have nothing to do with increasing knowledge. The hero who throws himself on a grenade is apparently doing what is right, but there is no net increase of knowledge.

Response 2: The person who is killed does not experience a net increase of knowledge, of course, but the people who are saved do. They now better appreciate life and how to preserve it. This is true of all instances of right action; the overall amount of knowledge is increased.

c. **Overall evaluation**   Now that you have evaluated the reasons in favor of and the quality of responses to criticisms, you can evaluate the theory overall. Look again at the criteria for theory evaluation in section E, and apply each to epistemism.

2. Everyone hears arguments, judgments, and other kinds of moral opinions expressed. Describe what you take to be the most common normative ethical theory with which you disagree, state the reasons in its favor given by its proponents and the usual criticisms and responses, and then offer your own evaluation of the theory.

3. Describe a disagreement you have had with someone about a moral matter, either about some specific situation or some general judgment or principle. Were there any normative ethical theories involved in the dispute? What, in your opinion, was the key element in the dispute?

4. There are some topics about which there is likely to be moral disagreement. Find one of the following on which there is a fairly even split in your class, and have each side present its reasons. You might want each side to appoint a secretary to write the reasons decided on by the group, then the criticisms of the other side's views, and then perhaps even the responses of the group to the criticisms offered of its own position. The list is meant to be suggestive; everyone should be asked to supply additional suggested topics.

    a. Capital punishment
    b. Abortion (on demand before the end of the twelfth week of pregnancy)
    c. Hunting for sport
    d. Marijuana laws

e. Euthanasia

f. Guaranteed annual wage for all adults, whether they work or not

Recommended reading

Frankena, William K. *Ethics,* 2d ed. Prentice-Hall, Englewood Cliffs, N.J., 1973. In chapter 1, Frankena proposes a different view concerning the nature of normative ethical theories than the one presented here.

Salmon, Wesley C. *Logic,* 3rd ed. Prentice-Hall, Englewood Cliffs, N.J., 1973. This book should supply you with any additional logic material and explanations you might need.

Warnock, G. J. *The Object of Morality.* Methuen, London, 1971. In chapter 1 Warnock presents three different views of what ethics is, none of which appears to be the view taken in this book.

Two

Chapter two

Egoism

Egoism is often the first view people adopt when they consciously attempt to formulate an ethical theory. It is tempting to say that the right thing to do is what increases my own good, or that everyone really wants what is best for themselves. We hear such statements as "Look out for yourself or no one else will" and "I'm number one when it comes to doing good." Unfortunately, the view most persons want to adopt is much more difficult to state clearly than it appears at first; usually it turns out that there are really two different kinds of theories mixed together—one an ethical theory and the other a theory of motivation. These two theories may be related, as we shall see shortly, but they are certainly not the same. In order clearly to evaluate egoism, we must first distinguish egoism as a theory of motivation from egoism as an ethical theory. The former view is called *psychological egoism* and the latter, *ethical egoism.*

To see the difference between the two views, consider them as represented schematically.

Psychological egoism
1. If any person *a* performs a voluntary action, then person *a*'s sole motive for performing that action is self-benefit.
2. Helping a little old lady across the street is a voluntary action performed by person *a*

Therefore,
3. Person *a*'s sole motive in helping a little old lady across the street is self-benefit.

Ethical egoism (one version)
1. If any person *a* performs an action that increases person *a*'s own good (benefit), then that action is right.
2. Eating proper foods is an action that increases person *a*'s own good (benefit).

Therefore,
3. Person *a*'s eating proper foods is a right action.

In the first set of statements, the claims are about motives; and in the second, about actions being right. There is a common element—benefit, or good, is mentioned in both statements—although it occurs in the consequent of the first statement representing psychological egoism and in the antecedent of the first statement representing ethical egoism. However, it is clear that in the statement of psychological egoism there is no term concerning such notions as *right, obligation,* or *duty.* In the statements representing ethical egoism there is no mention of motives at all, but there is a term in theory of obligation—namely, 'right'—which allows at least part of a theory of obligation. In the first statement of psychological egoism there is a proposed connection between *benefit for me* and *motive for acting,* whereas in the first statement of ethical egoism there is a proposed connection between *good* (benefit) *for me* and *right action.*

Since the second statements in each case are subsidiary, it will be simpler to refer to the first statements as the statement of the theory. The third statements are, of course, derived from the first two via the deductively valid argument of affirming the antecedent.

Most people who are inclined to be egoists adopt a certain strategy when the distinction between psychological and ethical egoism is pointed out. They suppose that indeed there are two different views, but that the psychological view offers the evidence for the ethical theory. If we use PE to stand for psychological egoism and EE to stand for ethical egoism, we can see the relationship proposed in the following argument.

If PE, then EE.
PE.

Therefore,
EE.

The defense of ethical egoism in terms of this model requires that we establish the truth of two different kinds of statements. The second premise requires that we establish the truth of a psychological theory of motivation, and the first premise claims that there is a relation between that psychological theory and an ethical theory. If either of the premises should turn out to be unjustified, then the conclusion is not warranted in the case of this argument. Of course, the conclusion may be warranted on other grounds; for when one shows that an argument fails, one does not thereby show that the conclusion of that argument is false. Since the above argument is valid (being an instance of affirming the antecedent), we must look into the truth of the premises. We shall begin with the second premise.

Therefore, the order of business in this chapter is as follows:
  A. Psychological egoism defined
  B. Nonempirical psychological egoism
  C. Empirical psychological egoism
  D. Ethical egoism

A. Psychological egoism defined

The first general statement of psychological egoism can be put informally
so as to make it more intuitive. We shall return to the formal statement
later for purposes of evaluation. Sometimes it is said that we are all selfish,
or that selfishness is the basis of all our actions. This is one way of stating
psychological egoism, although it is also misleading. Often we want to
contrast desirable and undesirable character traits, and we use the term
'selfish' to describe one undesirable character trait. Those who wish to
defend psychological egoism, however, use the term as descriptive of a fact
of human nature, something that is true of all human beings. So, it is not a
very good idea to use the term 'selfish' as part of an explanation of psychological egoism.

Another statement of psychological egoism might help us to understand the view more easily: "The sole or overriding motive that human
beings have is to increase their own interests." This is equivalent to the
first formulation; and if it is clearer, then you may want to work with it.

1. **Some phenomena for theories of motivation**   In keeping with the
methodology proposed in the first chapter, we must have some phenomena
before us as we begin our investigation into a theory of motivation. The
following short list is not in any way intended to be complete; anyone reading this will want to add further items. Additions are acceptable as long as
such items are not themselves theories of motivation.

1. Quite often we act for our own benefit.
2. Sometimes we act for the benefit of others.
3. Sometimes we act not for the benefit of any particular people but,
for example, for the benefit of the environment or to create beautiful
things.
4. Often we are mistaken about our motives.
5. Sometimes we change our minds about what our motives were at a
given time.
6. If there is a conflict between being able to benefit ourselves and
being able to benefit others, we sometimes choose to benefit ourselves
and sometimes we choose to benefit others.
7. The motives we have are influenced by what we take to be of
value.

Remember, to say that these are the phenomena of motivation is not in any way to say that they are truths or facts. It could turn out that the correct theory of motivation is incompatible with many of these phenomena; and consequently, they must be rejected as facts and no longer included even in the phenomena. The phenomena are the starting place of our investigation, not the stopping place. However, as part of our evaluation of a theory, we must see what kind of a job it does in explaining the phenomena. Even when a given phenomenon is rejected by a theory, it must be rejected without the use of ad hoc devices or illegitimate assumptions.

2. Benefit or good   The terms 'benefit' and 'good' were used in the formulation of egoism. 'Benefit' is used in a nontechnical sense and is probably clear as it stands. For this discussion, the term 'good' will not be specified any further—although it will be helpful to say something about how one would go about specifying it.[1] Many people think that the only thing that is good is pleasure, others think that power is the only good thing. More often, though, people are inclined to think that a variety of things are good—they suppose that pleasure is good, as well as power, freedom, love, friendship, and so on. If you maintain that the sole or overriding motive of all voluntary action is to secure for yourself what is good (or what is to your benefit), then you need not, in making this claim, commit yourself to any particular view about what, exactly, is good. At some point you may want also to take a stand on what is good, but you need not do that at this point. Since there is a separate chapter on good and value, it certainly would be premature and unwise to say much about this topic now. If, however, the nature of value is significant in terms of your stand on egoism, then perhaps you should skip ahead and read chapter 6 first.

Nevertheless, nothing will be supposed in the following discussion concerning the *nature* of good or other things that might benefit people. It will not be supposed that any given thing is or is not of value; and it will not be supposed that there is exactly one thing of value, or that there are a variety of things of value.

3. Sole motive   The theory of psychological egoism states that the *sole* motive anyone has is self-benefit. If, however, the claim is only that one of the motives we have in acting is to benefit ourselves, then the view is not psychological egoism. This expanded view is quite compatible with views that suggest that self-benefit is unimportant and frequently overridden by other motives, such as doing good for others (without regard for our own benefit). If psychological egoism is a correct theory, the claim has to be stronger than just that one among many motives is to benefit ourselves. For example, it could be claimed that there are other motives that either are

[1] The full discussion of theories of value occurs in chapter 6.

not primary motives or are always overridden by the motive to benefit ourselves.

Someone could claim that we have a motive to help others, but that it is not a primary motive. If we are on a bridge under which a drowning person floats and we could reach down and, without danger to ourselves, pull the person out, then we would do so. There is an example of a motive independent of self-benefit. However, should the motive to benefit ourself come into conflict with any of these other motives, then it would always override the other motives. In a conflict situation, the motive that determines our action is the egoistic one. This can be called the *primary motive version* of psychological egoism, but it is not widely held. Furthermore, and much more seriously, it cannot support ethical egoism. For this latter reason, we shall not interpret psychological egoism in this fashion.

In addition, there are some difficulties with this primary motive view. In almost every situation, even where nothing apparently is to be gained for ourselves, our reputation is at stake. It is barely possible, most people would concede, that a man saves a drowning child and before anyone can get his name slips away. However, if this did occur, there is reason to believe that most people would consider a certain amount of good lost to the rescuer. The good to the rescuer here is in the form of an enhanced reputation, personal satisfaction, not unlikely financial reward, and so on. If the overriding motive is always self-benefit, then we would expect that the rescuer would stay for his reward. It is not clear, then, that there would ever be a situation in which the egoistic motive was absent.

It would seem, therefore, that it makes no practical difference whether we say that the sole motive is self-benefit or that the overriding motive is always self-benefit. However, it is the sole motive version that offers support for ethical egoism, and that is the point of talking about psychological egoism.

4. Empirical claim   Those who claim that psychological egoism is a correct theory of human motivation are committed to the view that it captures *the* law of human motivation. It is a law of nature that if anyone performs a voluntary action, then the motive is to bring about good for oneself. It is a law of nature in the same way any law in, say, physics is a law of nature.

Psychological egoism is a claim about the nature of human motives. When we are told that this is the nature of human motives, we are also being told that we will always observe humans acting in this manner (when we are properly instructed) and that other views about human action are not correct. It is not like a claim concerning the nature of numbers or a claim about geometry. In those areas we need not observe anything in the world to determine whether a theorem is correct, we need only consult the appropriate axiom system and see if the rules of inference allow the derivation. The kind of claim made is more like the claim that the earth is a sphere, that there are nine planets in the solar system, or $E = mc^2$. This means that there is some evidence we can find from observing human behavior that can either confirm the view or disconfirm it. It is, therefore, a view that is falsifiable.

In spite of the fact that psychological egoism is a falsifiable view, there are many who offer what appears to be nonempirical evidence. Usually such people are willing to admit that the view is nevertheless falsifiable, and this enables the discussion to proceed without difficulty. In contrast, though, there are those who claim that the view is not falsifiable, that it is not an empirical theory, and that it is true simply because of human nature or the nature of the concepts involved in motivation. This kind of view will be examined more closely shortly.

5. Voluntary action   Nothing fancy or mysterious is meant by 'voluntary action'. In part, the term signifies those actions which, as we sometimes say, are willed by the person and not forced by external factors. A person who inadvertently steps off the edge of a cliff does not voluntarily perform the action of falling, nor does that person even perform the action of stepping off the edge voluntarily. The two actions are nonvoluntary, since the person did not act knowingly even if not forced into either action. Suppose, to continue, that electrodes are placed in your brain at certain strategic places, an electric current is run through causing certain muscles in your body to relax, and the result is that your bladder empties. Since this would be embarrassing at a party, it would be something that you would try mightily to prevent. However, if you failed to prevent it, then you would have performed an involuntary action. The "spring of action" would have come not from you but from whichever of your enemies was pushing the buttons—the action was willed perhaps, but by your controller and not by you.

The kinds of actions that you will and that are not performed as a result of someone else's willing or without any willing at all are the *voluntary actions*. Some of you may wonder whether there are really any such things as voluntary actions on the grounds that there are causes that result in our acting independently of anything we will. Others of you will be tempted to say that our own will is determined by events and factors beyond our own control, and so there are really no voluntary actions after all. These are legitimate concerns. For now, though, let us not raise these problems and instead stay with psychological and ethical egoism.

Summary of psychological egoism   *Psychological egoism,* in summary, is a psychological theory of motivation that is neutral with respect to which things will benefit us and which things are of value. It claims that egoistic considerations are the sole or overriding motive for all voluntary action, and that as an empirical view purporting to have discovered the law of motivation, it is falsifiable. In exception to this view, some people claim that psychological egoism is a correct theory of motivation; and in support, they provide nonempirical evidence.

B. Nonempirical psychological egoism

The statement of psychological egoism is the same regardless of one's grounds for holding the view, but the evidence in its favor and the willingness to consider counter-evidence are different. In what follows, a sampling of the arguments and the counter-arguments of psychological egoism as a nonempirical view will be presented.

1. **Willing and wanting**   Often we hear the claim that we always do what we want to, when the action is voluntary, and so we always act to increase our own good. If we didn't want to do something, then we wouldn't do it, it is claimed, and so we did it to satisfy our want. When we do something to satisfy our want, then we are doing something for our own good. Thus, it is concluded, psychological egoism is established.

The above argument is stated in a loose and informal way, but that is the only way the argument can have any plausibility at all. To see this, let us make some distinctions that are not very controversial, but that will help us to state the argument more precisely.

There are some actions we do because we will to do them, our voluntary actions, and some actions we do independently of any willing. Examples were given of such actions, but consider a few more. I write the word 'will' because I will to do it, but my eyes just blinked independently of any act of will on my part. So there are voluntary actions that we will and actions we don't will that are not voluntary. In addition to this distinction, there is also the distinction between those actions which follow our *inclinations* and those which do not. Many of you awake early, jump out of bed, and set about your tasks immediately, but many of you do not. You have to drag yourself out of bed with great effort when, apparently, your inclination is to sleep a bit longer. This is a common experience for human beings: often we act contrary to our inclination to do something.

In the informal statement of the argument, the claim that we always do what we want is ambiguous. It might mean any of the following:

1. We always will our voluntary actions.
2. We always will to do what we are inclined to do.
3. We always will to do what we calculate will benefit us in the long run.

If the argument, however it goes, is based on claim 2, it should not be accepted. Claim 2 is obviously not true: Very often we will to do something we are not inclined to do—something that is perhaps contrary to our inclination to act. At the moment this is being written, I am inclined to go for a walk in the bright sunshine of an early summer morning. However, I remain seated at my typewriter making the world safe for correct psychological theories. Many of you, as you read what I took such pains to write, are inclined to go to the movies, to drink beer, to read a novel, or to go to sleep; but if you have read this far, you have not acted on these inclinations. Our acting according to what we will rather than what we are inclined to do is a phenomenon that any theory of motivation, including theories not based on empirical evidence, must take into account and explain. Failure to explain this phenomenon adequately is evidence against the theory or against that part of it which makes the claim.

Some of you will, at this point, be inclined to say that perhaps claim 2 is really true, even though it does not seem to be true. This is always a possibility, but possibilities do not prove anything. There is the same possibility, just considering mere possibility, that claim 2 is true as there is that it is false. There is some actual evidence, though, that claim 2 is false. If you want to state that claim 2 is true, you must present some actual evidence that it is. It will do no good, by the way, to suggest that it is possible that the evidence showing that claim 2 is not true is not actually evidence at all. For, although this possibility is cheerfully admitted, as long as there is an equal possibility that the evidence *is* actually evidence, this possibility shows nothing.

Someone might claim, although I don't know how such a claim would be made good, that if psychological egoism is correct, then claim 2 can be shown to be true; that is, the claim would be that the truth of claim 2 follows from the truth of psychological egoism. Let us suppose, for a moment, that this is so. If it is so, then it requires that we establish the correctness of psychological egoism on some grounds other than claim 2. You cannot use claim 2 as an essential part of the evidence for psychological egoism and then defend claim 2 by using psychological egoism. If claim 2 is the evidence required to establish psychological egoism, then you don't have the psychological theory available yet to defend the claim when it is attacked. If you could establish the correctness of psychological egoism independently of claim 2, then, of course, you could use the theory to establish and defend claim 2. But if you could do that, then you wouldn't need claim 2 at all to establish psychological egoism.

There were three interpretations of "We always do what we want," the second of which has been considered. So now let us consider the first—"We always will our voluntary actions." There are two closely related problems with this statement as support for psychological egoism. First, it appears to have no content. And second, it appears to be neutral with respect to theories of motivation. When the notion of *voluntary action* was introduced, it was explained in part via the notion of *willing*.[2] In brief, voluntary actions are those actions which we will to do. If we substitute into claim 1 the analysis of voluntary action, then we have the following statement:

---

[2] Voluntary action could have been explained without using the notion of *willing*. We could have used the (ambiguous) term 'want' to express the notion of an action that is within our power. If this had been done, the ambiguity of claim 1 and claim 2 would still be present, but of course it would be phrased in different language.

1'. We always will those actions which we will.

Claim 1' is a statement that no one would quarrel with, for it says nothing about *what* we will, and it says nothing about whether we in fact will at all. In short, it doesn't say anything that appears to have any content. If it doesn't have any content, then it cannot be used to defend or support psychological egoism—a specific theory of motivation. Claim 1' does not disallow the possibility that we will some actions that are contrary to our own interests. If we will them, then they are voluntary actions not motivated by self-benefit. And if this is the case, we have shown that psychological egoism is not correct.

Once again the temptation will be to say that there are no voluntary actions in which we will anything other than what we suppose is to our own benefit. This is, however, simply another way of stating psychological egoism. If one could establish this claim independently of claim 1 and, as we have to, independently of claim 1', then we would be entitled to make that claim. However, again, this cannot be done if claim 1 is the basis for establishing psychological egoism. Similar considerations apply to any suggestions about the possibility of being mistaken.

Suppose we interpret the statement that we always do what we want as:

3. We always will to do what we calculate will benefit us in the long run.

Can this interpretation support psychological egoism? By itself, as it stands, it is compatible with the denial of psychological egoism, for it may be that we will to do that which will benefit us in the long run and we also will what will benefit others in the long run. The problem arises as to what happens if there is a conflict between the benefit to ourselves and the benefit to others. The psychological egoist must maintain that if there is a conflict, then we always will what is to our own benefit.

In evaluating claim 3, we can point out, first, that there is apparently no such calculation done by human beings. When we act to rescue someone who is drowning, we seem to think about the person and not about what the long-run effects might be. We don't calculate the chances of there being a hidden camera taking the whole rescue down for posterity or the likelihood of the person being saved rewarding us. Here again I can speak from my own experience. On two occasions I have rescued drowning people and on each occasion the lack of forethought was (or at least appeared to be) later on astonishingly evident. The same kind of experience is reported by most war heroes—they simply do not, as far as they can tell, think of the consequences of their action at all.

If the psychological egoist wishes to claim that all of us, on almost every occasion, do calculate in this way, then some positive evidence that this occurs must be presented. It is always possible, when we are speaking of motivation, to be mistaken. But this fact by itself does not support the claim of the psychological egoist any more than it supports the claim of someone who wants to deny that particular theory of motivation. So there is reason to suppose that claim 3 is false, and as yet no reason to suppose it is true. Furthermore, some supporters of psychological egoism use claim 3 as another way of stating the theory of psychological egoism. Of course, if we could establish that psychological egoism is correct, then we could establish that it is correct in that statement of it also. This is, though, precisely the task the egoist has to perform—namely, to present evidence that psychological egoism is indeed correct.

The conclusion of the above discussion of the three interpretations of "We always do what we want" is that one nonempirical argument fails to establish psychological egoism as a correct theory, and indeed provides no evidence at all for its correctness. We are not entitled to conclude that psychological egoism is not correct, for one does not establish that a theory is not correct, or even worse than another, simply by examining one proposed bit of evidence in its favor. We have to look at more evidence, and we also have to examine its competitors in the area of nonempirically based theories. The next argument to be considered does introduce a competitor for the first time.

2. Opposing views: psychological altruism   Some people defend psychological egoism by attacking another view. The other view, which we shall call *psychological altruism,* is seen by such people to be the polar opposite of psychological egoism.

> *Psychological altruism*
> 1. If any person *a* performs a voluntary action, then person *a*'s sole motive for performing that action is to benefit others.
> 2. Scratching his head when it itches is a voluntary action performed by person *a*.
> _____
> Therefore,
> 3. Person *a*'s sole motive in scratching his head when it itches is to benefit others.

This Scheme R for psychological altruism should be compared with the one for psychological egoism on page 38. In both cases, an example in the second statement was chosen that goes contrary to the phenomena. In each case, though, the person who wants to defend the theory in question should be able to explain why such cases are not an embarrassment. The psychological altruist can say that the person who scratches his head when it itches relieves a discomfort all right, but that is only the beginning of the story. It is known by everyone that if the itch is not scratched, then the discomfort would grow worse, the person would be unpleasant to others, and he would not do his job as well. All this would clearly reduce the amount of good that could be done for others. What this shows, so the psychological altruist claims, is that the action was done for the purpose of achieving the good of others.

Most of you reading this "defense" of psychological altruism won't know whether to be amused or outraged, for the defense simply consists of making the theory consistent with the phenomena, which can be done for any self-consistent theory. In fact, this is a "defense" of the same quality one often finds for psychological egoism. We are told that the reason the little old lady is helped across the street or, to take a real case, Rosen turns off the headlights of a parked car is that if he did not, then he would feel guilty. If he felt guilty, then he would suffer. Therefore, the action is done in order to avoid the suffering, that is, to benefit himself. In both cases, the explanation is imaginative but seems not to be supported by any external evidence. The temptation to use the psychological theory you are defending to provide the evidence for that defense must, of course, be overcome. The theory itself cannot be used to rescue evidence used to establish the theory as correct, nor can it be used to "refute" counter-evidence by asserting its own correctness and then stating that if it is indeed true, the counter-evidence would not really be counter-evidence. We'll return to this point again shortly.

Psychological altruism is not a very good theory of motivation. If we refer to the criteria for the acceptability of theories, we find that there are very few reasons in its favor. It can be admitted that there are some, perhaps many, actions we perform that are apparently performed to increase the good of others. The phenomenon of actions performed for the benefit of others must be explained by any adequate theory of motivation; and psychological altruism, by virtue of its attempt to deal with this phenomenon, merits some amount of support. However, there is at least an equally numerous set of actions that appear to be done not for the benefit of others but for our own benefit.

One of the criteria of acceptability is how well the theory can respond to criticisms. As pointed out above, one obvious criticism of psychological altruism is that there are numerous counter-examples. When I am alone in my room and feel thirsty, the fact that I drink some water does not suggest that the benefit of others was in any way in my mind. This counter-example constitutes a denial of psychological altruism, as can be seen in the following formulation:

> not-1. Drinking a glass of water when thirsty is a voluntary action of person *a;* and the sole motive in performing it is not to increase the good of others (instead the motive seems primarily or solely to increase person *a*'s own good).

This is a counter-example to the statement of psychological altruism as represented in the first statement of the Scheme R version of that view. It is called a *counter-example* because it is an example or instance of an action that falls under the theory but goes counter to it. If someone claims that any object when unsupported and near the surface of the earth falls, we can show a counter-example to this view if we can present one such object that does not fall. Such counter-examples are evidence against a theory—and, except in those situations in which the theory is still the best one around, one counter-example is usually enough to reject the theory.

The defender of psychological altruism can, as we have seen, make the theory consistent with the phenomena represented by the counter-examples. However, this is done only by employing ad hoc devices. Is there any reason to think that the person did think primarily or solely of others when he scratched his head or drank the water? There doesn't seem to be any, except the desire to make those instances of the phenomena consistent with the theory. It is only after such examples are presented that mechanisms such as unconscious desires or motives are brought in. If the psychological altruist claims that people have unconscious motives primarily or solely to benefit others, is there any reason (independent of trying to save the theory) for accepting such a claim? The answer seems to be no.

Therefore, psychological altruism does not seem to have very good reasons for acceptance. In fact, there are good reasons against psychological altruism; and it doesn't seem to be able adequately to respond to those criticisms without employing ad hoc devices. We, and the psychological egoist, are apparently justified in rejecting psychological altruism as an acceptable theory of motivation. Does this rejection, though, justify our acceptance of psychological egoism as a correct or even a better theory than psychological altruism? The answer to both parts of this question seems also to be no; but let us look at each part separately.

It is a general truth of logic that if a proposition is false, then its negation is true. The trick, though, is to select the correct statement as the negation. For example, the negation of the claim "If anything is human, then it is immortal" ("All humans are immortal") is "Some humans (for example, Socrates) are not immortal." The negation is *not* "If anything is human, then it is mortal" ("All humans are mortal"). The negation of the claim "If anything is a swan, then it is white" is "Some swans are not white" and not "If anything is a swan, then it is not white." Given that there are swans, it cannot be true that if anything is a swan, then it is white and also be true that if anything is a swan, then it is not white. However, from the falsity of one you cannot conclude the truth of the other—since, as is the case here, both statements can be false. There are some white swans; and there are some swans, in Australia, that are not white.

Psychological egoism and psychological altruism stand in relation to one another as do the two statements about swans. They both cannot be true, but they both can be false. Such statements, called *contraries,* do not allow you to conclude the truth of the one from the falsity of the other. Thus, even if we were to establish, as we apparently have, that psychological altruism is not correct, the correctness of psychological egoism does not follow. It may very well be that both theories are incorrect. For this latter reason we cannot conclude that psychological egoism is even a better theory than psychological altruism, for they may be equally bad in relation to a third and better theory.

3. Opposing views: psychological realism   The results of our discussion of psychological altruism should lead us to consider yet other theories. As was the case with the claims about swans, the truth, in terms of a theory of motivation, may lie somewhere in between the two theories we have considered thus far. It is true that some swans are white and some are not white but instead black. The corresponding theory with respect to motivation would be that some of our actions benefit ourselves and some benefit others. In addition, there may be motives that have nothing to do with benefiting ourselves or other persons at all. For example, we may be motivated to save certain animal species, to improve the wilderness, to love God, or to seek the truth; these are all phenomena, as much as any that concern benefiting ourselves or others. Because it allows for these other motivations, this third theory seems to do better than either egoism or altruism. However, this third theory, because it covers greater motivational possibilities, does not permit the simple explanations of the other theories. But since we are not considering these views as scientific theories, but rather as kinds of common-sense views that we formulate without doing formal empirical research, this is not much of a criticism.

Since we need a name for this third theory, let's call it *psychological realism*. This view, to repeat, does not pretend to do the job that psychologists want a theory of motivation to do. For the purpose of our discussion, however, this shortcoming is not so bad, for both psychological egoism and psychological altruism are equally weak—neither allows predictions, fruitful connections with other areas of science, and so on. All three of the theories are grossly deficient as scientific theories. So the fact that one of them is deficient from an empirical point of view is not sufficient reason to reject it and to accept one of the others.

The fact that we now have three theories to consider allows some comparisons that we could not carry out before. It has been argued that psychological altruism can be supported as well as psychological egoism. This is not to say that psychological altruism can be adequately supported, but rather that, however you assess the strength of psychological altruism, you should make the same assessment of psychological egoism. All the moves that the psychological egoists have open to them in defending their theory are open to the psychological altruists also. If the moves are effective in one case, they must be judged effective in the other. If, on the contrary, the moves are deficient in one area, then they must be judged equally deficient in the other. This allows us to suggest a scale of acceptability, as well as the place of both psychological altruism and egoism on it. Since psychological altruism is clearly recognized by us to be very close to the bottom of any scale, and psychological egoism is to be put in the same place, wherever that is, then it too is to be placed close to the bottom. Supposing that the scale is from 0 to 100, then we might indicate the placement of the theories considered so far as follows (PE stands for psychological egoism; PA, for psychological altruism; and PR, for psychological realism):

0	10	20	30	40	50	60	70	80	90	100
	PE									
	PA						PR			

The argument being presented can be put briefly as follows:

1. If two theories are equally placed on a scale of acceptability, and one of them is very low on that scale, then the other one is low on the scale of acceptability.
2. PE and PA are equally placed on a scale of acceptability, and PA is very low on that scale.

Therefore,
3. PE is very low on the scale of acceptability.

4. The end reached as a motive   Often one hears a defender of psychological egoism assert that whenever we do something such as turning off someone else's car lights in a parking lot, we gain satisfaction from it. Gaining this satisfaction, they claim, is the motive for performing the action. As usually presented, the evidence to support the claim that it was the satisfaction and not the benefit to the other person that motivated us is that we did indeed receive some satisfaction from our action. There are several points worth making about this set of claims.

First, it is not obvious that one always does gain satisfaction. In my own case, it seems false that when I turned off the lights I gained any satisfaction. Being as honest as I can, and reflecting as coolly as I can, I cannot say that I experienced any short-run or long-run phenomenon that can correctly be called satisfaction. This is not to say that introspection is the best method of determining one's motives, for I and others have been wrong in the past about motives introspected. It is to say, however, that someone who claims to know what my motives are in a given case, or generally, must come up with some reason to support that claim. By this time it should be clear that psychological egoism, the very theory to be supported by the argument we are now considering, cannot be used to support the claim that my motive was to secure my own satisfaction. The theory has not yet been established. In fact, we are considering this evidence precisely because we are attempting to establish this theory. Furthermore, if the theory had already been established, we wouldn't need the argument we are now considering.

Second, even if we suppose it to be true that every time someone performs a voluntary action they receive satisfaction, this would not, by itself,
establish that the motive in performing the action was to achieve that satisfaction. That action leads to many other states for me and for others—it
leads to a prevention of the unhappiness of the person whose lights were on;
it leads me to be about a half a minute later arriving at my office than
usual; it leads me to present the example to classes and then to write it
down here; and so on. Finally, every action leads indirectly to death.
What justifies the selection of only one of these ends and the claim
that it was *that* end which motivated me to perform the action? If the
only justification for that claim is psychological egoism, then the theory
cannot be supported by the argument, since the argument requires the
theory to support it.

Finally, every action leads to a large number of consequences for the
performer of the action as well as for the people and things upon whom and
which the action is performed. If the argument is any good, it establishes
that we are motivated to do whatever results from the action—whether we
had that consequence in mind or not. This would allow us to conclude that
expending energy is the motive for performing the action, that opening a
car door is the motive for performing the action, that pushing knobs is the
motive for performing the action, and so on. If one is justified in claiming
that satisfaction is the motive, then one is equally justified in claiming that
shutting a car door is the motive. Of course, one is not justified in the face-
tious claim that shutting a car door is the motive.

Often, when this kind of counter-argument is presented, the defender
of psychological egoism claims that our motive—to achieve satisfaction—is
unconscious, and that if we did not get satisfaction from this action, then
we would not perform it. However, whether the motives are unconscious or
not, there is no more reason to think we are motivated primarily to achieve
satisfaction for ourselves than primarily to achieve satisfaction for others.
This is just the kind of claim that the establishment of psychological
egoism as a correct theory would support. So it is difficult to see how the
claim can be used to support the theory. Also, there are other motives
alleged to move me to action—namely, the good of the other person. If
this is rejected as a motive, then some reason must be given for the rejection. The reason for the rejection could be that psychological egoism is the
best theory of motivation; but this has not yet been established. In fact,
this is precisely the task at hand for the psychological egoist, the one as yet
to be completed in any satisfactory way.

Summary   It has been shown in this section that if we use either nonempirical or not formally empirical methods (such as scientists use), we do not
seem to be able to establish psychological egoism as a correct theory of motivation. It does not compare favorably with at least one other such theory
of motivation—the theory here called psychological realism. There are, in
addition to the arguments and counter-arguments presented here, a large

number of other arguments you may want to examine.[3] Enough has been done, however, to show you the way such arguments move, as well as to prepare you to evaluate the next argument of this type you meet up with. Let us now turn to the empirical evidence for psychological egoism to see if the theory fares any better.

Exercises: Sharpening your critical skills
1. Present counter-examples to the following false claims.
   a. If anything is a human, then that thing is male.
   b. All women are mothers.
   c. If anything lives in the ocean and has a backbone, then it is a fish.
   d. If a proposition p is possibly true, then p is true.
   e. Whatever a person does immediately after deciding what to do is the explanation of that person's motive in acting.
2. Offer criticisms of the following arguments. What mistake is being made?
   a. Since the light was not green, it was red.
   b. This must be a triangle, since it is not a square.
   c. If students are not to be excluded from the University Senate, they must hold a majority of seats in that body.
3. There is no way to exhaust all the arguments that people present in favor of any view, especially a view that is as difficult to pin down as is psychological egoism. Present an argument, one that is different from any presented here, in support of the nonscientific version of psychological egoism, and critically evaluate it. (If you think it is a good argument, please send a copy of it to me so I can consider it in a later edition.)
4. What is wrong with the following claim? "Psychological egoism is correct, but not as stated. What is correct is that most of the time people are psychological egoists."

C.   Empirical psychological egoism

Remember that we are in the process of examining the evidence in support of psychological egoism. We are, as you recall, doing that because some people maintain that psychological egoism supports an ethical theory— namely, ethical egoism. They argue (with PE standing for psychological egoism and EE for ethical egoism) that:

If PE, then EE.
PE.
_____

Therefore,
EE.

We have examined the nonempirical evidence for psychological egoism and found that it offered no substantial support for that psychological theory of

[3] See the Recommended Reading at the end of this chapter.

motivation. Now we shall consider the kind of evidence that psychologists use in their work. We shall, in short, present a brief survey of the scientific evidence for and against this theory of motivation.

Psychologists and others in the social and behavioral sciences are frequently disturbed by what they take to be the intrusion of philosophers into an area in which they have no expertise. Everyone should rest assured that this author intends to do no more than report what psychologists have done. I do this not because psychologists are better at this kind of investigation than anyone else (although this is likely to be true), but because they are the ones who have in fact done the research.

A survey of the literature reveals a preponderance of experimental evidence in support of the claim that there are altruistic motives; that is, in the terms introduced so far, there are other motives for action than simply to increase one's own benefit. One of these motives, as indicated by the studies examined, is to increase the benefit of others. Since this is not a psychology book, this section will be brief; you should examine the literature identified in the list of recommended reading at the end of the chapter for greater detail.

Justin Aronfreed is a good person to begin with, for he develops clear distinctions between psychological and ethical egoism and also sets up understandable experiments. "When we say that an act displays altruism, we assert that the choice of the act, in preference to an alternative act, is at least partly determined by the actor's expectation of consequences which will benefit another person rather than himself."[4] However, Aronfreed also agrees that this fact, if it is one, is compatible with the act having some beneficial consequence for the actor. That is, he is not committed to the view that we earlier called psychological altruism. Aronfreed also specifies that there is a need for reinforcement of altruistic behavior. This requirement is the same as for any other kind of learned behavior, but it does not warrant the conclusion that the action is performed solely for the sake of the reinforcement. If you are inclined to think that reinforcement is the motivation, then you should see the section on nonempirical psychological egoism for a discussion of this point.

Aronfreed describes many experiments, but a fairly lengthy explanation of one will satisfy our needs. In this experiment, a group of 125 girls was divided into three groups, one containing 57 girls, one containing 37 girls, and one containing 31 girls; the girls in the largest group

> were exposed repeatedly to a very close temporal association between the agent's expressive cues of pleasure and their own direct experience of the agent's physical affection. Whenever the agent's choice between the levers activated the red light, the agent smiled while staring at the light, and at the same time uttered one of four exclamations in a pleased and excited voice. All of the exclamations were roughly

[4] Justin Aronfreed, *Conduct and Conscience,* Academic Press, New York, 1968, p. 138.

equivalent to *"There's the light!"* The agent then hugged the girl as if expressing a pleasurable reaction to the light. In the group of 57 there were hugs, in the 37 only the expression of pleasure and in 31 no response to the light.[5]

Next, each girl was given a choice of pulling a lever that would produce candy for herself or the red light for the agent.

The [child is] . . . in a situation where her empathetic and altruistic dispositions could be tested by her repeated choices between an act that produced candy for herself and an act that produced only observably pleasurable consequences for another person. . . . The majority of the children who had been exposed to the basic social conditioning paradigm actually chose to produce the light for the agent more frequently than they chose to produce candy for themselves; whereas children from both of the control groups typically chose the candy-producing lever more frequently.[6]

Aronfreed stresses the importance of empathy as a requirement for altruistic behavior. If the girls did not see the agent as having the kind of experience they had when they were pleased, then it is likely they would not have chosen to bring about what they thought pleased the agent. We are able to empathize readily with other people, and perhaps even with many types of animals. It is, however, more difficult to empathize with mosquitoes and amoebas.

Hopefully this experiment is clear. It indicates, says Aronfreed, that children sometimes act from altruistic motives. If this is true, then they don't always act from the motive of self-benefit. The girls always could have chosen candy for themselves, but on many occasions they did not. This voluntary action denies the claim of the psychological egoist that the only motive in voluntary action is self-benefit. As indicated in the bibliography and below, this denial results not from just one experiment, but from many experiments of the same type. This would indicate that psychological egoism, taken as a scientific theory of motivation, does not fare very well; the experimental evidence shows that the theory is not acceptable.

However, psychological egoists, whether of the empirical or nonempirical variety, will not accept this evidence as sufficient. They will say that the reward for each girl was the pleasure of the agent, that the alternative of getting the candy for herself would have produced less benefit (in the form of pleasure) than the action of activating the red light. This kind of move should be quite familiar, for it is just the move made earlier in the nonempirical discussion. On the one hand, it is certainly possible that the girls acted solely or primarily because they received pleasure from the fact that the agent received pleasure. On the other hand, it is possible they did

[5] *Ibid.,* p. 144.
[6] *Ibid.,* p. 145.

not, but instead acted to secure the benefit of the agent. In terms of possibilities alone, the two views are the same. However, in terms of what we observe in the experiment, there is at least some reason to suppose that the first possibility is not supported by the evidence. Moreover, the usual way of supporting the first possibility is to use psychological egoism as evidence. However, once again, psychological egoism is the view in question, so we cannot assume its correctness in the middle of the argument. Finally, those who work in the field give an interpretation of the results of the experiments that appears to be inconsistent with psychological egoism. This does not necessarily show that the experimenters are correct, for it would not be the first time that experimenters badly interpreted the experiments they constructed and carried out. The burden of proof, however, lies with those who make the claim that the experimenters are mistaken. Until such time that the experimenters are proven wrong, we would be justified in maintaining that they are correct and that altruistic motives do indeed exist.

In *Altruism and Helping Behavior,*[7] seventeen contributors discuss a variety of studies, from controlled laboratory experiments to the observation of people acting in noncontrolled environments. On the whole, these authors find that altruistic behavior, in the sense discussed here, does exist. Some of the authors allow the possibility of entirely egoistic explanations of the same phenomena, but they suggest that such explanations are implausible. Many of the authors find that a variety of motives direct altruistic actions. In a study on kidney donors, for example, the authors, Carl Fellner and John Marshall, suggest that the donors were motivated by:

(a) their belief in the "good" they were doing for the recipient, saving a life, (b) their positive relationship with their physician, both actual and symbolically, (c) the positive emotional reinforcement from the recipient and family, and (d) the considerable attention paid to them by friends, acquaintances, news media, etc.[8]

This pair of authors suggests that there are at least four different kinds of motivation. The first motive is most clearly identifiable as altruistic; and if any is egoistic, the last is the most likely candidate. Psychological egoists contend that all the motives are actually egoistic, even though they may not appear to be so at the time. However, once again, it is up to the psychological egoist to establish the truth of that claim. The burden of proof lies with the challenger.

Scientists working in this area sometimes take notice of the kind of moves mentioned here, but more often they do not. Sometimes, though, the language used by psychologists seems to be more applicable to the kinds of claims made here. Consider the following as an example:

[7] J. Macaulay and L. Berkowitz, eds., *Altruism and Helping Behavior,* Academic Press, New York, 1970.
   [8] *Ibid.,* p. 280.

A wealth of recent laboratory experiments on altruistic behavior clearly indicates that, under certain circumstances, people will help others who are in need, despite the absence of an externally administered reward for the altruistic person. We now find that people will actually learn an instrumental conditioned response, the sole reward for which is to deliver another human being from suffering.[9]

These authors are clearly saying that there are some solely altruistic actions, the motives involved apparently having to do only with rewards for other people. In case anyone doubts that these authors had philosophical positions in mind, the following passage should dispel any questions.

Classical political philosophers, such as Hobbes, Locke, Rousseau, and Comte, as well as their modern descendants, have found it essential to address themselves to the problems of selfishness and altruism in human nature. Ample psychological evidence is available to indicate that man is neither wholly selfish nor wholly altruistic in his behavior. It has not previously been demonstrated, however, that the roots of altruistic behavior are so deep that people not only help others, but find it rewarding as well. . . . Our research demonstrates that instrumental behavior can be learned and maintained solely through the rewarding function of altruism.[10]

Once again, a statement such as this from psychologists should not be expected to clear away empirical psychological egoism. Egoism's defenders will claim that the motive in performing the action is the reward or the pleasure received from seeing another person benefited. By now, however, the response to a statement like this should be clear to everyone.

Summary   This ends the presentation of empirical evidence. For more detail, you may want to follow up some of the items in the bibliography. This section, though, allows us to conclude that empirical evidence does not support psychological egoism. Furthermore, given that many psychologists agree that motives vary, what we have called psychological realism seems to be the most supportable theory. The nonempirical case for psychological egoism is discredited; and now, so is the empirical case.

Exercises: Theories of motivation
1. Choose some recent general work in psychology and read the entries under motivation in the index or table of contents. Does what is said address itself to the issue of psychological egoism? What is the position taken?
2. In the discussions of psychological egoism and altruism, nothing was said about motivation toward bad consequences for oneself or others. If we suppose bad conse-

[9] R. F. Weiss, W. Buchanan, L. Alsstatt, and J. P. Lombardo, "Altruism is Rewarding," *Science,* 171, 3977 (March 26, 1971), 1262.
[10]*Ibid.,* p. 1263. The authors will be relieved to hear that there are very few philosophers who follow any of the cited authors in their theory of motivation.

quences to be the polar opposite of good consequences, or benefit, then we can construct two additional principles of motivation:

> *Psychological masochism:* If any person *a* performs a voluntary action, then person *a*'s motive for performing that action is self-harm.

> *Psychological maltruism:* If any person *a* performs a voluntary action, then person *a*'s motive for performing that action is to harm others.

If we consider these two principles as each representing a theory of motivation, they can be evaluated in the same way as were the other theories considered. Present such an evaluation.

3. Argue either in favor of or against the following claim: "Psychological masochism and psychological maltruism each explain some phenomena. Those phenomena are not explained by psychological realism, and thus we have to adopt another theory of motivation or else fix up psychological realism." In part this exercise requires that you address the issue of whether or not human beings are sometimes motivated to do harm to themselves or to others.

4. Evaluate the truth of, and indicate the place of, the following proposed principle: "If something reinforces action, then that something is a motive of action." Is the principle acceptable? If it were acceptable, would it support psychological egoism more strongly than psychological altruism?

D. Ethical egoism

Since the examination of psychological egoism is now complete, it is time to see if there is any relation between it and ethical egoism. Egoists usually claim that psychological egoism supports ethical egoism; and accordingly, the psychological view is presented first to provide the required support for the ethical theory. However, the ways in which the psychological theory support the ethical theory are not clear, partly because of the multiplicity of views that have gone under the title of ethical egoism. The first task is thus to state clearly what ethical egoism is, so we may then consider any relation of support between it and psychological egoism. This consideration is worthwhile for two reasons, even though the last section concluded that psychological egoism does not fare well as a theory of motivation. First, further evidence might very well change our views about psychological egoism. Second, when we see what kind of relation there is between the two kinds of egoism, we might not want to offer psychological egoism as a support for ethical egoism.

As stated at the beginning of this chapter, ethical egoism is schematically represented as follows:

1. If any person *a* performs an action that increases person *a*'s own good (benefit), then that action is right.
2. This particular action increases person *a*'s own good.

Therefore,
3. This particular action is right.

This representation, however, is not sufficiently general either to capture all the versions of ethical egoism or to represent a complete theory of obligation. A theory of obligation covers not just actions that are right, but also actions that are obligatory (duties), actions we have a right to do, actions that are morally better than others, actions that are morally worse than others, and so on. These different predicates represent different kinds of judgments about actions; and as such, they are some of the phenomena a theory of obligation will attempt to explain. To indicate that as broad a range of phenomena as possible should be explained by our ethical theory, we can say that we need to have a more complete ethical theory. If we let MO represent any term in our theory of obligation, including 'right' and 'obligatory', we can generate the following more general statement:

1. If any person a performs an action that increases person a's own good (benefit), then that action is MO.
2. This particular action (whatever it is) increases person a's own good (benefit).

Therefore,
3. This particular action of person a (whatever it is) is MO.

In keeping with the function of a theory of obligation, this general statement of the theory of ethical egoism allows us to arrive at justfied singular moral judgments (instances of statement 3). This is the main function of a normative theory of obligation; and a theory should be judged in terms of how well it performs this function.[11] Let us now explain some of the crucial terms in this general statement.

1. **'Increases'**   The statement establishes a distinction between an action that does in fact increase a person's own good and one that only seems to

---

[11] The most general scheme for an ethical theory is:

If any x is F, then that x is M.
This x is F.

Therefore,
This x is M.

The F is replaced with whatever the theory suggests as the appropriate nonmoral predicate, and the M is replaced with what is claimed to be the appropriate moral or value predicate. The actions of persons are referred to by x; F refers to the characteristics of those actions that increase the good of the people performing them; and M, to some term of obligation, such as 'right' or 'obligatory'. The logical terms 'if' and 'then' are never replaced. For those who demand a more symbol-laden general scheme, the following is offered:

$(x)\ (Fx \rightarrow Mx)$
Fa

$\therefore$ Ma

The first symbolized line captures the first statement of the general scheme.

that person to do so. It may seem to someone that it will be beneficial to take a shortcut across a field on the way home. However, if the person sinks into a quicksand pit, then it's obvious that the person made a mistake. We don't want to saddle anyone with the view, for example, that it is obligatory to do what merely appears to be of self-interest. If this were the case, it would be obligatory for the person to take the shortcut, to take the turn that leads into the quicksand, or, in the case of a student, to write in "none of the above" on a true/false exam, even when none of these actions is to the interest of the person—even when they are contrary to the person's interests. This is certainly one way to interpret ethical egoism; but since it results in such a weak position, it will not be interpreted that way here.

There is another reason to avoid interpreting the statement as claiming that what appears to be in your interest determines, say, obligations. The usual way of interpreting ethical egoism is as a *teleological view*—that is, as a theory that restricts the information in the antecedent of the first statement to consequences of actions. Specifically, for egoism, this means the consequences of an action insofar as they affect me. The problem with talking about what seems to be a consequence of an action is that a seeming consequence is often not an actual consequence; and moreover, no *seeming* consequence of an action is a consequence of that action at all.

A consequence of an action is something that occurs as a result of that action. For example, one usual consequence of drinking water, under normal circumstances, is that the water quenches your thirst. This occurs whether it seems to you, beforehand, that it will or not. The consequence is independent of what seems to you to be a consequence. What seems to you to be a consequence is not regularly related to an event in any causal way and can occur independently of any cause of that event. A seeming consequence is something that is true of a person; it seems *to Jones* that the water will kill her. If a seeming consequence is true of a person, and a consequence is true of the world, then we have good evidence that a seeming consequence (of an action) is not any kind of consequence (of the action) at all. If it is not, then we do not want to classify an ethical theory that concerns only seeming consequences as a teleological theory.

However, we do not want to say that the increase in benefit is limited only to what actually does occur independently of what the agent knows and has evidence for. There are many actions that have consequences a person does not know about and could not reasonably be expected to know about. Suppose, for example, you are walking along a beach and pass over a fortune in Spanish gold buried long ago by a pirate. If you had dug a hole at that place and recovered the gold, this would no doubt have been to your advantage, since, under most circumstances, the discovery would have benefited you greatly. However, we would not be justified in claiming that you failed to fulfill your obligations by passing by without digging, for there is no reasonable way that you could have known the gold was there. There are many actions that could be beneficial to you but that are not obligatory. The same kinds of examples could be generated for other moral predicates in theory of obligation. For example, suppose you step on a fly that, if it had lived, would have fatally bitten you. There is no obvious sense in which you have performed a morally right action.

It seems, therefore, that if we are to be fair to the egoist, we must find some position between the seeming interests and what in fact turn out to be the real interests of a person. One good candidate for such a middle ground is the set of actions likely to lead to beneficial consequences for you, given what you know. Each of us is in possession of a certain amount of knowledge; and each of us has to act on what we know at that moment. (Keep in mind that you may want to restrict our knowledge to those items we are justified in accepting at a given time, given the evidence on hand. Nothing fancy is meant by 'knowledge'.) The egoist's claim, for example, is that obligatory actions are those actions likely to benefit the person, given the knowledge available to that person. So the general statement's reference to 'increasing the benefit' will be understood in this manner, and not as referring either to what the person merely believes will increase his interest or to what in fact will increase the person's interests.

2. 'Good' or 'benefit'   Once again, the terms 'good' and 'benefit' will not be further specified. What is to your benefit may be restricted to power, or it may include pleasure as well as power, or only pleasure, or these plus freedom, and so on. You may, for the time, plug in whatever you suppose is of value or whatever you suppose does benefit you. Later on, in chapter 6, we shall examine theories of value and draw some specific conclusions about what is good.

3. MO   In the consequent of the general statement of ethical egoism, MO is only a partially specified term, since it refers to some predicate or other in the area of theory of obligation. There are a number of terms that can replace MO and mean quite different things. To claim that one has a right to express whatever opinions one wishes is far different from saying that it is right to express whatever opinions one wishes. You no doubt have the right to claim that milk tastes best when chocolate syrup is added, but you are not ordinarily doing something morally right when you express this opinion. You have the right to drink milk with scotch whiskey and chocolate syrup, but this does not turn the action into one that is right. Each person has the right to get up at night to get a drink of water, but this is not usually an action that is right. In general, different roles are played by different predicates of moral obligation.

Even though different roles are played, this does not preclude significant relationships among such predicates. There have been many attempts to define all the moral predicates of obligation via one that is taken as a *primitive*. This is a common phenomenon in all areas. Of course, such definitional theories must be seen as attempts to provide a simpler theory of the relation of moral predicates to one another and should be evaluated accordingly.

Our purposes now will be served by noting two things: first, some predicates cannot serve as the primitive for defining all others; and second, insofar as an ethical theory cannot allow for the use of a predicate or predicates, that theory is deficient—especially if there are other theories that can account for the applications of those predicates. One predicate that apparently cannot be used to define all the other predicates is 'right to'. However, there is a way of defining this predicate in terms of 'obligation' that enables us better to understand both predicates.

> Person a has a right to do action B[12] =df Person a has no obligation not to do action B.

Supposing that we understand, for the moment, roughly what we mean when we talk about obligations, the above definition does help. To say that person a has a right to take a drink of water in the middle of the night is equivalent to claiming that he or she has no obligation not to take such a drink. If I don't have a right to cut off the head of the person in front of me at a movie so that I can see better, then I have an obligation not to do so. If you have a right not to attend a Prohibition Party lecture, then you don't have an obligation to do so. If a mother has no right not to buy food for her children, then she has an obligation to buy the food for them. These four examples expand the definition and exhaust the possible combinations. More abstractly, the combinations are as follows:

> right to =df no obligation not to
> no right to =df obligation not to
> right not to =df no obligation to
> no right not to =df obligation to

This is one way to show that 'obligation' and 'right to' can be interdefined. It would not matter which of the notions we took to be primitive in terms of generating out the other. However, neither of these notions can be used to define the notion of *right action*. A simple proof of this consists of presenting some right actions that are neither obligatory to do nor obligatory not to do. Consider the class of actions that, as it is said infor-

---

[12] There are a number of different moral notions that go under the heading of *rights*. If the claim is that a person has a right to scratch his or her head, this is one sense of the term, the one we shall concentrate on in this section. However, when we claim a right to free speech, this is not the same sense of 'right to'. Here we mean that if anyone prevents us from speaking, they are doing what is wrong; whereas in the other use of 'right to', interference is sometimes acceptable and sometimes not. I have a right to win the race, but all my competitors have a right to win the race also. The competitors are not violating obligations or being immoral if they win.

Moral rights that require others to act or to forbear are, in a sense, stronger than the ones that do not. The former involve *right action* or *obligation.* It will be assumed that those alternative terms can be used in place of 'right to', and this procedure will be used to prevent confusion.

mally, are over and above the call of duty (or obligation). (In more formal language such actions are called *supererogatory*.) The soldier who throws himself on a grenade in order to save the others sharing his foxhole is doing something that has positive moral worth. It is an action that is apparently right; but it is not apparently obligatory. If the soldier scrambled out of the foxhole instead of throwing himself on the grenade, this would not justify a claim that he had failed to fulfill an obligation, for he does not have an obligation to sacrifice himself for his soldier colleagues. This example shows that a definition (df) of the following sort is mistaken because it does not adequately take into account all phenomena.

Person *a*'s action B is right =df Person *a* has an obligation to do B.

This proposed definition is not acceptable because supererogatory actions do exist. When you stop to help someone who has a flat tire, open a door for someone whose arms are full, go out with someone who is lonely, or turn off someone's car lights, your actions are right; but they are not, apparently, obligatory. The name may be fancy, but actions of this sort are familiar to us all.

There is another kind of counter-example that purports to point out obligatory actions that are not right. Suppose you agree to meet someone at the Empty Wallet restaurant at 8 P.M., and you're there on time. Here, it seems, a kind of low-level obligation has been fulfilled; and yet the action doesn't have enough positive value for it to be called morally right. When you fulfill what we might call your ordinary obligations, there is no reason as yet to call such actions right. It may be that if you fail to meet your obligations, you are doing what is wrong; but it does not follow from there that if you do meet your obligations, you are doing what is right. This can be captured, again more formally, as follows.

1. If person *a* is obliged to do B, then not doing B is wrong.
2. It is not true that if person *a* does B and B is obligatory, then person *a*'s doing B is right.

These examples are included here to show that there is no way to derive the rightness of an action from its being obligatory, even if it is true that not to act in this instance would be wrong.[13]

[13]One cannot define *right action* via the negation of *wrong action*. A proposed, but incorrect, definition of that sort would be the following:

Person *a*'s action B is right =df Person *a*'s action B is not wrong.

There are, of course, numerous counter-examples to this. It is not wrong to tie your left shoelace before your right, but it is usually not morally right to do so. It is not wrong to put ketchup on pea pods and beef served with brown rice, but it is not morally right either. It is not wrong to take a deep breath of clean air when you walk in the woods, but it is not morally right to do so. There are, as everyone can easily see, many more examples of this sort.

If this line of reasoning is correct, then there is a whole area in theory of obligation that cannot be explained or accounted for by use of the notions of *right to* and *obligation*. Thus, as shall be argued later with respect to ethical egoism and its basis in psychological egoism, if a theory can only account for part of the phenomena, it is to that extent deficient. Furthermore, if there is another theory that can account for these "extra" phenomena, then the first theory is seen to be yet more deficient and most likely unacceptable.

Summary   A brief summary at this point might be helpful. There are a variety of notions in theory of obligation; some of these notions can be taken as basic and others can then be defined in terms of them. Some notions, though, cannot be used to define all the rest. One that cannot is *right to,* and another is *obligation*. It will be argued that the only version of ethical egoism that can be supported by psychological egoism is one that replaces MO with *right to.* This will show, in turn, that insofar as you hold ethical egoism because of psychological egoism, your ethical theory will be deficient. It is not an endorsement of psychological egoism to argue that it can support ethical egoism; it is only to say that *if* psychological egoism is correct, then one version of ethical egoism is correct.

Exercises: Definitions of moral notions
1. This section suggested that the consequences of actions be specified as the likely consequences, given what a person *a* knows. Contrast this view with the specification of consequences as "the consequences person *a* calculates will occur, given what person *a* knows."
2. Show what is wrong with the following proposed definitions of moral terms.
    a. wrong action = df a nonobligatory action
    b. obligatory action = df action we have a right to do
    c. right action = df action that is not wrong *and* that we have a right to do
3. Explain what 'wrong' means in the first line of exercise 2.

E.   The connection between psychological and ethical egoism

The usual strategy for the egoist is to attempt to establish psychological egoism and then to show that the psychological theory supports the ethical theory. In the most general form this strategy is represented as:

If PE, then EE.
PE.

_____

Therefore,
EE.

So far the second premise has been examined, and the conclusion is that psychological egoism is found wanting as a psychological theory of motivation. The first premise, the purported connection between the psychological and the ethical theory, is what we will now examine.

It was earlier shown that psychological egoism purports to have discovered the law of human motivation. Such a law would be a law of nature and, insofar as it is, any conclusions we can draw about other laws of nature apply to it. For example, it is often said that if someone is an unsupported body near the surface of the earth, they *must* fall, or it is *impossible* for them not to fall. Terms such as 'must', 'possible', 'impossible', 'can', 'may', and the like are *modals*. The sense of the modal and the justification for its use in such statements is almost always, if not always, dependent upon the corresponding law. In fact, the significance of the modal seems to be exhausted by referring to the appropriate law. When we say that a person must fall, we do not in such contexts suggest the person has a moral obligation to fall or that it would be prudent to fall. If a person loses his grip on a tree limb and falls, there is nothing the person can do either to stop the falling or to alter it in any significant way. It may be strange to use modals in connection with laws that describe the way the world is, but it is a common enough practice and does no harm as long as we continue to understand that natural laws *describe* the world and do not prescribe how it *ought* to be.

It has been argued that psychological egoism is not a correct theory. But if psychological egoism is correct, then people can no more refrain from acting in what they perceive to be their own interests than an unsupported body can refrain from falling.[14] This fact suggests the following argument in support of the "right to" version of ethical egoism:

Argument A
1. If psychological egoism is correct, then no one can ever do anything except act in his own interest.
2. Psychological egoism is correct.[15]

Therefore,
3. No one can ever do anything except act in his own interest.

Argument B
4. If (3) (that is, if no one can ever do anything except act in his own interest), then no one has an obligation to do anything not in his own interest.
5. (3). (No one can ever do anything except act in his own interest.)

Therefore,
6. No one has an obligation to do anything not in his own interest.

---

[14] You must supply the fuller context for the falling example. You are an unsupported body near the surface of the earth; so you aren't in orbit, you are not resting on a helium-filled balloon, and so on.
[15] Contrary to what has apparently been established.

Argument C

7. If (6) (that is, if no one has an obligation to do anything not in his own interest), then each of us has the right to do what is in our own interest.
8. (6). (No one has an obligation to do anything not in his own interest.)

Therefore,
9. Each of us has the right to do what is in our own interest.

This series of arguments may look imposing at first, but it is actually only three separate affirming-the-antecedent arguments. In each of the arguments after the first, the second premise—the one that affirms the antecedent—is the conclusion of the argument above it. (The numbers in parentheses indicate where the statement is to be located in the earlier argument so that you can find your way more easily.) The real difficulty, though, is not to present a *valid* argument but to present a *sound* argument, an argument that has true premises as well as being valid. You will be able to work through the preceding series of arguments and convince yourself of its validity in a relatively short time, but something has to be said about the truth of the premises.

The first premise, (1), claims that if the law presented by the psychological egoist is an actual law of nature, then, just as is true of any law of nature, things that fall under it *must* act in the way described. In this instance, people must act in their own interests.[16] That is, they can do nothing except act in their own interests. Premise (2) is the assertion that psychological egoism is the correct theory of motivation. This assertion is one that has been questioned; and in fact, it has been argued that psychological egoism is not at all acceptable. Premise (2), however, should not be taken as an affirmation of psychological egoism, but rather as an illustration that on the *assumption* of the correctness of psychological egoism one can establish one version of ethical egoism. The value of this is great, even though the argument can only be a hypothetical one based on the (mistaken) assumption that psychological egoism is correct.

In argument B the first premise, (4), uses the conclusion of argument A as the antecedent and, for the first time, introduces a term of obligation into the consequent. The justification for this premise is part of the "ought implies can" principle. Very simply put, if you are obliged to do something, then you must be able to do it. The complementary principle is that if you are obliged to do something, then you must be able to refrain from doing it. Some examples will help. If someone claims that you are obliged to be a champion swimmer, you can show that you are not so obliged by

---

[16] Remember, though, that the sense of 'interest' is not what might in fact turn out to be a person's interests, but the interests of the person, given the knowledge the person has.

presenting evidence indicating that you have a limited endurance. More clearly, you can show you are not obliged to save a drowning person by establishing that you can't swim. You cannot be obliged to love your neighbor as you love yourself if human nature does not allow this. The complementary principle involves essentially the same considerations. If you cannot stop your hair from growing, then you have no obligation. to stop it. Suppose you fall from the balcony of a theater and notice that you will land on a small child if you continue to fall. No one can accuse you of failing to meet your obligations when you do indeed land on the child, for you could do nothing other than fall in just that way.

The second premise of argument B is the conclusion of argument A. Its justification is that it is the conclusion of a valid deductive argument, even though, because of the second premise of argument A, that argument is not sound.

The third argument, argument C, contains the definitional connections between the notions of *obligation* and *right to* noted on page 62. The second premise of that argument is the conclusion of argument B.

The three arguments together constitute an argument showing how one can move from psychological egoism to ethical egoism—even if the ethical view is an incomplete one. And this is the main problem such a defense of ethical egoism has—namely, it results in a theory of obligation that leaves out all phenomena having to do with right and wrong actions. If this point has become obscured, then you should review section 3 in part D.

There is another criticism of this stance—that is, there are no positive obligations in the resulting theory. To get a positive obligation from a right to do something, you would need to establish that no one has a right not to do something (see the definitions in section 3). Do you have an obligation to feed your child? This could be established only if we could show that you have no right not to do so. However, this can't be done by showing that you can't do anything other than feed your child. This would show only that you have a right to feed the child, not that you have no right not to do so. Since the only thing one can show, given the strategy of using psychological egoism to support ethical egoism, is that one has a right to do something, then the whole area of phenomena involving positive obligations is left unexplained.

One can say, of course, that such phenomena as right and wrong actions, supererogatory actions (those above and beyond the call of duty), and positive obligations are all illusory. This may be so, but if it is, then one needs some positive evidence to support this claim. The need for positive evidence becomes very pressing indeed when there are other competing theories that can account for the phenomena and do themselves have some reasons in their favor. The desire for this kind of superiority has led egoists to adopt a broader version of ethical egoism—in fact, many different versions of ethical egoism have been suggested. Now that we have looked at how one version of ethical egoism may be supported by psychological egoism, we shall examine some other versions of ethical egoism independently of any support they might derive from psychological egoism.

F.   The most plausible versions of ethical egoism

There are a large number of possible views that could go under the title of ethical egoism, but we need examine only the most plausible versions, the ones people have been most inclined to hold. Hopefully, plausible versions and ones most commonly held are the same; but if there is a view not examined here that you think is more plausible, you will find here the mechanism whereby that view can be stated and evaluated.

It has been argued that egoism presents at least two different sets of moral notions, those having to do with obligations and rights and those having to do with right actions. The difference was established through a presentation of actions that are right but not obligatory, and vice versa. One clear way to proceed, then, is to establish these two areas of egoism as the minimum number that should be included in a theory of obligation.

> If any person *a* performs an action that increases person *a*'s own good (benefit), then that action is right.

> If any person *a* performs an action that increases person *a*'s own good (benefit) more than any other available action, then that action is obligatory.

In addition to the use of 'right' versus 'obligatory' in the preceding statements, another difference has been built in. Right actions are those likely to benefit you, given the knowledge you have. Accordingly, many actions in a given situation are right, but only one such action is obligatory. The obligatory action is the one most likely to maximize what benefits you, given the knowledge you have. By stating the difference in this way, we can incorporate both *right* and *obligation* into one egoistic theory and arrive at a more complete view.[17]

---

[17] There is a drawback. From certain points of view, this way of accounting for obligations seems deficient. A couple of examples will illustrate this. For example, when playing records, you may find that you would enjoy the music more if you turned up the volume a bit. If there are no decompensating factors, such as great inconvenience, in turning the volume up, then the preceding rules would suggest an obligation to do so. Obviously, no such obligation exists. Furthermore, how wide does the consideration of our interests have to be? Suppose it casually occurs to you as you read the paper that it is quite certain that the stockmarket will go up in the next few months and that auto stocks in particular are quite likely to go up. Are you then obliged to buy such stocks? More examples of this type later in the text.

Supposing that these two rules together represent a reasonable statement of ethical egoism, we still must take into account the distinction between direct moral rule theories and indirect or meta-moral rule theories. Recall that a direct moral rule allows the derivation of a singular moral judgment, whereas a meta-moral rule allows the derivation of a direct moral rule. Put into the general scheme, the rules concerning *right* for the two positions are contrasted as follows:

Direct moral rule ethical egoism
1. If any person *a* performs an action that increases person *a*'s own good (benefit), then that action is right.
2. This particular person *a* performs this particular action that increases person *a*'s own good.

Therefore,
3. This particular action is right.

Indirect or meta-moral rule ethical egoism
1. If any person *a* performs an action from a rule R that, when regularly acted from by person *a*, increases person *a*'s own good (benefit), then R is a direct moral rule of moral rightness.
2. This particular person performs an action from a rule R that, when regularly acted from by person *a*, increases person *a*'s own good (benefit).

Therefore,
3. R is a direct moral rule of moral rightness.

The preceding contrast is more easily understood in terms of examples. Suppose for a moment that ethical egoism is a correct ethical theory and that some person is faced with a decision about whether to lie about why he was late. The truth is that our friend, *a*, was engrossed in reading magazines at the drug store and forgot about his date with *b*, until, with a start, he came back to reality and saw that he would be an hour late. Should he tell *b* the truth, or should he tell her that he stopped to help an accident victim to the hospital? On the one hand, using direct moral rule ethical egoism he can conclude that lying would be right, for by lying he will avoid all the unpleasantness as well as the decline of his status in *b*'s eyes. On the other hand, if a person regularly acted on a rule R of the form "If you have broken a promise or not fulfilled an obligation to someone, then lie about what happened," it is not likely that he would thereby increase his own good. Such people are usually found out—usually sooner than later. This results in distrust and rejection of subsequent explanations, and leads, in turn, to all manner of damage to that person's interests—in ways that are obvious to all. Thus you could conclude that even though in a particular instance it might be to your advantage to lie, it is nevertheless not in your interest to adopt a rule to that effect. On the contrary, it is to your advantage to adopt a rule that requires truth-telling, for then the bad consequences will not come about. In their place will be the good consequences of an enhanced reputation, an increase in the likelihood of your attaining a respectable and secure place in society, and so on.

Someone might suggest that this distinction is really just the distinction between long-run and short-run interests. It might be in your short-run interest to lie, but not in your long-run interest. However, this is really not that distinction, for in certain cases you may be able to get away with lying, and thus, insofar as that individual action is concerned, it would be in your long-run interest to lie. However, it is not in your long-run interest to adopt such a policy when it is likely that you will be found out. In this sense, it is in your interest in the long run to be an indirect ethical egoist rather than a direct ethical egoist.

The ethical egoist will want to explain as much of the moral phenomena as possible, so we will want to allow for explaining wrong actions—those we have an obligation not to do. So far we have talked only about actions that are right and actions that are obligatory. It is relatively easy though, to provide the principles that cover negative notions once we understand that *right* and *wrong,* for example, are contrary notions. The principles concerning right and wrong actions would appear as follows:

If any person *a* performs an action that increases person *a*'s own good (benefit), then that action is right.

If any person *a* performs an action that decreases person *a*'s own good (benefit), then that action is wrong.

There are interesting and important questions about the relationship between a decrease of benefit and a concept of *positive disbenefit,* but such questions need not be answered to understand these relations. Similarly, the principles concerning obligation and obligation not to perform some action would appear as follows:

If any person *a* performs an action that increases person *a*'s own good (benefit) more than any other available action, then that action is obligatory.

If any person *a* performs an action that decreases person *a*'s own good (benefit) more than any other available action, then that action is obligatory not to do.

In spite of the number of different notions and the different-looking principles in which they occur, only one kind of consideration is really involved in these principles—self-benefit. Since this is so, we shall say that the ethical egoist has only one principle, although perhaps a more precise statement would be that there is only the one source of obligation, right, wrong, and so on. In the text we shall concentrate on only one or two of the notions on the assumption that the same kinds of things would apply to the others in an appropriately modified form.

Summary   Ethical egoism seems to require at least two different rules, one having to do with *obligation* and its related notions and the other having to do with *right* and its related notions. At least two kinds of positions can be generated after we have interpreted all the variable and unclear parts of the statement—namely, the direct and the indirect (meta-moral) rule versions. An apparent but unstated assumption is that the various forms of egoism are rule theories; rules are required, it seems, to justify the singular moral judgments that fall under them.

G. Ethical egoism evaluated

Now that the main positions are before us, let us evaluate them by use of the criteria of acceptability. We cannot use psychological egoism as a support for ethical egoism because psychological egoism does not fare well as a theory of motivation. Thus we must look elsewhere for support. It is apparently true that there are at least some actions that are right because they increase our own interests. Insofar as there are such phenomena and the theory before us accounts for them in a direct manner, we have some evidence in favor of that theory. Admittedly, this does not constitute a great deal of evidence, especially if the theory cannot account for certain phenomena and other theories can. This seems to be the position so far of the two versions of ethical egoism previously laid out.

In the following, I will present and evaluate some of the standard criticisms of ethical egoism, doing my best to avoid ad hoc assumptions, and avoiding any examination of competitors. If some of the criticisms do not apply to both the direct and the indirect versions, then I will make that very clear.

1. Other people   What about other people? This question results in a series of puzzles that egoists must face and a series of questions they have great difficulty in answering. Is it true that other people should, if they want to hold the correct ethical theory, hold one of the versions of ethical egoism? The answer to this question must be "yes" for the following reasons. If the theory were true for only one person, then it would scarcely recommend itself as a theory covering all or a significant part of moral phenomena. Moral phenomena extend backward in time and across the whole planet, wherever and whenever there have been human beings. In the face of this, it is an odd suggestion, to say the least, that the only phenomena worth explaining are those concerning one person. This would be the same as saying that there is a correct theory of motivation—perhaps psychological egoism—but that it applies only to one person. Such a theory would fare very poorly when compared with other theories possessing a range wider than just one person.

Furthermore, if you are *the* person, you would have to explain why other people are excluded. Suppose your neighbor also adopts ethical egoism and then claims you have chosen the wrong person—it should be him instead of you. There seems to be no more reason why you should be the person rather than he. It is probably an entirely arbitrary choice on your part, with nothing to justify such a limit.

This would lead the ethical egoist to agree that the first statement in the general scheme should be read as it is written, 'If *any* person *a* . . .'. We have, therefore, a moral standard for *all* human beings. Only in this way can the ethical egoist present a theory that will even be in the running when a final decision is made as to which of the competing theories is best. In this form, the theory is more reasonable; but now, other problems arise.

One such problem concerns actions that advance the interests of one person at the expense of the interests of another. Suppose, for example, that a race is to be run in which only one person can win. It is in the interest of person *a* to win; and thus, the winning of the race by person *b* is not right. However, since the theory is equally accessible to person *b* he can say the same thing. Thus, the winning of the race by person *b* is right, and person *a*'s winning is not right. This allows us to conclude that the same action, for example, person *a*'s winning the race (coming in first), is both right and not right. Now, a situation such as this is an extreme embarrassment to a theorist and cannot be allowed to stand. If this situation isn't remedied, the theory will never rank very high among ethical theories. Ethical egoists have attempted to respond to this criticism in a variety of ways. One common response is to say that it is true for person *a* that his winning the race is right but that it is also true for person *b* that *his* winning the race is right. This response, though apparently clear, is ambiguous between the following two different claims.

1. Person *a* accepts (believes) that his winning the race is right (as does person *b* for himself).
2. Ethical egoism is a correct ethical theory when it applies to person *a* but not correct when it applies to anyone else.

Let us consider the first response. Earlier, in chapter 1, the notion of *acceptance,* or *belief,* was discussed in connection with *knowledge* and *truth.* It was argued there that neither acceptance and truth nor acceptance and knowledge can be equated because there are many items that people accept that are not true and many they accept that they are not warranted in accepting. You may accept that Calcutta is the capital of India, but you would be mistaken. It is not true that Calcutta is the capital of India nor can anyone justifiably claim to know that it is.[18] If someone claims to accept ethical egoism, he or she can be saved from a contradiction in the following way.

When person *a* claims that the action is right, he is saying only that he accepts that it is right, and person *b* is making the same kind of claim. It can be true of both persons *a* and *b* that they each accept different propositions:

1. Person *a* accepts that his winning the race is right and that person *b*'s winning the race is not right.
2. Person *b* accepts that his winning the race is right and that person *a*'s winning the race is not right.

These two statements can both be true, for now their truth is dependent on what the people accept as true and not what really is true.

To see this more clearly, consider two other claims that persons *a* and *b* might disagree about:

1. Person *a* accepts that the earth is a sphere.
2. Person *b* accepts that the earth is pie shaped.

Both these claims can be true as long as they are what persons *a* and *b* really do accept. This can be discovered by administering a lie detector test, or by some other appropriate means. One thing, though, that would not be relevant would be to establish whether or not the earth is a sphere. This fact is totally irrelevant to the truth or falsity of either of the two preceding statements.

The two claims are not part of a theory about the shape of the earth; they are about the mental states of people. In a similar manner, acceptance claims about morality are themselves not part of an ethical theory.[19] In terms of this model, the interpretation of ethical egoism results in something that is not primarily an ethical theory.

Furthermore, if we persist, claiming that all an ethical theory does is tell us what we accept, it would be difficult to explain why any such theory is needed and what light it sheds on any of the moral phenomena. Such a

---

[18] Some circumstances exist under which you could conceivably be justified in making such a knowledge claim, but such occurrences are very rare indeed. You may have purchased a defective world atlas or have been told that Calcutta was the capital of India by a drunk geography teacher. However, these occasions are rare; and even in these cases, the proposition is not true.

[19] Of course, this is not to say that theories about the shape of the earth and ethical theories are the same in any essential respect. They may or may not be the same, but that need not be discussed here. Beliefs are something theories may have to explain, but they are not part of a theory's statement or any part of its working apparatus. Comparisons of different kinds of theories with ethical theories will be made later on, but not here.

theory cannot help us arrive at any justified singular moral judgments, for there are apparently no such things. There are only the judgments we accept. Thus there can be no actual disputes between people. Once it is pointed out that each person is merely calling attention to what he or she believes when making a moral judgment, then each person can agree that the discussion is over. While this may indeed be the situation, it does not appear to be the case. Anyone maintaining that it is the case must provide us with some reasons, independent of the theory, to support the claim.[20] Such a theory appears to provide us with little or no explanation of the phenomena; and in the absence of any reasons to accept it, we would be foolish to do so. Finally, there are some judgments that people make (and accept) that apparently are not correct. Therefore, contrary to the theory, judgments do exist in addition to those merely accepted by a person.

For example, Hitler accepted that he was doing what was morally acceptable, if not right, when he killed six million Jews and Slavs in World War II. The same is true of at least some of the National Guard troops at Kent State University when they shot at the students there. This is especially true of many slave owners in the United States in the seventeenth, eighteenth, and part of the nineteenth century. What seems to be true is that such people were *mistaken,* not merely that they and we had different beliefs.[21] The fact that we can argue with such people and provide support for our own views supports this interpretation to some degree. Later, in chapter 7, we shall examine the question of what kind of support moral judgments can have; for now, we can report that they seem to have some kind of support and that this apparent support is one of the phenomena to explain. A theory that simply rejects a whole range of phenomena without any reason is in trouble.

This brief discussion raises a whole range of questions, such as "Who is to say which person is correct when moral judgments differ?" and "How can I tell if I am correct?" These are the very questions with which we began our substantive discussion, and they are a few of the questions that an ethical theory is supposed to handle. The fact that they naturally arise here is not surprising. But their appearance does not mean that there is not an answer. There may be no answer, and perhaps we shall wind up holding a theory similar to the one being examined. But such a choice should be made only when all other major theories have been examined and found not to be as good as this one. Until that happens, we can tentatively say that this theory doesn't seem to be a very good one.

Finally, to end the discussion of 'true for me' interpreted as acceptance, consider what an individual might mean by the claim, "I am an ethical egoist." Sometimes a person making such a claim means that he or

---

[20] Much later, in chapter 7, such a theory will be examined at greater length. In reality, it is a theory in meta-ethics and will be discussed further in that context.

[21] Remember, though, that what *seems* to be so is not *always* so. We may finally conclude that there are no moral disputes in this sense, and something like ethical egoism is correct.

she accepts some version of psychological egoism; and, as we know, it takes a while to straighten that out. However, if you have made it this far, you can do that for yourself or your friends without any great difficulty. Sometimes, however, the person claiming to be an ethical egoist may mean that she or he always tries to act in such a way as to maximize self-interest. This is an interesting claim for someone to make, but what is gained by making it is not clear. No psychological or ethical theory is supported by it or related to it in any understandable way. If someone makes this claim, you can simply point out his or her many actions that are not directed primarily toward self-interest. All of us have opened doors for strangers whose arms were loaded with packages, given directions to people we never expected to see again, and so on. Of course, anyone who makes this kind of claim will reject these as counter-examples, but the rejection is usually made on the basis of some general theory of motivation. Which one do you suppose is likely to be used?

A person who claims to be an ethical egoist may express a great determination to stick to that point of view, or a firm belief that it is a correct ethical theory no matter what. In either case, the claimant must come forward with a defense of his or her theory, especially in relation to other theories. What we must do, as scrutinizers of ethical theories, is examine the kind of defense the person presents. If no defense is forthcoming, the person must be placed with that group of people who maintain a view regardless of how good or bad it is and regardless of how good or bad rival views are. These are difficult people to deal with in any area, so no special problem is posed in moral philosophy by their existence. However a geologist would appropriately treat such people when they stubbornly hold a geological theory is the appropriate way to treat them when they stand by their theory in moral philosophy.

Let us now consider the interpretation of 'true for' as an attempt to escape inconsistencies—namely, that ethical egoism is a correct ethical theory when it applies to person a but not correct when it applies to anyone else. This claim, if substantiated, would allow us to escape an inconsistency, for it would show that person $b,$ for example, is mistaken when he claims that his winning the race is right. Only person a is correct in making this claim. So while it is right for person a to win the race, it is not right for person b to win. Thus we have avoided a situation in which it is both right and not right for person a to win the race.

There are several problems with this interpretation; but since such mistakes are by now familiar, they will be covered quickly. First, it is difficult to see how person a or any other person could justify choosing himself as the only person whose interest has to be taken into account. Without such a justification, the choice appears arbitrary and capricious. If all others are equally justified, then the original problem of an inconsistency reappears. Second, interpreted in this way, the theory becomes very narrow, covering only a small part of the total area a theory can cover. It would leave out all the phenomena involving relations among people other than person $a.$ It would, for example, provide no basis for judging that if person *b* tortures person *c* for no reason, that such an action is not right. It would make it impossible to make judgments about events that occurred before person *a* was born; and after person *a* dies, so will all of morality.[22] At this point you should be able to supply additional criticisms that will add to the evidence discrediting this interpretation.

To summarize this section, the various senses of 'true for' arose in the context of wondering how the ethical egoist would handle other people. In allowing everyone to use the theory as correct, we found ourselves accepting inconsistent claims. To get out of this difficulty, we introduced the expression 'true for'. However, this expression does not seem to be able to save the day; the criticism generated by the problem of other people (justifiably) using the theory remains. This criticism, in brief, poses a dilemma. If the theory applies to all people, then apparently inconsistent judgments are equally justified. If the theory applies to only one person, then it is woefully incomplete, and the choice of the person who gets to use the theory cannot be justified. Such arguments are complex because the various interpretations of key notions have to be taken up. If you got lost the first time through, you may wish to go through again, now that you have the overall strategy in mind.

2. Counter-examples   Counter-examples are examples drawn from the phenomena that go counter to a general claim. The general claim "If anything flies, then it is a bird" can be shown to be false by the justified claim "This thing flies, and this thing is a bat." The general claim "If anything is a human, then it is male" can be refuted by showing that "Elizabeth is human, and Elizabeth is female." What we shall be looking for are counter-examples to one or more of the direct moral rules or the indirect or meta-moral rules that the egoist maintains are part of the correct ethical theory. Let us consider first the direct moral rule version.

> If any person *a* performs an action that increases person *a*'s own good (benefit), then that action is right.

> If any person *a* performs an action that increases person *a*'s own good (benefit) more than any other available action, then that action is obligatory.

Let us consider the rule concerning *right* first. The United States endorsed the institution of human slavery from its inception until 1865. Before the United States was founded as a country, slavery was permitted in

---

[22] As usual, there is always a possible response. Person *a* could say that such actions are wrong because they make him feel bad when he hears about them (or some such move). However, no doubt you can handle such ad hoc moves at this stage.

the colonies for about 150 years. There were hundreds of thousands of slave owners and millions of slaves during that time. Some of these slave owners, no doubt, did not do very well as managers of plantations, factories, or other businesses in which their slaves worked. Others, though, did very well indeed, living a life of luxury and enjoying the best and tastiest fruits available. Not only did they live well and prosper, but many families did so for generations. The reference group for our counter-examples will be that considerable group of slave owners who lived very well indeed, became respected members of their communities, and died still being honored by their fellow citizens. There is little question that the activity of keeping slaves was to their interest. This enables us to state the following counter-example(s).

> This person *a* (and thousands like him) performed the action of keeping slaves, which increased person *a*'s own good (benefit), and that action is not right.

If this claim is accepted, then we have a strong reason for thinking that the egoistic rule concerning *right* is not acceptable. Notice that it is not just one case that is being relied on, for then the force of the counter-example would not be nearly so great. In addition, there are many counter-examples involving different kinds of actions and additional millions of persons. It is to the interest of generals, usually, that they wage war, but war is not usually right. It is to the interest of the pimp that he solicit for his prostitute, but in a large percentage of such cases it is not right. It is to the interest of the seducer who is not at all interested in his or her sex partner as a person to practice the art of seduction, but it is not usually right. You can join in at this point and add many more such counter-examples.

The counter-examples, if they are effective, are strong evidence against the acceptance of direct rule ethical egoism. As presented, the proposed counter-examples address themselves to the rightness of actions, but the same counter-examples apparently apply to the "ought" rule also. It is not obligatory for the slave owner to keep slaves, even though it may be, given the alternatives available to him at the time, the one that would maximize his interests. If the action is not right, then it would appear that it is not obligatory. In this instance, to make the point even stronger, it appears obligatory not to keep slaves. The same kinds of comments apply to the other proposed counter-examples. Once again, you are advised to construct your own counter-examples so as to begin actively to do philosophy.

Egoists will deny the validity of the proposed counter-examples. They will want to claim that such apparent counter-examples are not counter-examples at all. Indeed, one expects that a certain number of proposed counter-examples will turn out not to be counter-examples. However, the responses to your counter-examples must be to the point; they cannot simply assume the correctness of the theory and then dismiss the counter-examples because they are not compatible with the theory. If the proposed counter-examples were not incompatible with the theory, they couldn't be used as counter-examples. As a reminder, if this procedure could be used freely, then any theory whatsoever could be "defended." Someone might claim, for example, that all humans are male. When we present Elizabeth as a proposed counter-example, that person could claim that Elizabeth cannot be a human being because she is not a male. Given the correctness of the theory "If anyone is human, then that person is male," such a response would indeed be perfectly plausible and effective. However, when we are examining whether or not such a view is correct, the view itself cannot be brought into play to counter a proposed criticism. If this were permissible, then any theory could be shown to be immune to criticism.

So, if the ethical egoist wishes to show that the proposed counter-examples are not actually counter-examples, something positive must be done, independent of the theory. Failing this, the egoist should admit the counter-examples as powerful criticisms of the theory. There is no time limit on responses to criticisms, so we cannot say the counter-examples are absolute, indisputable proof that egoism is incorrect. This is especially true if all the other theories we shall consider do a worse job than egoism in responding to such criticisms.

Finally, you are reminded that counter-examples are drawn from the phenomena. They are not God-given, intuitive, final truths that we must all accept. They are, instead, simply those items that appear to be facts when we begin our investigation. We should all be prepared to give up any one phenomenon that can be shown to be unreasonable, given other things we know. The other side of that is that we would be foolish to give up something as part of the phenomena simply because it is inconsistent with an unestablished theory.

Do the kinds of counter-examples proposed apply to the indirect rule theories as well as to the direct rule theories? If they do, then we are saved a great deal of time and trouble in our evaluation. And it does seem that with a small amount of modification the same examples can be used. Consider the rule a slave owner might adopt for himself: "If buying and keeping slaves will make me rich and a respected member of the community, then it is right." In many parts of the United States in the eighteenth century, this rule, if acted from, would have significantly benefited the actor. Recall that one of the indirect rules of such a version of ethical egoism is the following:

> If any person a performs an action from a rule R that, when regularly acted from by person a, increases person a's own good (benefit), then R is a direct moral rule of moral rightness.

The rule proposed above that the slave holder can adopt and act from seems to fit the indirect or meta-moral rule. On these grounds, it is a direct

moral rule. However, as was established, it is not acceptable as a direct
moral rule of moral rightness.[23] What it means to say that it is not acceptable, once again, is that there are a significant number of counter-examples
that can be directed against it. To remind you once more, the means of
response of the egoist cannot be to point out that the proposed counter-examples are not consistent with the theory and must, for that reason alone,
be rejected. If the counter-examples are not to be accepted—if they are to
be rejected—then some reason on the part of the egoist must be given.

3. Too wide a theory   The two kinds of egoist theory, the direct and the
indirect or meta-moral rule versions, apparently allow all manner of actions
to be called right or obligatory that are not. Simply put, the theory seems
to turn every prudent action into a right action, and the most prudent action into an obligation. This point, as with most others, is best understood
via actual examples. It will most likely benefit each of us if we continue to
breathe; and yet, that does not seem to be an action that is morally right.
However, using the direct moral rule version of ethical egoism, that action
is right. This kind of counter-example can be multiplied by instances that
each of us can supply. For example, it will benefit most people if they keep
both eyes open when they walk down the street, if they don't eat too fast, if
they look to the right and to the left before they cross the street, if they
have health insurance, if they determine fairly accurately the balance in
their checking account, and so on. In most circumstances, though, these
actions are not morally right. The same kinds of examples can easily be
generated with respect to *obligation*.

The earlier counter-examples show that apparently wrong actions exist
that, in terms of the theory, would be called right. The preceding examples
illustrate some morally neutral actions that, in terms of the theory, would
be called right. To achieve a kind of completeness you may want to find a
class of apparently right (or obligatory) actions that, in terms of the theory,
would be classified as morally neutral or wrong. To do this you might want
to examine common courtesy. We have some obligation, it would seem, to
treat others in a courteous manner and not to cause them needless suffering.
If treating someone this way would not likely lead to some benefit for ourselves, then according to ethical egoism this kind of action would either be
morally neutral or wrong (if it actually led to some decrease in benefit to
ourselves). At this stage, since evidence has piled up against ethical
egoism, this exercise can be left to those who have a special interest in
counter-examples of this type.

[23] An alternative way of putting this discussion would have been in terms of
correct direct moral rules. This was not chosen as the best way to phrase the
problem, for it would make for a more awkward discussion. However, nothing
would be lost if that mode of presentation were used.

H. A summary of egoism

The discussion of egoism requires a distinction between the psychological view—psychological egoism—and the ethical theory. The psychological theory is thought to support the ethical theory, although the method of support beyond the following general scheme is difficult to determine:

> If psychological egoism is correct, then ethical egoism is correct.
> Psychological egoism is correct.
> _____
> Therefore,
> Ethical egoism is correct.

> If PE, then EE.
> PE.
> _____
> Therefore,
> EE.

The first task was to state, as clearly as possible, the psychological theory. Next, the two different kinds of proposed support for it, the nonempirical and the empirical, were examined. It was found that the nonempirical support is not adequate; that at least one other theory is better supported, psychological realism; and that at least one other theory was as well supported, psychological altruism. The theory of psychological altruism was found unacceptable; and if psychological egoism is no better a theory of motivation than psychological altruism, then it is not acceptable either. The empirical evidence available does not support psychological egoism. Experimental evidence exists that illustrates nonegoistic or altruistic primary motives in human beings, even though it may be true that no one would come to have altruistic motives if they were not rewarded for so acting.

Even though psychological egoism was found wanting as a theory of motivation, the relation of support between that psychological theory and ethical egoism was explored. A connection was found between psychological egoism and the part of theory of obligation that deals with the notions of *right to* and *obligation*. This connection does little good for the ethical egoist, though, for the psychological theory is apparently not justified, and the ethical theory supported by it is not a complete theory.

The examination of ethical egoism completed the chapter. First, that view was more carefully described and explained. It was pointed out that there would have to be at least two sets of rules, one having to do with *right to* and *obligation,* and the other with *right* and its attendant notions. There is also a difference between an egoistic theory that applies its rules directly to actions and situations—direct rule egoism—and one that applies its rules to other rules—indirect or meta-moral ethical egoism. Three broad types of criticism were levied, one arising from the problem of other people, one having to do with counter-examples, and one stemming from the egoist's apparent inability to distinguish between prudence and morality.

In response to many of the criticisms, especially the counter-examples, the temptation will be to claim that the counter-examples work only because we have restricted the interests we are considering to just one person. If, instead of considering just the interests of the slave owner, we had included the interests of the slaves as well, it might be suggested, then the counter-examples would not work. When we consider the sorry state of the slaves, then we see that, overall, the interests of everyone are not furthered by slavery. This may be, but if we were to extend the range of consequences to include everyone, then we should have given up egoism in favor of another teleological view—namely, utilitarianism. This is a natural move for people to make when egoism appears deficient. These people still want to maintain that consequences—and only consequences—are what counts, and yet they want to consider the consequences for everyone. In a very rough way, that is the statement of utilitarianism. To get a more precise statement and to evaluate that position, let us next turn our attention to that ethical theory.

Exercises: Practice in critical analysis

1. "If an action is not right, then it is not obligatory" ("If an action is obligatory, then it is right"). Present considerations for or against the truth of this claim, in either of the forms presented.

2. One difficult matter is learning how to expose inadequate responses to criticisms, and especially inadequate responses to proposed counter-examples. Show what is wrong with the responses to the proposed counter-examples in the following.

   a. *View:* If I accept an action as right, then that action is right.
   Proposed counter-example: The action of my rescuing a child from a fire was right, and you did not learn about it until much later.
   Response: It was right then only because I was going to accept it as right later.

   b. *View:* If any person is a woman, then that person is a mother.
   Proposed counter-example: Martha Graham is a woman, but she is not a mother.
   Response: Martha Graham is not really a woman because she is not a mother.

   c. *View:* If any book is more than 500 pages long, then it is worthless.
   Proposed counter-example: The Columbus, Ohio, telephone book is useful, and it has more than 1000 pages.
   Response: The telephone book is useful, but it is actually a large number of different books: one consists of all the listings under 'A'; one consists of all the listings under 'B'; and so on. None of these books is more than 500 pages long.

3. Each of the following theories proposes exactly one direct rule of obligation. Criticize them.

   a. If any action consists of reducing disease (directly or indirectly), then that action is right.

   b. If any action maximizes jobs (directly or indirectly), then that action is right.

CHAPTER TWO: EGOISM

4. Each of the following theories proposes exactly one indirect rule of obligation. Criticize them.
  a. If any person *a* performs an action from a rule R that, when regularly acted from by person *a* increases the number of walls in the world, then R is a direct moral rule of moral rightness.
  b. If any person *a* performs an action from a rule R that, when regularly acted from by person *a* increases the Gross National Product of the United States, then R is a direct moral rule of moral rightness.
5. Many more different versions of ethical egoism exist than have been presented in this chapter. If you know of a version that is significantly different from any of the ones discussed here, present and evaluate it.
6. Suppose we change one thing about ethical egoism—either the direct or the indirect view—stipulating that when you calculate what will be of benefit to you, you don't know anything about yourself except that you are a member of our society: "No one knows his place in society, his class position or social status, nor does any one know his fortune in the distribution of natural assets and abilities, his intelligence, strength, and the like" (John Rawls, *A Theory of Justice,* Harvard University Press, Cambridge, 1971, p. 12). Now attempt to formulate ethical egoism, and then describe what differences have been made in the theory. Are there any criticisms that are now answerable? Are there any new ones that occur to you?

Recommended reading

Aronfreed, Justin. *Conduct and Conscience.* Academic Press, New York, 1968. This book presents some empirical data about egoism from a philosophically sophisticated psychologist.

Gautier, David P., ed. *Morality and Rational Self-Interest.* Prentice-Hall, Englewood Cliffs, N.J. 1970. A selection of articles.

Macaulay, J., and Berkowitz, L., eds. *Altruism and Helping Behavior.* Academic Press, New York, 1970.

Milo, Ronald D., ed. *Egoism and Altruism.* Wadsworth, Belmont, Calif., 1973. Among other essays, both for and against egoism, you will find the work of Bishop Butler, a must reading for any serious student of egoism.

Rand, Ayn. *The Virtue of Selfishness.* New American Library, New York, 1964.

Schlitz, Moritz. *Problems of Ethics.* Translated by David Rynin. Dover, New York, 1962. The author attempts to defend ethical egoism. See especially chapter 2.

Three

Chapter three

Utilitarianism

At the end of the last chapter it was noted that one way to make up a deficiency of ethical egoism is to extend the range of consequences to more than just one person. We could not establish that the general's waging war was wrong when we took into account just his interests and benefits, but we could when we considered what would be in the interest of everyone and what would benefit everyone. We could then see that war is not, usually, right at all. This is a natural extension of egoism, for we still restrict the range of considerations to the consequences of actions—we have only made the range of consequences broader. If we state the most general utilitarian view in the manner chosen so far, it appears as follows:

> *Direct utilitarianism* [1]
> 1. If any person *a* performs an action that increases the good (benefit)[2] of the greatest number, then that action is right.
> 2. Person *a* performs this particular action that increases the good (benefit) of the greatest number.
>
> Therefore,
> 3. This particular action of person *a* is right.
>
> 1. If any person *a* performs an action that increases the good (benefit) of the greatest number more than any other available action, then that action is obligatory.
> 2. Person *a* performs this particular action that increases the good (benefit) of the greatest number more than any other available action.
>
> Therefore,
> 3. This particular action of person *a* is obligatory.

[1] What are here called *direct* and *indirect rule utilitarianism* are usually called *act* and *rule utilitarianism*. The usual set of terms has two disadvantages: it is not as descriptive and it will be confusing when the discussion of act and rule deontology is presented in chapter 5.

[2] The curious reader will wonder about the use of the term 'utilitarian' and its relation to the term 'utility'. J. S. Mill, who brought the term into wide use, says, "The creed which accepts as the foundation of morals, Utility, or the Greatest Happiness Principle, holds that actions are right in proportion as they tend to promote happiness, wrong as they tend to produce the reverse of happiness" (J. S. Mill, *Utilitarianism,* Bobbs-Merrill, Indianapolis, 1957, p. 10).

It would not be too misleading to say that what is useful or has utility is the same thing as what benefits someone or has value; that is, what is good and what has utility are the same thing. Mill supposes that only happiness has value—at least only happiness has value underivatively. We shall further explore questions concerning *value* in chapter 6.

Indirect utilitarianism

1. If any person a performs an action from a rule R that, when regularly acted from by person a,[3] increases the good (benefit) of the greatest number,[4] then R is a direct moral rule of moral rightness.
2. Person a performs an action from a rule R that, when regularly acted from by person a, increases the good (benefit) of the greatest number.

Therefore,

3. R is a direct moral rule of moral rightness.

1. If any person a performs an action from a rule R that, when regularly acted from by person a, increases the good (benefit) of the greatest number more than any other available action, then R is a direct rule of moral obligation.
2. Person a performs an action from a rule R that, when regularly acted from by person a, increases the good (benefit) of the greatest number more than any other available action.

Therefore,

3. R is a direct rule of moral obligation.[5]

[3] The phrase 'by person a' should give us pause, for there is an alternative that should be considered—namely 'generally'. We don't want to give the impression that there is something idiosyncratic about a particular individual such that he alone, when acting, brings about the greatest good for the greatest number. In this sense 'generally' might be less misleading. However, in the statement we are referring *not* to some particular person but rather to 'any person a'. This carries the generality we wish to include without our having to write in a special term.

[4] If we wanted to restate the phrase 'increases the good (benefit) of the greatest number' so as to emphasize the teleological nature of utilitarianism, we could use 'has good maximizing consequences', or 'has good maximizing consequences for the greatest number'. However, this phrasing does not make for a clear parallel with egoism and would be more difficult to work with later on.

[5] Mill should be taken as the model of what a utilitarian is, for it seems clear that he was the most influential philosopher in that tradition. In my opinion, Mill remains the best philosopher within that tradition. There is some evidence that Mill held a version of indirect utilitarianism; and although it is not the purpose of this chapter to argue about how best to interpret Mill, the following passage seems to lend support to the view that Mill held an indirect version of utilitarianism: "The corollaries from the principle of utility, like the precepts of every practical art, admit of indefinite improvement, and in a progressive state of the human mind, their improvement is perpetually going on. But to consider the rules of morality as improvable is one thing; to pass over the intermediate generalizations entirely and endeavour to test each individual action directly by the first principle is another. It is a strange notion that the acknowledgement of a first principle is inconsistent with the admission of secondary ones" (Mill, *Utilitarianism,* p. 31).

These general statements of the two main types of utilitarian theory will not be a total mystery if you have worked your way through chapter 2. However, it will help to remind you of some of the distinctions already made, and to interpret other parts of utilitarian theory that are in some way ambiguous. The examination of utilitarianism is made simpler than that of egoism because there is no psychological theory of motivation that utilitarians have used to support their ethical theory. It is true that Mill thought that people desire only happiness as an end, though he hedged even on this claim. However, he does not make use of this supposed fact to argue that we have a right to desire our own happiness as an end. There is a great deal of controversy about how Mill used the supposed psychological fact of what people desire in chapter 4 of *Utilitarianism,* but we shall not get involved in that controversy here. We shall be able to discuss the view of utilitarianism, and specifically the position of Mill, without discussing any psychological theory of motivation.

In this chapter we shall employ the same strategy used in chapter 2: first, offer clarified versions of the view to be considered, and then evaluate the view as clarified. The topics to be taken up are as follows:

A. Direct and indirect utilitarianism
B. Nature of the good, whose good, and who acts
C. Calculating the greatest good
D. Utilitarianism evaluated
E. Egoism and utilitarianism

A. Direct and indirect utilitarianism

The general statement of the two forms of utilitarianism contains two separate parts for each version. Both the direct and the indirect versions of the theory require one rule for the notions of *obligation* and another for those concerning *right.* Accordingly, both the direct and the indirect versions require two rules, one having to do with each of those notions. The direct rule theory applies the principle of utility, as we shall call it, directly to the actions that are to be judged right or obligatory; the indirect rule theory applies the principle of utility to rules and not directly to actions that are to be judged. The same distinction was made in chapter 2 with respect to egoism, and should be somewhat clear. A few examples will serve as a reminder.

Consider just the rules regarding *right,* the first rule in each of the pairs—where the rule is the first statement in the general scheme. Suppose a person is given 5 dollars too much change by the clerk-owner of a small grocery store, and there is little likelihood this will be noticed. Suppose also, as is not unreasonable, that the overall good that will result if the money is kept is greater than if it is returned. The grocer will miss it, but, again in our story, the person who has it will benefit more from having it since she or he will treat it as a windfall. The grocer will not know specifically that the 5 dollars was given out by mistake, the profits for that week will be 5 dollars less, but profits fluctuate and the grocer does not know beforehand what the profit is going to be. In this set of circumstances, the greatest good for the greatest number seems to be reached by keeping the money. (We shall have to suppose the person receiving the 5 dollars will spend it in very much the same way whether it comes from the grocer or some other source.) If we apply the direct utilitarian rule concerning right ("If any person *a* performs an action that increases the good (benefit) of the greatest number, then that action is right"), then we are led to conclude that keeping the money is right.

In contrast, the rule from which the person acts, "If you are given too much change, then keep it," probably would not lead to the greatest good (benefit) for the greatest number. If people generally acted from this rule, then clerks would have to be much more careful, they would have to be much more suspicious of their customers, the customers would by annoyed at not being trusted, fewer people would get away with any of the overpayment, and so on. All these are bad consequences of generally acting from the rule and would enable us to reject, on utilitarian grounds, the rule as one that can justify the singular moral judgment that taking the 5 dollars is right.

B. Nature of the good, whose good, and who acts

Once again, the nature of what is good or of benefit to a person need not be specified precisely. Many utilitarians claim that the only thing of value is pleasure; but then many others claim that there are indeed other things of value. Some items listed are knowledge, virtue, friendship, love, beauty, and freedom. In chapter 6 we shall take a much longer look at the nature of value and what things, if any, have value. For now, if you require a more specific view, plug in your own favorite candidates as we consider the usual distinctions necessary for proper examination of a theory.

The expression 'greatest number' seems fairly clear, but there have been some astonishing interpretations of it. One fairly common move is to limit those who are to count as part of the numbers, and then to do your calculating. Many Nazis claimed that they were increasing the amount of good in the world, even though they were causing great suffering among the Jews, Slavs, and many more millions of people. Their claim was that such creatures were not really, or fully, human, and thus their benefit need not be taken into account when they (Nazis) determined the morality of their actions. The same kind of response was found among slave owners and many nineteenth- and early twentieth-century factory owners. In times of war, it is fairly common not to view the enemy as fully human. This may make it easier to fight wars, but it is a difficult move to defend rationally.

Recall that the egoist could not justifiably select the one *person* whose good should be increased; and similarly, no one can apparently justifiably select the one *group* whose good should be increased. It would then follow that we cannot justifiably restrict the range of whose good is to be considered. The good of all human beings, at least, must be taken into account. If we become aware of additional sentient creatures besides humans, we'll have to include them also.

One great advantage of utilitarianism over egoism is that it clearly applies to everyone, in terms of both whose interests have to be taken into account when we calculate the consequences and which people are morally enjoined to act or not. According to the utilitarians, the consequences affecting all people are to be taken into account, and all people have rights and obligations. One problem for egoism arises when there is a conflict between two individuals, each trying to achieve self-benefit. This is not a problem for utilitarianism, though, for each of us is asked to seek not the benefit of ourself alone but of all. This advantage of utilitarianism over egoism is, when we compare the two theories, a strong reason for preferring the former theory to the latter.

C. Calculating the greatest good

Most utilitarians talk about calculating the greatest good for the greatest number, but very few such theorists have ever supposed that there can be some kind of precise and completely quantitative process of calculation. Those who restrict what is of benefit or value to pleasure, such as Jeremy Bentham, are inclined to think that there is a strict calculus. They suppose that one could add up the pleasures resulting from some action, subtract the pains and discomforts, and then arrive at a figure that would allow you to conclude either that the action is right or wrong, obligatory or not. Bentham puts it in the following way:

> Sum up all the values of all the *pleasures* on the one side, and those of all the pains on the other. The balance, if it be on the side of pleasure, will give the *good* tendency of the act upon the whole, with respect to the interests of that *individual* person; if on the side of pain, the bad tendency of it upon the whole.
>
> Take an account of the *number* of persons whose interests appear to be concerned, and repeat the above process with respect to each.[6]

1. The problem of quantifying what's valuable   Most utilitarians, however, do not think that there is a strict calculus. They avoid a calculus because, for one thing, there is no quantifiable standard of what is valu-

[6] Jeremy Bentham, *An Introduction to the Principles of Morals and Legislation,* Hafner, New York, 1948, p. 20.

able. The standard meter stick is used to determine whether or not anything is a meter long, but no such standard unit exists for, say, pleasure.
Furthermore, most philosophers do not want to restrict things of value or
of benefit to human beings to pleasure. Once you include other candidates,
such as happiness (as a long-run state in contrast with the short-run state of
pleasure), freedom, love, and friendship, then you have added more items
that are even more difficult to quantify. We talk about quantities of love,
but it is only in the grossest sense. No one supposes that there is a calculus
of love available for precise figuring.

Since we want to consider only the strongest views, we shall suppose
that there is no strict calculus, nor need there be such a calculus for utilitarianism to be workable. We must assume, however, that we are able to
estimate or calculate in some rough way the relative desirability of ends.
For example, we have to agree that someone could consider the value of his
or her freedom as opposed to the amount of security he or she desired. If a
person is offered either a life with great security but with little material
goods or a great deal more in the way of material things but also much
more insecurity, then we have to suppose that a decision between the two
can be arrived at. The person making the decision would have to know
more about the circumstances, for example, the kind of insecurity. But
allowing the possibility for a decision is not difficult; in fact, it seems to
suggest that we make this kind of decision frequently.

2. The problem of knowledge   When the problem of determining what
was in a person's own interest arose in the discussion or egoism, we decided
to suppose neither that the person merely believed an action would be of
benefit nor to limit consideration to those consequences which would in
fact benefit the person. If we did not do this, on the one hand, we would
have the absurdity of claiming that an action is obligatory or right simply
because a person believes it will benefit him—even when there is good evidence to show that the action will be harmful to that person. On the other
hand, we would be asked to suppose that a person is obliged, say, to perform an action about which he is completely unaware because, in fact, the
performance of that action would maximize the benefit of that person.[7]
This same problem arises with respect to utilitarianism. We do not want to
say that when a person performs an action that he merely believes, perhaps
even without evidence, will bring about the greatest good for the greatest
number, that action is right. Suppose someone believes, for example, that
it is in everyone's interest to die as quickly as possible so as to join God in
heaven—and to this end, poisons the water supply of as many cities as possible. Or, to take a less fanciful case, suppose someone believes that Caucasians are superior to all other types of people and sets about to enslave all
non-Caucasians so as to maximize the greatest good for the greatest
number—even, as this person believes, for the non-Caucasians. Is this person performing an obligatory action? This is an apparently clear instance,

[7] If this discussion has slipped your mind, turn to page 61 in chapter 2.

drawn from the phenomena, of an action that is not obligatory, but one that would be said to be obligatory if we were to interpret utilitarianism in terms of *belief* in the good-maximizing consequences of an act as the determiner of obligation.

Recall, also, that a supposed or believed consequence of an action is not a consequence at all. It is true that someone believes something when that belief exists. Whether, in our example, people will be happier when Caucasians are the master race is another matter, one that may very well be irrelevant to the fact that someone holds that belief. You may want to say that the belief itself is false, but that is irrelevant to whether or not the person holds the belief. If the obligation attached to an action is a function of what someone believes the consequences to be, then the actual consequences are irrelevant to the obligation attached to that action. However, utilitarianism is usually held as the second of the two main teleological theories of obligation—theories that see obligation as a function of the consequences of actions alone. However, if obligation is seen as a function of what are believed to be the consequences of an action, then the theory is not teleological. So if we interpret the consequences to be what a person believes the consequences to be, then numerous counter-examples exist to point out that the view, which is supposed to be a teleological theory of obligation, is not a teleological view at all.

The other extreme—that obligation or rightness is a function of what the consequences actually are—is also unacceptable. Suppose you take a crucial multiple choice examination on which the answer to number 17 is: "*d.* Either none of the above or the denial of the conjunction of (a) and (c)." The action of circling *d* is, we can easily suppose, the one that in these circumstances will maximize the good for the greatest number. You will do well on the examination, your family will be proud, your chances of getting a good job will be increased, and so on. (Suppose also, to "lock up" the case, the grading is done on a noncomparative basis so that others will not suffer on the examination if you do well.) In this set of circumstances, supposing that obligation is a function of what the actual consequences are, then you are morally obliged to circle *d.* However, again, this is a pretty clear instance of an action that is not obligatory. It is bad luck not to circle *d;* you may curse yourself for not having done so; but it would apparently not be correct to accuse you of moral laxity for not doing so.

Frequently, more fanciful examples help to fix the point more firmly than realistic instances. Suppose that unbeknownst to you a new antibiotic drug is growing in the small piece of mold on your toothbrush. If you were to take that toothbrush to the biochemistry laboratory at 10:45 A.M. on Tuesday when professors Behrman and Royer are discussing the relative merits of touch football and chamber music as methods of relaxation for faculty, those two, in a desire to stop the conversation, would ask you what you had in your hand. The rest would be history—for this antibiotic will wipe out all diseases, and no one will be allergic to it. In terms of the view being considered, you would be obliged to perform the action of going to the biochemistry department with toothbrush in hand, whether you knew where the biochemistry department was or not. However, once again, this is an apparently clear instance of an action that is not obligatory.

There are countless actions that, if carried out, would maximize the greatest good for the greatest number. This seems to be an incontrovertible truth. However, if obligation is a function of the actual consequences of an action (if it is performed), then all those actions are obligatory; and all those who are in a position to perform the actions except for their ignorance of the nature and significance of that action are to be morally blamed for not fulfilling their obligations. This is a consequence that a theory of obligation would have great difficulty overcoming, and there is no reason to saddle utilitarianism with this consequence if we can avoid it. Since there is another interpretation that allows utilitarians to escape both this problem and the results of replacing consequences with what are *believed* to be consequences, we shall use that interpretation.

The middle ground, chosen both for egoism and for utilitarianism, specifies consequences in terms of what is likely to occur given the knowledge that is available. For example, given the knowledge available, you cannot predict or even have an inkling that the mold on your toothbrush is a new and important antibiotic. Thus, you have no obligation to take the toothbrush to the biochemistry laboratory, for the knowledge available to you does not contain that item.

Generally, the knowledge available is what we can reasonably expect people in that culture to have. This is not meant to be a complicated notion, but to approximate the legal requirement and definition of what one can reasonably expect people to know. This means that sometimes a person will fail to fulfill an obligation because of a lack of knowledge and yet will still be held morally accountable and judged to have failed to fulfill an obligation. Suppose a father knows that if he is aware of the needs of his children, then he will know what his obligations to them are, such things as the obligation to buy them shoes, to take them to the doctor, to buy adequate food, and so on. This person cannot escape his responsibility by deliberately keeping himself in ignorance, for he is obliged, as we say, to know these things. His obligation stems from his general obligation as a parent; and the kind of knowledge he is attempting not to have is just the kind required in order that he fulfill that general obligation. A principle is sometimes invoked here to capture this point: We are obliged to know all those things which are required for us to carry out all our genuine obligations. This principle may, at first, seem strange to you; it may even seem to oblige people to do all manner of things. However, if you apply it in a few simple cases, you will see that this is not so.

Some people, because of special knowledge, have obligations most of us do not have. If three people watch a man stagger and subsequently collapse on the street, and one of them is a physician, then it seems clear that the physician has a special obligation to help the person that stems from his or her medical knowledge. A teacher in a classroom has a special obligation to help someone who has a learning disability, whereas people passing in the street outside do not. By contrast, some people, because of knowledge *dis*abilities, have few obligations. If someone is mentally retarded and cannot know or cannot, with any reasonable effort, come to know something, then that person has no obligations with respect to that knowledge. A mentally retarded person who cannot master the notion of a pressure point can hardly be obliged to stop the bleeding of someone who is severely injured. A case such as this is a simple application of the "ought implies can" principle; for if the person cannot perform the action (because of a lack of knowledge in this case), then that person is not obliged to do so.

The position being developed will also allow the utilitarians to explain a good deal of the phenomena often lumped under the name of "relativism." Some cultures provide information not available in others, training not given in others, and general knowledge not provided in others. One cannot reasonably be expected to know about how to treat those who have received back injuries if that knowledge is not available in one's culture. Thus obligations will vary from person to person because of different knowledge and abilities, and also from culture to culture because of the differences in the availability of knowledge and the possibility of acquiring skills. This does not make utilitarianism the same as some relativistic view, as we shall see later, but it does allow it to explain many of the same phenomena as a relativistic view. Much more will be said on this topic in chapter 4.

3. Limiting the notion of *consequences*   One last point about the extent of consequences will complete this section. There is a sense, understood by us all, in which the U.S. involvement in Indochina in the '60s and '70s is a consequence of the Revolutionary War in the eighteenth century. If the latter event did not successfully occur, then the former event would not have occurred, because there would have been no such country as the United States of America. We can capture this by saying that the Revolutionary War was causally necessary for the U.S. involvement in Indochina almost two centuries later. This may not appear to be a very strange claim; but the claim that U.S. involvement in Indochina is a consequence of the beginning of life on earth, some two billion years ago, no doubt seems much stranger. However, let us restrict our examples to consequences that occur as a result of actions performed by human beings. Some person or people were crucial to the ancestors of those who made the Revolutionary War successful. The actions of these people in reproducing, making use of the sense already explained, can be called causally necessary for the success of the war. In that same sense, then, the successful prosecution of the war is a consequence of the actions of such people in reproducing.

This sense of 'consequence', however, is too broad to be used by the utilitarians. It would require us to calculate, in a rough sense of 'calculate', the roots and effects of actions indefinitely into the past and future. Even if we could somehow come to know what the consequences of an action would be, and what the effects of it were, this would make the practical task of arriving at singular moral judgments impossible. Furthermore, even though there is a sense of 'consequence' and 'effect' in which we can talk about remote events, both in the past and the future, as consequences, there are other senses of those terms in which it is not appropriate. We usually use shorter-run notions of *cause* and *consequence* in our daily lives. We say that someone died of head injuries, not that the death was the consequence of that person's birth or of the production of a certain car with a bolt that, as a result of lack of service, would fail at a crucial time and bring about the accident. We say that the consequences of a person's flunking a course include having to take the course over again, but not that 20 years later the person would tell a certain joke at a cocktail party.

Let us limit the consequences of actions to those events which result from the actions that one could reasonably predict and that are relatively important in terms of the histories of the people involved. Admittedly this is not a very precise notion, but since it relies on an everyday notion of the limits of consequences, its use seems legitimate. It should be made clear that this notion of limiting the consequences to what one could reasonably predict and the relative importance of the prospective consequences is closely related to another kind of limitation. In a common-sense way, there is a temporal and spatial limitation to the actual consequences of actions.[8] The ripples in a pond caused by a rock thrown into the middle spread out but then subside; so, too, do we suppose the causal consequences of actions to fade out. It may be true, theoretically, that the causal consequences extend indefinitely into the past and the future; but practically, we do not view the situation that way. When we talk about the consequences one could reasonably predict, it will never turn out that what can reasonably be predicted is greater than the practical limit of the consequences of an action. Thus we have a connection between what one can reasonably know to be the consequences and the practical limit of those consequences.

You may think, however, that even though we do not have to calculate indefinitely into the future and the past, there is still the practical problem of calculating in each set of circumstances. For example, when we are in a position to invite someone we don't like very much to join us at a table in a bar, it is very difficult on the spur of the moment to calculate the benefit to all the parties involved. Action is called for then, and we must act. Many of the really important moral decisions in our lives, as well as many of the trivial moral decisions, have to be made without any time to calculate, and often in circumstances in which calculation is impossible. This problem is an old one for utilitarians; and Mill responds to it by pointing out that although an individual may not have time to calculate or

---

[8] This kind of notion has received attention from philosophers—it has even been given the fancy name of the "ripples in the pond postulate." See, for example, J. J. C. Smart, *An Outline of Utilitarian Ethics,* Melbourne University Press, Victoria, 1961, pp. 19–23. Just as the ripples caused by a stone thrown into a pond have an effective limit, even though they may have no theoretical limit, so do the consequences of actions. This image will perhaps help to fix the notion of the *limit of consequences* a bit better.

think very much about an individual action, there really has been enough time.

> There has been ample time, namely, the whole past duration of the human species. During all that time mankind have been learning by experience the tendencies of actions; on which experience all the prudence, as well as all the morality of life is dependent. People talk as if the commencement of this course of experience had hitherto been put off, and as if, at the moment when some man feels tempted to meddle with the property or life of another, he had to begin considering for the first time whether murder and theft are injurious to human happiness.[9]

The utilitarians, along with the egoists, think that consequences alone count in determining the rightness of actions. This is not to say that they think motives unimportant. Motives, though, are not important in determining whether an action is right or wrong. One might want to say, along with Mill, that people who have motives of a certain sort are good people, but that is not to say that their actions are *right*. People with good motives may nevertheless perform wrong actions frequently, and those with bad motives may perform right actions almost all the time. Later in the chapter we shall return to this issue, and question whether that assumption is correct. For now, however, simply note the difference for the utilitarian in the evaluation of the moral worth of an action and the moral worth of the individual who performs that action. The former is a function of consequences alone and not motives, but the latter is a function of motives.

Summary   Utilitarians require that we be able to calculate what is of value; and they especially require us to be able to determine that one end or course of action is more valuable than another. This does not, however, require a strict calculation, but only that we be able to make a determination in most cases without great difficulty. Just as was true of egoism, what is of value or benefit will not now be specified. It may be limited to one thing, such as pleasure, or it may include any number of other things, such as love, freedom, and friendship. When the utilitarians talk about what is in the interest of the greatest number, they do not mean what someone *believes* is in the interest of the greatest number. Instead, they mean that consequences are those which one could reasonably predict will occur given the knowledge that is available. Finally, consequences are not to extend indefinitely into the future, the past, or, for that matter, into space; they are to be limited to results that could reasonably be predicted and that have a certain degree of importance to the people involved. This, in brief, is how we should understand the key notions of utilitarian theories of obligation.

[9] Mill, *Utilitarianism,* p. 30.

Exercises: Applying utilitarianism
1. Choose an incident within your own experience in which you or some other person made a singular moral judgment (of obligation, right, wrong, and so on).
Show how the application of direct egoism and direct utilitarianism to this situation would allow the derivation of the judgment, even though it is likely that neither of the theories was actually used in the set of circumstances. If the application of the theories gives different results, give reasons for preferring one to the other.
2. Suppose you could choose to be more intelligent or better-looking but not both. Which would you choose? How did you make your choice? What kind of calculation did you make?
3. What are (were) the consequences of the U.S. involvement in the Vietnam war? What are (were) the consequences of Gerald Ford's pardon of Richard Nixon? Does the method of determining consequences in these instances support or undermine the proposed method of determining consequences in this chapter?
4. The utilitarian suggests that we divorce the evaluation of actions from the evaluation of agents performing those actions. Without reading ahead, present reasons for agreeing or disagreeing with this position.

D. Utilitarianism evaluated

1. **Reasons in favor**   Now that we have some better idea of what utilitarian theories of obligation are, it is time to see why anyone would want to hold such theories, in addition, of course, to their ability to explain moral phenomena.

> 1. The theory has universal scope.
> 2. It is held and used by people either directly or indirectly when they consciously and explicitly do moral reasoning.

These two reasons will be explained in detail shortly, but before that, two things must be pointed out. First, no psychological theory of motivation is used to support utilitarianism. The second claim, which is an empirical claim, requires some explanation about how it supports utilitarianism. Second, it should be remembered that most theories have few positive reasons for acceptance in their favor; they win out by being able to best explain the phenomena, to answer adequately any criticisms, and to avoid ad hoc explanations. These are the other criteria of acceptability, the most important reasons for accepting a theory.

One of the problems with egoism, you will recall, was that it was too limited in scope; there seemed to be no way in which the theory could reasonably be applied to other people. A theory of obligation gains acceptability insofar as it can account for such phenomena wherever they occur. This is something utilitarianism is explicitly designed to do, especially as it is interpreted here. Utilitarianism suggests that right action, for example, is a function of the likelihood of good-maximizing consequences for everyone.

You may be tempted to say this is just a special instance of accounting for the phenomenon better than the rivals, and indeed you have a good point. However, since the reason is very important in terms of comparing utilitarianism with egoism, it seems worth stating as a separate, positive point. I would not be upset, though, if someone whose philosophic sense is disturbed by this special placement put it in the category of better explanation or better account of the phenomena than the rivals.

2. Counter-examples   At this point we have more carefully specified the nature of utilitarian theories of obligation and have given a brief summary of the reasons in their favor. Now we shall examine some of the objections to utilitarianism. The counter-examples selected will apply to both the direct and indirect varieties of utilitarianism, although it will be shown, in each case, how the counter-example applies.

Suppose, as evidence indicates, that we can provide fresh produce to the American public (and by extension to everyone) if we but pay those who pick the produce a very low wage. This wage allows the pickers to live only at a low standard of living, but it does allow them to live without starving or suffering any fatal diseases. It is true that they do not live with much dignity and the chances of their children escaping such a life are very small, but these are negative factors that must be weighed in with the positive. On the positive side we have several million people whose quality of life is increased by a small amount as a result of being able to buy produce for a very low price. While the amount of benefit each person receives is small, there are so many millions of people that the resulting amount of benefit is very great indeed.

Although the amount of disbenefit or disutility that each farm worker receives more than offsets the benefit each individual consumer receives, there are very few workers in comparison with the entire population that receives the benefit. Suppose there are about 50,000 farm workers and, again roughly, about 100 million people who consume the products they pick. In order to match the utility produced by the millions, there would have to be 200 times as much disutility to each picker. It is plausible to suppose that there is not that much disutility. Each farm worker gets enough to eat, has a place to sleep, clothes to wear, and all the other basic necessities.

Even if we suppose the amount of utility and disutility is about the same, the example would still work as a counter-example; for then it would, on utilitarian grounds alone, be morally indifferent which way we acted. It would not matter whether we paid the farm workers more or continued to keep the produce prices low. However, let us illustrate this with respect to specific utilitarian views.

Consider, first, direct utilitarianism—the view whose principle of obligation is "If any person *a* performs an action that increases the good (benefit) of the greatest number more than any other available action, then that action is obligatory." The complementary principle concerning right is "If any person *a* performs an action that increases the good (benefit) of the greatest number, then that action is right." The suggestion is that paying the farm workers the low salary does increase the good or benefit of the greatest number. If this is so, then the action is morally right. You must not misunderstand the claim; it is not that it is good business to pay low salaries, or that it is the American Way, or that it is necessary—none of those. The claim is that it is morally right to pay low salaries. Whatever one thinks about farm workers, it is pretty clear, insofar as we report the phenomena, that it does not appear morally right to pay such workers low salaries.

Of course, if one could establish, independently of any of these considerations, direct utilitarianism as a correct theory of obligation, then one could establish the surprising conclusion that paying the farm workers low salaries is right. However, there are no overwhelming reasons in favor of utilitarianism; and thus, this conclusion is not justified.

It would be a sufficiently powerful criticism of direct utilitarianism to describe actions that are apparently not right but that, according to that view, are right. It would be a stronger conclusion yet to establish that the action of paying low wages to the farm laborers was obligatory. Now, it is not clear that one can establish this, but it is worth a short discussion. One would have to establish that paying low wages is the action that among all the alternatives, given what we know, is most likely to maximize the good or benefit of the greatest number. This is difficult to establish, for we have to consider the alternatives available to us. On the one hand, we could invest in mechanical pickers that, in the not-too-distant future, would replace hand pickers. In the short run, the venture would be costly, for the development costs would be very high; but within a fairly short period of time this money would be retrieved by the savings on labor. On the other hand, it is not at all clear, given the lack of success in developing such machines in the past, that such machines either could be developed or that when developed would result in any savings. Furthermore, given the unskilled nature of the labor involved, and the nature of our society, if the farm workers were unemployed, it would work a great hardship on them. This disutility would also have to be included in our calculations. When we add the positive and the negative benefit, it is not clear that this alternative would increase the benefit of the greatest number more than paying the farm workers low wages. You are invited to consider other such alternatives and to decide whether there is a reasonable case to be made that the alternative of paying low wages is the one most likely to maximize the greatest good of the greatest number among all the alternatives available. According to direct utilitarianism, not only is the action of paying low wages right, but it is also apparently obligatory.

Remember, however, that this last criticism is not necessary for the counter-example to be effective. But should the last criticism be effective, it would be very powerful.

A single counter-example, by itself, does not provide a very strong criticism of direct utilitarianism, or any ethical theory for that matter. In this instance, the counter-example represents a large class of actions of the same type. The same kinds of considerations apply to paying women lower wages than men for the same work, to paying blacks lower wages than whites, to laying off blacks and other minority groups before whites, and so on. The reader is asked to flesh out and construct the counter-examples of this type that seem most plausible. As can be seen, moral philosophy is not something esoteric, but something that we all can and must engage in.

Since counter-examples always meet with mixed reception, it is wise not to depend on just one kind, but to offer a variety of kinds. There are people, alas, all too many of them, who find the greatest good and benefit in the suffering of others or in cheating others. Suppose, for example, that a person receives immense benefit, in the form of pleasure and enough psychic energy to last the rest of the day, from cheating the paper boy out of his money. The paper boy, we shall suppose, does not find this out, for the customer is very clever. The action affects no one but the two of them; and since we can calculate the amount of benefit and disutility in just the two instances, it is easy to see that more overall utility results when the boy is cheated out of his money. You can fill in more details, such as the fact that the paper boy has 100 customers, as you wish.

The action of the cheater is, on direct utilitarian grounds, morally right—and yet it appears to be a pretty clear instance of an action that is not morally right. The same case can apparently be used for the indirect utilitarian view, for the general adoption of the rule "If an action of cheating one person a small amount will benefit the cheater much more than the cheated is harmed, then cheat that person" would apparently increase the good or benefit of the greatest number. Remember, though, that the action does not affect very many people.

The presentation of just one person of this type would not be much of a criticism of utilitarianism, but it is the existence of very many such people that provides a serious problem. There is the sadist who gets enormous kicks from sticking pins into people on the subway, the teacher whose day is "made" if one student can be humiliated, the petty bureaucrat who can make it through the whole week by frustrating the aims of a few customers with tons of red tape, and so on. Once again you are invited to try your hand at constructing such counter-examples from your own experience. The minimal hints given above should enable all of you to remember instances of this sort from your own experience.

Now we will consider a third counter-example. In this case, the action involves a very small amount of benefit that does not thereby seem to render it morally right. Suppose a young man whispers, just loud enough for the young woman in front of him to hear, "Isn't that girl attractive." Mightn't this make the young woman feel somewhat better than she would have that day had she not heard the compliment? Now suppose someone does this complimenting as a matter of course and adopts as a rule of action "If you can compliment someone without incurring any responsibilities onto yourself but at the same time cause some benefit to the person complimented, then make your compliment." This kind of action although it may involve only a few people, results in an increase in the amount of good for the greatest number and thus, on the utilitarian standard, would have to be judged morally right. Yet this kind of action, even if we say that it is kind, is apparently not a morally right action.

Other examples of this type might include scratching someone's back when it itches, returning 3 cents in overpayment to the neighborhood grocer, smiling at the little boy who is nervously taking a short cut through your yard, and complimenting your host's food when you are invited to dinner (even when it isn't very good). Doubtless, you can once again supply still other examples from your own experience, for kindly, relatively uncomplicated actions of this sort are abundant.

Finally, as the fourth type of counter-example, consider actions that do increase the benefit of the greatest number but profit the actors in such a way that we are prompted to withhold the judgment that they have done something morally right. Suppose for a moment that putting the mass-produced automobile within the reach of most citizens in many countries has increased the benefit of the greatest number of people. Certainly, the private car has enlarged people's horizons, provided mobility, freed many from dependence on local merchants, created jobs, provided increased social opportunities and a place to pursue such opportunities in private, and so on. The person whose actions are probably most responsible for this great— and we're saying, beneficial—change in society is Henry Ford, the man who made the assembly line work. It's probably safe to say that Henry Ford's motive in making the assembly line work was not to increase the greatest good of the greatest number, but to make a lot of money. According to the utilitarians, the motive for an action is irrelevant to whether it has positive moral worth,[10] so Ford's action of mass producing cars, to the utilitarian, would be morally right. However, while we may admire Ford for his cleverness, or despise him for his lack of social awareness, his action of perfecting mass production methods does not seem to be a morally right action.

This same kind of counter-example can be constructed wherever someone has benefited greatly from an action that has also benefited a larger number *and* the person did not have the increase in the benefit of others as a primary motive in acting. This would apply to Fisk and Gould and the others who developed the railroads in the United States in the nineteenth century, John D. Rockefeller's development of the oil industry, those who made fortunes in armament manufacturing while supporting the justified side in war, and so on. You should work out a counter-example of this type that is most convincing to you.

If the utilitarians are correct, then motives are not relevant to the rightness of actions but only to the goodness of persons, and the above

[10] "Utilitarian moralists have gone beyond almost all others in affirming that the motive has nothing to do with the morality of the action, though much with the worth of the agent. He who saves a fellow creature from drowning does what is morally right, whether his motive be duty or the hope of being paid for his trouble" (Mill, *Utilitarianism*, pp. 23–24).

purported counter-examples are not actual counter-examples. However, to remind you, utilitarianism has not been established via any strong independent evidence as yet, so the construction of counter-examples from the phenomena is perfectly legitimate. Someone could, of course, provide a strong defense of utilitarianism or work out some new arguments in favor of the view; then we would be justified in rejecting the proposed counter-examples. For now, though, these counter-examples have to be seen as negative evidence, as examples that tend to show that utilitarianism is not a correct theory of obligation. Even though there is this evidence against utilitarianism, and more criticisms will be presented as we go on, you are asked not to make any final decision about utilitarianism until all the main theories of obligation are examined.

The counter-examples proposed above are constructed for direct utilitarianism, but it would save us considerable trouble if the same kinds of counter-examples also applied to indirect utilitarianism. With very little change it does seem the counter-examples do apply to the indirect form of utilitarianism. To show this, consider how just a few of the counter-examples would have to be changed to apply. Consider the rule "It is morally right to pay low wages to farm workers" or, as we have been saying it, "If any action is one of paying low wages to farm workers, then it is right." Is this a rule that, when acted from by most, leads to the greatest good for the greatest number? If the answer is "yes," then we are entitled, given indirect utilitarianism, to conclude that the rule is a direct moral rule. The rule, along with the appropriate second premise, would enable us to derive a singular moral judgment to the effect that paying this group of farm workers low wages is right.

The kind of reasoning offered above, which attempts to establish that it is for the greatest good that we pay low wages to farm workers, would also establish, then, that the cited rule, when acted from, leads to the greatest good for the greatest number. This is not to say that whenever an action, for example, keeping the 5 dollars the clerk overpaid you, would lead to the greatest good for the greatest number, you are justified in concluding that acting on the general rule that corresponds to that action would lead to the greatest good. In this instance, it does not. However, the examples presented here were chosen because they do seem to apply both to the direct and the indirect version of utilitarianism. Hopefully, this is clear enough from the discussion, and you can fiill in the details of the other kinds of counter-examples to make them apply also to the indirect versions of utilitarianism.

Supposing that the above claims are justified, then we do not have to construct completely different counter-examples to indirect utilitarianism since, with appropriate changes, the same criticisms apply.

3. The problem of justice   The problem that causes utilitarians the most difficulty is distributive justice. *Distributive justice* is usually contrasted with *retributive justice.* The latter concerns theories of punishment;

and the former, theories of the morally proper manner of distributing the things of value. The expression 'things of value' is what is at stake when we talk about benefit, good, utility, and disutility. The utilitarians tell us a right action is one that increases the benefit or value for the greatest number; but, according to most philosophers, they are not adequately able to distinguish among different distributions of the value that is created.[11] To see this difference, let us begin by distinguishing among various notions of distribution. One distinction exists between the *greatest amount* of value and the *greatest amount for the greatest number.* It might be that we could increase the amount of value by killing some of the people in our society. If, having a barely adequate amount of food, we killed off certain nonproductive old people, we would have fewer people, but these fewer people would eat better. The amount of value would increase, but it would not increase for the greatest number of people. One criticism of utilitarianism has been that it cannot distinguish between these two situations—that, in fact, it would have to allow that it is morally permissible to kill nonproductive elderly people in the name of justice.

Even if we suppose that we do not kill people, and that the number of citizens of alternative societies stays constant, there are still other kinds of distributions of things of value that give rise to problems. Imagine a society that has ten people to whom the things of value are to be distributed. Suppose that the things of value are measured by some unit of value V and that there are a total of 100 V's to be distributed in this society. The first of the columns that follow represents the distribution of V's in this society.

Society 1	Society 2	Society 3
10	15	15
10	15	15
10	15	15
10	15	15
10	15	15
10	5	5
10	5	5
10	5	5
10	5	5
10	5	6

[11] For now, things of value can be considered something tangible, such as a bag of rice, or nontangibles, such as love or freedom. When we ask, "How shall we properly distribute the things of value?" we are asking how much rice each person should get, whether all or only some of us will be free, and so on. Even when we consider the distribution of nontangible things of value, the question of how properly to distribute them is an important and practical one. Depending on the answers, we will choose certain governments and economic systems. (At the risk of boring you, I ask you to recall that no specific theory of value is being presupposed in this discussion.)

The second column shows the distribution in a society that, like the first one, has 100 V's to distribute but that parcels them out differently. The third column shows a distribution like that in society 2 except that it involves 101 V's.

If we compare society 1 with society 2, we see that the total amount of good is the same, 100 V's. However, we all recognize the difference between the two cases. The difference is not in the average amount of V's people receive, for the arithmetical average is the same, 10 V's. It is the distribution that is different.[12] We can characterize the difference in a technical way (see footnote 12), or we can draw attention to relevant differences via nontechnical examples. Suppose that V is food and that the twenty people that make up societies 1 and 2 require roughly the same amount of food. It would seem that in society 2 half the people would be on the edge of starvation and half would live very well, whereas in society 1 this would not be so. Most of us would say there is a moral difference in the way the V's are distributed in the two societies. But utilitarians, so the argument goes, cannot make this distinction with their theory of obligation.

This point is made even more dramatically if we consider society 3 and society 1. Because the total amount of V's is greater in society 3 than in society 1, some would certainly claim that on utilitarian grounds alone, the former is actually preferable to the latter.

The three cases represent three different distributions of things of value; in two of them, the total amount of value is the same. In spite of the same value being present, the choice of a method of distribution will often make a moral difference. If we are asked whether society 1 or society 2 is morally preferable, we all recognize the significance of the question; the societies *are* morally different. As citizens, we would perform such actions as voting, sending money to political candidates, supporting revolutions, writing books and pamphlets, fighting wars, and the like on the basis of our choice of which of these societies is best.[13] When we oppose some of the options, we sometimes do so because we believe them to be morally wrong or to include morally unacceptable (that is, unjust) ways of distributing society's things of value. For example, society 2 might describe a slave society and society 1 a free society. No one, I think, would say the choice between these two societies is morally indifferent. How the amount

[12] We could use what are now fairly standard technical terms to make these same distinctions. "*Pareto improvement* upon an initial distribution [is] . . . any alternative distribution according to which every participant fares no worse than (i.e., fares better or as well as) he does on the initial distribution. We arrive also at the idea of a Pareto *optimal distribution* within a set of alternatives as any distribution within the set that is such that none of the other distributions in the set effect a Pareto improvement upon it" (Nicholas Rescher, *Distributive Justice,* Bobbs-Merrill, New York, 1966, p. 13).

[13] There are, of course, many more options than these three. These three are chosen, however, because they are fairly clear and allow the general point to be made.

of good in those societies is to be distributed is not a morally indifferent choice. Well, you ask, who says it *is* morally indifferent?

The answer to this question highlights the major criticism of utilitarianism. If utilitarianism cannot adequately distinguish the moral worth of different distributions of the things of value, then it cannot adequately account for an important area of our moral life and a significant part of the moral phenomena. Suppose, as do utilitarians, that as long as the amount of value created is the same, it does not matter whether we choose the distribution of society 1 or that of society 2. If society 2 turns out to be a slave society, that, according to the utilitarian, is irrelevant.

Furthermore, suppose it turns out that a certain kind of slave society produces a slight amount more of good than a corresponding free society. That is, suppose society 3 represents a slave society that will allow the production of the greatest amount of good—even more than in society 1. This is not incredible. Since we must often make decisions about which kind of society we want to build in the future, and if the only considerations we can use are utilitarian ones, we would conclude that society 3 is the best possible society, since it results in more overall good than any other possible alternative. The creation of this society would, on utilitarian grounds, be obligatory; and, of course, it would at least be morally right.

It has traditionally been argued that utilitarianism is silent on these questions, for it only calls for the maximization of things of value and has nothing to say about the distribution. But utilitarians often say that the method of distribution does makes a difference in the total amount of good produced; and some, especially Mill, try to show that a principle of the just distribution of things of value follows in some way from the principle of utility. However, as the case now stands in the philosophical world, the evidence indicates that the utilitarian is in trouble because of the problem of justice. There is no reason to think that the greatest total amount of good will be produced in a society when there is a just distribution. Societies exist in which that is not true. Before advanced technology, more good probably was produced by having the institution of slavery than by not having it. The action of keeping slaves would then, on utilitarian grounds, be morally right.

In chapter 5 of *Utilitarianism,* Mill makes a valiant attempt to save utilitarianism from this criticism; but, again, it is generally thought that he did not succeed. (At the end of this chapter there will be a brief presentation of Mill's view.)

If the criticism is restated in terms of which of two competing societies we should morally prefer, or which is morally better, the point can be made in a sharper way. Of course, we are not in a position to set up a society; as individuals, we do not have the resources or power. However, as members of a democratic society, we are constantly making decisions about which society is best and which one we should create. One of the important considerations in setting up or maintaining a society is the determination of morally preferable actions, and one of the important moral questions concerns the distribution of the things of value in our society. A theory of obligation that cannot provide adequate help with this question is deficient.

Apparently, there is a moral difference between two societies—one, a slave society; the other, a free society—that create the same amount of value. If there is a moral difference, then there is a moral difference in the worth of the action of setting up one of these societies rather than the other. Most of us would say that in most circumstances the creation or selection of the slave society is morally wrong. However, since the total amount of value created by either action (of creating either society) is the same according to utilitarianism, our choice of a society to work for is morally indifferent. If it *is* morally relevant that we distribute value in one way rather than another, and utilitarianism cannot account for that difference, then as an ethical theory it is essentially incomplete.

The temptation is to use some nonutilitarian grounds to determine which of the distributions is morally preferable. However, if this is done, utilitarianism, as it is usually understood, has been abandoned as a theory of obligation. Some philosophers suppose a theory of obligation should consist of some version of the principle of utility *and* a principle of justice.[14] Such people do not think a principle of justice can be reduced to, or derived from, a utilitarian theory of obligation. They believe that a theory of justice is independent of what we have called utilitarianism.

Exercises: Critical analysis of utilitarianism

1. Choose some moral issue in which it would make a difference in your final (singular) moral judgment if you adopted utilitarianism rather than ethical egoism. Show how the application of each of the theories leads to your making different judgments. Now choose an issue in which the application of the different theories would make no difference in the singular judgment arrived at.

2. Critically evaluate the following argument: The counter-examples against the various forms of utilitarianism presuppose some other theory that is incompatible with utilitarianism. Of course, if we suppose the correctness of that incompatible theory, we can show that there is something wrong with utilitarianism, but that is true of any theory. So the counter-examples are not effective.

3. Present a utilitarian argument either in favor of or against Gerald Ford's pardoning of Richard Nixon (see page 26 for a description of that action).

4. J. S. Mill supposes that ordinary people actually do use utilitarianism as a theory in their moral reasoning, although they frequently do not recognize this fact. "It would, however, be easy to show that whatever steadiness or consistency these moral beliefs have attained, has been mainly due to the tacit influence of a standard not recognized. . . . The principle of utility . . . has had a large share in forming the moral doctrines even of those who most scornfully reject its authority" (*Utilitarianism,* p. 6). Critically evaluate this claim.

[14] William K. Frankena holds a version of that theory that we shall examine in the next chapter. William K. Frankena, *Ethics,* 2d ed., Prentice-Hall, Englewood Cliffs, N.J., 1973.

E.   Egoism and utilitarianism

The astute among you will have noticed that the criticisms of utilitarianism involving justice also apply to ethical egoism. In fact, there is no reasonable way egoism can generate out a theory of justice, whereas Mill at least presents some arguments in an attempt to show that utilitarianism accounts for the phenomena of justice. On this score, then, utilitarianism fares better than egoism. To the extent that utilitarianism can account for the rightness of actions that involve more than one person without any problem of inconsistency, it is also more acceptable than egoism. Evidence suggests that people use some kind of utilitarian standard more frequently than an egoistic one. Furthermore, you should consider what usually happens when the two kinds of considerations clash—when there is an irreconcilable conflict between your own good and that of the rest of your fellow human beings. Whichever way the resolution of this conflict turns out, it will provide evidence for one or the other of the two teleological theories.

In terms of the number and seriousness of criticisms, utilitarianism fares better than egoism. However, remember that so far we have examined only two theories of obligation, both of which are teleological; that is, both the egoist and the utilitarian suppose obligation and rightness are a function solely of the consequences of actions. They do disagree about the range of consequences that must legitimately be taken into account: the egoist limits the consequences to one person, while the utilitarian extends the range to all human beings. In the next chapter, we shall begin the examination of nonteleological theories of obligation.

Recommended reading

Acton, H. B., and J. W. N. Watkins. "Negative Utilitarianism." *Proceedings of the Aristotelian Society,* Supplement XXXVII (1963), 83–114. Do we have more of an obligation to relieve suffering than to bring about positive good? If your answer is "yes," your utilitarianism will take a different form than otherwise.

Bentham, Jeremy. *An Introduction to the Principles of Morals and Legislation.* Hafner, New York, 1948. Bentham's work most influenced Mill, though the latter's views are not always the same as Bentham's.

Brandt, Richard B., ed. *Justice and Equality.* Prentice-Hall, Englewood Cliffs, N.J. 1962. Brandt presents a variety of essays on a variety of topics concerning justice.

Lyons, David. *Forms and Limits of Utilitarianism.* Oxford University Press, London, 1965.

Mill, J. S. *Utilitarianism,* ed. Samuel Gorovitz. Bobbs-Merrill, Indianapolis, 1971. The text of Mill's *Utilitarianism* is reprinted along with many excellent articles about that work and its problems.

Narveson, Jan. *Morality and Utility.* Johns Hopkins, Baltimore, 1967.

Rescher, Nicholas. *Distributive Justice.* Bobbs-Merrill, Indianapolis, 1966.

Sidgwick, Henry. *The Methods of Ethics,* 7th ed. Macmillan, London, 1962. This is a very detailed and carefully worked out utilitarian position by a late nineteenth-century author.

Smart, J. J. C. *An Outline of Utilitarian Ethics.* Melbourne University Press, Victoria, 1961.

Appendix

Justice

While we cannot fully treat the topic of justice, we should at least outline the main rival theories in order to better understand the issues raised in chapter 3. The accounts of each theory must be brief, so if you wish to examine the views in greater detail, you should read from the works quoted or from the ones listed in the recommended reading. Since this is a chapter on utilitarianism, let us begin with J. S. Mill's views on justice.

Mill's strategy should be quite familar to us. First, he lists a set of phenomena that people generally believe to fall within the topic of *justice;* then he attempts to show that utilitarianism can account for these phenomena. For example, he notes that we suppose it unjust to deprive someone of liberty, property, or "any other thing which belongs to him by law." [1] When we know that certain laws are unjust, this highlights the injustice of "taking or withholding from any person that to which he has a *moral right.*" [2] We think it unjust for a person to "obtain a good or be made to undergo an evil which he does not deserve." [3] We suppose it unjust to "break faith with anyone . . . [and] to be *partial*—to show favor or preference . . . [where these] do not properly apply." [4]

These phenomena are, so Mill claims, explained by his view:

> Duties of perfect obligation are those duties in virtue of which a correlative *right* resides in some person or persons; duties of imperfect obligation are those moral obligations which do not give birth to any right. I think it will be found that this distinction exactly coincides with that which exists between justice and the other obligations of morality. . . . Whether the injustice consists in depriving a person of a possession, or in breaking faith with him or in treating him worse than he deserves, or worse than other people who have greater claims—in each case the supposition implies two things: a wrong done, and some assignable person who is wronged. Injustice may also be done by treating a person better than others; but the wrong in this case is to his competitors, who are also assignable persons. It seems to me that this feature in the case—a right in some person, correlative to the moral obligation—constitutes the specific difference between justice and generosity or beneficence. Justice implies something which it is not only right to do, and wrong not to do, but which some individual person can claim from us as his moral right. [5]

[1] Mill, *Utilitarianism,* p. 54.
[2] *Ibid.,* p. 55.
[3] *Ibid.,* p. 55.
[4] *Ibid.,* p. 56.
[5] *Ibid.,* pp. 61–62.

If, as Mill supposes, he can give his standard utilitarian analysis of the notions of *obligation* and *right,* then he will have given an account of justice without bringing in some principle independent of the principle of utility. Mill is very careful to give a psychological explanation of how it has happened that justice has a different "feel" to it than ordinary obligations. However, this is not essential to our discussion.

Has Mill succeeded? It is not at all clear how this account of justice adequately responds to the criticisms in the chapter, but that will be left up to you to determine. Now, in very brief fashion, here are some other accounts of justice.

One view which is popular in the United States we can call *competitionism.* "The ethical principle that would directly justify the distribution of income in a free market society is, 'To each according to what he and the instruments he owns produces.' "[6] This principle, as applied here, by Milton Friedman, is directed to income policy alone, but, without difficulty, we can extend it to the level of a general principle of justice. So stated, it might appear as follows:

> If any distribution of things of value is a result of competition in the economic system, then that distribution is just.

There are many problems with an unrestricted principle of this sort. For example, should we allow those who cannot compete (the sick, the mentally handicapped, and so on) to starve? What do we do about those forms of competition that lead to the absence of competition? What provisions do we make for national defense? Do we set aside some supplies independently of the market mechanism? These adjustments would require a more complex principle, and it is not at all clear what such a principle would look like. We can say that as it stands the principle is inadequate as a theory of justice; we must await a further statement of it before any final decision can be made.

A view that is also popular would make distribution a function of merit. A general statement of this view might be:

> If any distribution of things of value is on the basis of merit, then that distribution is just.

Most people who hold a theory such as this realize the need for some test or further specification of merit. The problem has been that many of the proposed tests of merit are apparently not morally acceptable. Some have claimed that you have merit when you are an Aryan, or a member of the Central Committee, or of noble birth. Obviously, this indicates the need for a test to determine which standards of merit are morally acceptable. One test that might work is to determine if the distribution of things of

[6] Milton Friedman, *Capitalism and Freedom,* Univ. of Chicago Press, Chicago, 1962, pp. 161–162.

value under the standard resulted in a just distribution. This, of course, cannot be done because merit is supposedly being used to explain the notion of *just distribution*. Furthermore, we cannot leave the notion of *merit* unspecified because there are competing notions, some of which, at least, are clearly unacceptable.

As Mill points out in his listing of the moral phenomena, equality is one thing we are concerned about when we discuss justice. A general principle of justice in the equalitarian tradition might be:

> If any distribution of things of value is equal, then that distribution is just.

There have been many attempts to specify *equality*. Some have used numerical equality: we each take numerically the same amount and take turns when there isn't enough to go around. This approach runs into difficulty in a way pointed out by Aristotle long ago. The amount of food that an active woodsman needs is more than that needed by a sedentary clerk, so a numerically equal amount of food for each would sometimes be unjust. Such considerations led Aristotle and others to introduce some notion of *proportional increase* in the amount of value in a person's life.

> Treating people equally does not mean treating them identically; justice is not so monotonous as all that. It means making the same relative contribution to the goodness of their lives (this is equal help or helping according to need) or asking the same relative sacrifice (this is asking in accordance with ability).[7]

This statement by Frankena is representative of the sort of position equalitarian philosophers are inclined to move toward. A number of questions about the term 'same relative contribution' remain unanswered, however. Do we accept the judgment of each person as to what his or her own relative contribution should be? Do we accept each person's judgment of what each needs in order for there to be a proportional increase in the good of each? This doesn't appear to be acceptable. So we must also await some further specification of this view.

Is there a communist theory of justice? Those who claim there is begin with these words of Marx:

> In a higher phase of communist society, after the enslaving subordination of the individual to the division of labour, and with it also the antithesis between mental and physical labour, has vanished; after labour has become not only a means of life but itself life's prime

[7] William K. Frankena, *Ethics,* 2d ed., Prentice-Hall, Englewood Cliffs, N.J., 1973, p. 51.

want; after the productive forces have also increased with the all-round development of the individual, and all the springs of co-operative wealth flow more abundantly—only then can the narrow horizon of bourgeois right be crossed in its entirety and society inscribe on its banners: From each according to his ability, to each according to his needs![8]

Marx obviously has a certain context in mind when he proposed this principle. It seems clear that we have not reached the point he describes before the principle of distribution can be put into effect. Shall we conclude that all distributions are now not just? The principle, taken from its context, would be:

If any distribution of things of value follows the rule "From each according to his ability, to each according to his needs," then that distribution is just.

If we attempted to apply this principle now, before the "springs of co-operative wealth flow more abundantly," either nothing would be just, or severe difficulties would arise. We cannot use 'need' in the sense that individuals now have need, for that would not result in any just distribution. What do we do when some supposed or even real needs are incompatible? These questions would have to be answered in order for Marx to have a complete theory of justice.

As a result of the work of John Rawls, contemporary writers have recently taken up the topic of justice with enthusiasm. Rawls's position is as follows:

First Principle
> Each person is to have an equal right to the most extensive total system of equal basic liberties compatible with a similar system of liberty for all.

Second Principle
> Social and economic inequalities are to be arranged so that they are both:
> (a) to the greatest benefit of the least advantaged, consistent with the just savings principle, and
> (b) attached to offices and positions open to all under conditions of fair equality of opportunity.[9]

[8] Karl Marx, *Critique of the Gotha Programme*, Foreign Languages Press, Peking, 1972, p. 17.
[9] John Rawls, *A Theory of Justice*, Harvard University Press, Cambridge, 1971, p. 302.

Rawls's theory is quite complicated, and a full explanation would require much more time and space than we have. For now, we shall have to be content with this exposure.

In this short appendix you have seen some of the theories of justice that are available. It is not necessary for you to choose one to continue in the investigation of which normative ethical theory is best. You may finally say, as Mill does in effect, that whatever turns out to be the best normative ethical theory will also tell us what is the morally proper way to distribute things of value. However, should that not be so, you may wish to return to this topic later.

Four

Chapter four
Rule deontology

In chapters 2 and 3 we examined two teleological theories of obligation, theories that restrict the considerations relevant to *rightness* and *obligation* to the consequences of actions performed by people. The following general form of a theory of obligation will help us to contrast this kind of theory with another.

> If any x is F, then x is M.
> This x is F.
> ─────────────────────────
> Therefore,
> This x is M.

Teleological theories restrict the substitution instances of F to consequences of actions, such as leading to more good for one individual or for the greatest number of individuals. *Deontological* theories of obligation are the negation of such theories, those which do not restrict the substitution instances of F to consequences. For example, one such theory has the following moral principle: "If any action would be judged by the majority of persons living in a culture as morally right, then in that culture the action is morally right." This form of ethical relativism is not concerned with the consequences of actions; in fact, for it, consequences are irrelevant. Another view, one we shall call *agapism,* maintains that the correct moral principle is "If any action is performed out of love, then it is morally right." Once again, this principle has no reference to consequences.

Not all deontological theories ignore consequences entirely. Some claim that consequences do matter, but only as one of many factors relevant in determining the moral rightness of an action. William Frankena, for example, suggests that we should use two considerations to determine whether an action is right—the amount of good or value resulting from the action, and the way in which that value is distributed. For such views, there are at least two rules and, correspondingly, two different kinds of instances of F that are relevant to rightness of actions. In contrast, egoism and utilitarianism claim that only the amount of value that is a consequence of an action is relevant. The complication of bringing in more than one kind of substitution instance of F will require considerable explanation before we can evaluate such deontological theories. In fact, the number of different kinds of rule deontological views is so great that we will need a fairly complicated set of distinctions in order to know which view is being discussed. Fortunately, one set of distinctions has already been introduced, and the others can be set out without great trouble.

The sections in this chapter will be arranged as follows:
- A. Distinctions old and new
- B. Multiple categorical rule theories
- C. Multiple prima facie rule theories
- D. Single categorical rule theories
- E. A look back; a look ahead

A. Distinctions old and new

In chapter 1 the distinction between a categorical and prima facie rule was drawn. A rule that holds no matter what else is true of the action or thing to which it applies is a *categorical rule.* In contrast, a rule that can be overridden by a rule of the same type is a *prima facie rule.* "If you have made three outs, then your side is no longer at bat" is a categorical rule of baseball. No matter what else is true of your team and no matter what else happens, you are no longer at bat. When the antecedent of "If an enclosed plane figure has three straight sides, then it is a triangle" applies to a figure, then no matter what else is true of that figure, it is a triangle. It may be green, drawn in the sand, exist only in your mind, or whatever; but if the antecedent is fulfilled, then so is the consequent, no matter what other predicates apply to it. A prima facie rule is always one of at least two such rules; for one rule can't override another unless there is another to be overridden. One theory we shall look at shortly maintains that there is a principle of justice and a principle of beneficence [1]—the second enjoins us to bring about good, and the first, to distribute it in a certain manner. There will be a further explanation of 'prima facie' when such theories are examined later in this chapter.

Egoism and utilitarianism not only limit the values of F to consequences but also limit the consequence to only one kind that is to count in the determination of the rightness or obligation associated with actions. The egoist claims that the only factor is the amount of benefit that I, an individual, receive, whereas the utilitarian claims that the benefit to all is what is important. Even though each of the theories has a rule concerning obligation and another concerning rightness, they agree that the difference between rightness and obligation is not of the kind of consideration—the consequences for someone or some group—but rather of which action will

[1] For our purposes, it would not be misleading to call it a version of the utilitarian principle.

bring about the most of those consequences. There are not two kinds of considerations, such as bringing about good and distributing it in a certain way, but only one kind of consideration. Theories maintaining only one kind of consideration will be called *single rule theories,* and those maintaining more than one will be called *multiple rule theories.* So a theory that maintains both a rule of justice and a rule calling for the maximization of benefit is a multiple rule theory. As we know, both egoism and utilitarianism are single rule theories.

The two sets of distinctions—categorical versus prima facie and single rule versus multiple rule—cross to generate the chart shown as Figure 4-1. This figure will be useful in reviewing this chapter, and it will assist you now as you begin each section; it charts the different views to be discussed and indicates why certain views are put together. However, don't try to memorize it as a means of understanding the views to be discussed, for that will be fruitless.

The discussion begins with multiple categorical rule theories because they are the most obviously flawed and will allow a clear presentation of the strategy we will use in discussing deontological theories.

B. Multiple categorical rule theories

A theory that maintains that there are at least two categorical rules of obligation or right is a multiple categorical rule theory. Two such theories will be examined briefly: one is an attempted combination of egoism and utilitarianism, and the other is an interpretation of the Ten Commandments taken as an ethical theory.

1. Egoism and utilitarianism combined   Many who have read the first three chapters will understand quite well the flaws of egoism and see also some of the difficulties in utilitarianism. Some of you will be tempted to try to make up the deficiencies of the theories by combining them. If one argues, loosely, that egoism has a defect on the side of benefit for oneself,

	Single		Multiple	
Categorical	Direct	Indirect	Egoistic utilitarianism	
	Agapism	Agapism Kantianism Relativism	A Ten Commandments theory	
Prima facie			Direct	Indirect
			Ross	Frankena

Figure 4-1   A classification of ethical theories according to the types of rules involved

then it seems to make some sense to suggest a theory that simply incorporates both egoism and utilitarianism. If we consider just the direct versions of these theories with respect to *obligation,* then we would have a theory with the following two rules:

> If a person *a* performs an action that increases person *a*'s own good (benefit) more than any other available action, then that action is obligatory.

> If any person *a* performs an action that increases the good (benefit) of the greatest number more than any other available action, then that action is obligatory.

A problem immediately arises when we consider those actions to which the two rules apply that give different results. There are times when an action would maximize your own good, but only at the expense of the good of the greatest number. Consider the typical "con man" who increases his own good only at the expense of others; it may be that certain business people and generals are in a similar position. If such people consider the first rule (egoism), then they are allowed to conclude that an action is obligatory. However, when the second rule is activated, that same action is seen as not obligatory. This is most embarrassing, for when the theory is used to help us arrive at a singular moral judgment to guide our actions, we are told that a certain action is both obligatory and not obligatory. In short, the theory leads to a contradiction—a fatal flaw for any theory.

How could this happen? It happens because the two rules are taken as categorical rules; once the antecedent applies to some situation, the consequent also applies, regardless of what else is true of that set of circumstances. When we activate the first rule, then we, as "con men," conclude that cheating a pensioner out of his or her monthly paycheck is obligatory; and when we activate the second rule, the conclusion is that the action is not obligatory.[2] We are not justified in qualifying the conclusion by saying

---

[2] The two rules are to be used, of course, with an appropriate second statement of the general scheme to arrive at a singular moral judgment. For example, the "con man," when he is considering cheating the pensioner and uses first the egoism part of the rule, would, we are supposing, reason as follows:

> If any person *a* performs an action that increases person *a*'s own good (benefit) more than any other available action, then that action is obligatory. Cheating this pensioner out of his or her monthly paycheck will increase my good (benefit) more than any other available action.
>
> Therefore,
> Cheating this pensioner out of his or her monthly paycheck is obligatory.

Since exactly the same reasoning can be used with a version of the second rule to conclude that the action is not obligatory, we arrive at a contradiction. ("If any person *a* performs an action that fails to increase person *a*'s good more than any other available action, then that action is not obligatory" is the relevant principle.)

that the action is obligatory (only) if the rule does not apply, for the rule is categorical.

It is easy to see that such a theory won't work; this is especially easy to see in the theory just examined. However, exactly the same problems arise for any theory having more than one categorical rule. When this is the case, conflicts are bound to occur; and since no provision is made for such conflicts, the theory is saddled with contradictions.

2. The Ten Commandments   A theory popular among nonphilosophers seems to call for ten different categorical rules. This theory, as you can guess from the discussion of the above egoistic-utilitarian theory, would be subject to many more sources of contradiction. In fairness to those who hold this theory, it should be said at the outset that there is undoubtedly a stronger version of that theory—and I shall suggest what it is at the end of the following discussion. At any rate, here are the Ten Commandments, thought by some to capture a theory of obligation:

1. Thou shalt have no other gods before me.
2. Thou shalt not make unto thee a graven image, nor any likeness of anything that is in heaven above, or that is in the earth beneath, or that is in the water under the earth; thou shalt not bow down thyself unto them, nor serve them; for I Jehovah thy God am a jealous God. . . .
3. Thou shalt not take the name of Jehovah thy God in vain. . . .
4. Remember the Sabbath day, to keep it holy.
5. Honor thy father and thy mother. . . .
6. Thou shalt not kill.
7. Thou shalt not commit adultery.
8. Thou shalt not steal.
9. Thou shalt not bear false witness against thy neighbor.
10. Thou shalt not covet thy neighbor's house, thou shalt not covet thy neighbor's wife, nor his manservant, nor his maidservant, nor his ass, nor anything that is thy neighbor's.

The list is no doubt familiar to most of you, but the form is not quite correct for this context. Therefore, let's transform a few of the commandments into moral rules of the form discussed here. The numbers before the transformed statements refer to the original numbers in the list.

5. If any person *a* honors (is in a position to honor) his mother or his father, then that action is obligatory.
6. If any person *a* kills (is in a position to kill), then person *a* has done what he or she is obliged not to do.
7. If any person *a* commits adultery, then person *a* has done what he or she is obliged not to do.
8. If any person *a* steals, then person *a* has done what he or she is obliged not to do.

9. If any person *a* bears false witness against a neighbor, then person *a* has done what he or she is obliged not to do.[3]

You should now be able to see how to transform the other commandments into the form of the first statement of the general scheme. The transformed statements, in conjunction with an appropriate second premise, would allow the derivation of a singular moral judgment. It should be noticed that I have translated the 'shalt nots' and the 'shalts' into 'obliged not' and 'obliged'. The context seems to indicate that obligations are being laid upon us, and not just that we are being told which actions are morally right. However, the same kinds of criticisms can be made regardless of the interpretation; so if you want to work with 'right' and not 'obligation', you should be able to modify the discussion in a relatively easy and straightforward manner.

First, because each of the rules is a categorical rule of moral obligation, we are entitled to offer counter-examples of the same sort presented against utilitarianism or egoism. The only difference is the number of rules against which we can offer counter-examples. Since the theory maintains that these are all rules of moral obligation and together they constitute a theory of obligation, then a counter-example to one of them is a counter-example to, and a criticism of, the entire theory.

There are some kinds of killing that are apparently not obligatory not to do; in some instances we have a right to kill. For example, we apparently have a right to kill a maniac who is shooting people from the top of a building and who cannot in any practical way be stopped short of death. (This very situation occurred in the University of Texas incident a number of years ago.) We seem to have a right to fight and kill in a war that is itself just (as was apparently the case with World War II). There are more controversial examples that might appeal to some of you—for example, whether you have a right to kill an aged parent who is suffering from terminal cancer. As usual, you are asked to join in and construct your own counter-examples.

Some people maintain that no matter what the set of circumstances and no matter who is involved, no one ever has the right to kill. This is a difficult issue to resolve here; and fortunately, it is not necessary for our discussion that we resolve it. All we need is enough counter-examples for enough of the rules that there is something for everyone, or that you are prompted to construct effective counter-examples from your own experience.

Suppose a mother steals a loaf of bread to feed her hungry children when there is no other way for her to get food and the society has more than enough to feed all its members. Does that person not have a right to

---

[3] The rules apply, of course, to contemplated actions—"If person *a* were to kill, then person *a* would do what is obligatory not to do," or to state this in another way, "If person *a* is in a position to kill, then person *a* is obliged not to kill." This kind of clarification can be carried out for all the rules.

do that? Consider the theft of a weapon from a person you know is going to use it to rob and maim somebody. Do you not have a right to do that? Suppose you are engaged in a just war and have an opportunity to steal secrets from the enemy. Is there any doubt that you have a right to do so? If not, then some occasions do exist on which you are not obliged not to steal, as Commandment 8 claims; and these represent counter-examples to that purported moral rule.

In addition to counter-examples, of which there are abundant numbers, the theory can be charged with inconsistency in the same way as the egoistic-utilitarian theory was. Suppose, as many Christians, Jews, and Muslims did, that you believe God orders you to convert the "heathen" by force. As history reveals with little coaxing, this requires the killing of large numbers of people. In other words, there are circumstances in which one or more of Commandments 1, 2, and 3 are inconsistent with Commandment 6. If you are to honor God and not take His name in vain, then if He commands you to do something that requires killing, you are obliged to do it. Activating the sixth moral rule (Commandment 6), though, you are entitled to conclude that you are obliged not to kill.

Commandment 6 is a fertile source of inconsistency. For example, depending on what it is to honor your parents (Commandment 5), if your parents ask you to honor them by providing a human sacrifice for their anniversary, you can't both fulfill this and not kill. Similarly, suppose that honoring your mother requires you to be at her birthday party, but to do so requires that you travel on the Sabbath. So you can't keep the Sabbath day holy and honor your mother both.

By this time, you should be able to construct situations from your own experience in which two of the rules apply resulting in an inconsistency. There are problems with interpreting some notions, such as *covet* and *vain,* but there should be enough clear examples to satisfy even the most scrupulous observer.

Must we conclude, therefore, that people who believe that the Ten Commandments have anything to do with our moral life are idiots? No, of course not! However, anyone who accepts the Ten Commandments literally as ten *categorical* moral rules is attempting to maintain a very awkward ethical theory. Such people are well advised to give up the Commandments as categorical rules; rather they should be interpreted as *prima facie* rules.

Exercises: Working with rules

1. Suppose we try to save the egoistic-utilitarian view by specifying what is to happen when the two rules conflict—for example, we say that the utilitarian rule is always to prevail. State what such a theory must say, what the principles would look like, and what kind of rule the conflict-resolution rule is. (That rule, the one that will tell us to follow the utilitarian principle when the two conflict, is obviously not a direct moral rule. What kind is it?)
2. Give some examples of categorical rules from sports or other games. Are there other types of rules within these games? Describe those rules, and try to say what kind of rules they are.

3. The laws that govern our society are often called *civil laws*. Such laws, as are found in criminal codes, traffic laws, and corporate law, are rules for behavior. Are any of them categorical laws? Are any of them clearly not categorical? Does the Bill of Rights pose any special problems?

C. Multiple prima facie rule theories

First, we must state clearly what a prima facie rule is. In the very brief treatment thus far, it has been said that a prima facie rule, as opposed to a categorical rule, can be overridden by other rules of the same type. Prima facie rules are designed, so to speak, to account for situations in which more than one rule can apply. Prima facie rules are such that a conflict between rules can occur and yet we can continue to hold both (or all) rules as moral rules. If we state more formally the nature of a categorical rule, then we can do the same for a prima facie rule.

> A rule R of the form "If any x is F, then x is M" is *categorical* =df Given that x is F, then no matter what other characteristic x has, it is M.

A consequence of this definition is that given that x is G, then as long as G is not simply not-M, it always follows that x is M. This can be seen clearly if we consider simple examples in plane geometry, as we did earlier. Once we establish that x is an enclosed-plane figure with three straight sides (F), then, no matter what other G we add (red, sides of 5 inches, drawn in ink, etc.), it is still true that x is a triangle.

We can now define what it is for R1, a member of a set of at least two rules, R1 and R2, to be a prima facie rule.

> A rule R1 of the form "If any x is F, then x is M" is *prima facie* =df When x is F, x would actually be M (for example, an actual duty) if R1 were the only rule, but R1 can be overridden by R2 and so x may not actually be M even though it is F.[4]

[4] Since we have divided rule theories into two types, categorical and prima facie, there are correspondingly two slightly different ways in which someone can come to have an actual duty. According to the categorical rule theories, someone has an actual duty to perform an action when that action falls under a categorical moral rule. In contrast, according to a prima facie rule theory, someone has an actual duty to perform an action when that action falls under a prima facie moral rule and there is no other prima facie moral rule overriding that one.

To get a less technical explanation of a prima facie rule, let us call upon W. D. Ross, the philosopher who introduced the notion in its modern sense:

> I suggest *'prima facie* duty' or 'conditional duty' as a brief way of referring to the characteristic (quite distinct from that of being a duty proper) which an act has, in virtue of being of a certain kind (e.g., the keeping of a promise), of being an act which would be a duty proper if it were not at the same time of another kind which is morally significant. Whether an act is a duty proper depends on *all* the morally significant kinds it is an instance of. The phrase *'prima facie* duty' must be apologized for, since (1) it suggests that what we are speaking of is a certain kind of duty, whereas it is in fact not a duty, but something related in a special way to duty. Strictly speaking, we want not a phrase in which duty is qualified by an adjective, but a separate noun. (2) *'Prima' facie* suggests that one is speaking only of an appearance which a moral situation presents at first sight, and which may turn out to be illusory; whereas what I am speaking of is an objective fact involved in the nature of the situation, or more strictly in an element of its nature, though not, as duty proper does, arising from its *whole* nature.[5]

This characterization, even though it may not be overly technical, does not present a clear and intuitively understandable explanation of 'prima facie'. To do that, we'll need to have some actual rules before us and then show how such a theory works. Let us continue with Ross's view.

> (1) Some duties rest on previous acts of my own. These duties seem to include two kinds, (a) those resting on a promise or what may fairly be called an implicit promise, such as the implicit undertaking not to tell lies which seems to be implied in the act of entering into conversation (at any rate by civilized men), or of writing books that purport to be history and not fiction. These may be called the duties of fidelity. (b) Those resting on a previous wrongful act. These may be called the duties of reparation. (2) Some rest on previous acts of other men, i.e., services done by them to me. These may be loosely described as the duties of gratitude. (3) Some rest on the fact or possibility of a distribution of pleasure or happiness (or of the means thereto) which is not in accordance with the merit of the persons concerned; in such cases there arises a duty to upset or prevent such a distribution. These are the duties of justice. (4) Some rest on the mere fact that there are other beings in the world whose condition we can make better in re-

---

[5] W. D. Ross, *The Right and the Good,* Clarendon Press, Oxford, 1930, pp. 19–20. All quotations from *The Right and the Good* that appear in this chapter are reprinted by permission of the Oxford University Press.

spect of virtue, or of intelligence, or of pleasure. These are the duties of beneficence. (5) Some rest on the fact that we can improve our own condition in respect of virtue or of intelligence. These are the duties of self-improvement. (6) I think that we should distinguish from (4) the duties that may be summed up under the title of 'not injuring others'. No doubt to injure others is incidentally to fail to do them good; but it seems to me clear that non-maleficence is apprehended as a duty distinct from that of beneficence, and as a duty of a more stringent character.[6]

Ross supposes that there are six prima facie rules of obligation, although he uses the term 'duty' to capture pretty much what we mean by obligation. He thinks he has discovered all the rules of moral obligation, although he would be willing to admit as many more rules as someone could reveal by producing counter-examples that show other sources of obligation. Here is a translation of the rules into the familiar form of the first premise of the general scheme:

1a. If any person *a* promises (explicitly or implicitly) to perform some action or to abstain from performing some action, then person *a* is obliged to perform that action or to abstain from that action. (fidelity)

1b. If any person *a* performs a wrong action with respect to person *b*, then person *a* is obliged to "undo" the wrong to person *b*. (reparation)

2. If any person *a* performs some service (favor) for person *b*, then person *b* has some obligation to person *a*. (gratitude)

3. If any person *a* merits a distribution of pleasure or happiness and person *b* can bring that distribution about (or prevent such a distribution that is not merited), then person *b* is obliged to distribute what is merited (or prevent what is not merited). (justice)[7]

4. If any person *a* can make some person *b* better with respect to virtue, intelligence, or pleasure, then person *a* is obliged to do so. (beneficence)

5. If any person *a* can make himself better with respect to virtue or intelligence, then person *a* is obliged to do so. (self-improvement)

6. If any person *a* is in a position to avoid hurting person *b*, then person *a* is obliged to do so. (nonmaleficence)

By this time everyone should know how each of the rules works to derive singular moral judgments. All that is required to derive singular

[6] *Ibid.*, p. 21.
[7] Ross has a specific theory of justice he supposes is correct. Elsewhere he defends the theory, but it is not now necessary to consider various theories of justice. One could put in any theory of justice and the theory of obligation would remain intact as representative of a certain kind.

moral judgments is appropriate second statements of the general scheme to go with the first statements presented above. For example, an appropriate second statement to go with rule 1a might be "I promised to pay George the 10 dollars I borrowed from him." This allows us to conclude that I am obliged to pay the money back to George.

Even though the derivation of singular moral judgments may be clear, some of the rules contain parts that are unclear. For example, it is not clear precisely what one is to do when a wrong is 'undone', as rule 1b requires; nor is it clear in rule 2 what kind of obligation person *b* has to person *a*. One would expect that the context would, in most circumstances, allow us to conclude what kind of obligation person *b* has. Thus, if someone rescues you from drowning, you probably would not say that you had an obligation to give that person your entire library or to become an indentured servant for 10 years. Similar contextual considerations will have to hold for the other rules and how they are to be understood. For our purposes, though, some lack of clarity will not hurt. Few of the criticisms trade on such unclarities; and when specific rules are involved in such criticisms, they will be explained more fully.

The rules are not categorical. From the fact that you promised to pay George back the 10 dollars we cannot conclude that no matter what else is true, you are obliged to pay back the 10 dollars.[8] Suppose that George is a fairly wealthy friend who does not need the money right away, and you meet someone on Christmas who cannot buy his children gifts because he has no money. This activates rule 4; and since he can buy the gifts with the 10 dollars and make himself and his children happy, you are obliged to give him the 10 dollars. Obviously, you cannot give him *and* George the 10 dollars, and you cannot be categorically obliged to do so—it is impossible to be obliged to do both at the same time. In this set of circumstances, according to Ross, we escape the puzzle by showing we have a prima facie obligation to pay George back the money and a prima facie obligation to give the money to the poor father. In this set of circumstances, the prima facie obligation to give the money so that Christmas presents can be bought is stronger than the prima facie obligation to pay the money back to George. So your actual obligation is to give the money for the Christmas presents.

This is not to say that you are no longer under a prima facie obligation to pay the money back to George. Even as you give the poor man the money, it is true that you have the prima facie obligation to give the money to George. This obligation, though, is overridden by the obligation to make the others happier. The next 10 dollars you have is George's, but he will hopefully understand that your obligation to him was not as strong as your obligation to increase the happiness of these other people. This is not to say that no matter who the others were, and no matter who George

---

[8] Since the rules are not categorical, from the simple fact that a prima facie rule applies, you cannot conclude that you have an actual duty to pay back the 10 dollars.

was, rule 4 would override rule 1a when they conflict.[9] One of the positive features of a prima facie rule theory is that it doesn't commit you to saying that one of the rules is always stronger than another; there is no need to specify a hierarchy of moral rules. One of the problems, as we shall see shortly, is explaining how one knows when one of the rules is stronger than another. About this problem, Ross has this to say:

> For the estimation of the comparative stringency of these *prima facie* obligations no general rules can be, as far as I can see, laid down. We can only say that a great deal of stringency belongs to the . . . duties of keeping our promises, of repairing wrongs we have done, and of returning the equivalent of services we have received. For the rest, "The decision rests with perception." This sense of our particular duty in particular circumstances, preceded and informed by the fullest reflection we can bestow on the act in all its bearings, is highly fallible, but it is the only guide we have to our duty.[10]

However, as indicated, we will discuss this in more detail later.

In any given set of circumstances, one or more of the prima facie rules may apply. The trick is to know which ones do apply and then, as a separate problem, decide which is the more stringent. Ross believes he has discovered all the sources of prima facie obligation, so we should not worry at all about whether there is yet another source. However, even if there should turn out to be additional rules of obligation, this would not be embarrassing to anyone holding a prima facie rule theory of obligation. All that would be needed would be the addition of the new rule to the list. Once we have the list of rules, next determine which ones apply in a given set of circumstances; and finally, determine which of the rules that do apply are stronger. Then we'll know what our obligations are in that set of circumstances.

This may seem like a lot of trouble, but it is a fairly easy procedure. Other philosophers have thought that two prima facie rules were enough. One such view, held by William Frankena, maintains that the two prima facie principles are those of beneficence and justice:

> What does the principle of beneficence say? Four things, I think:
> 1. One ought not inflict evil or harm (what is bad).
> 2. One ought to prevent evil or harm.
> 3. One ought to remove evil.
> 4. One ought to promote good.[11]

---

[9] Two prima facie rules conflict when, if each was the only one that applied, the person would have incompatible actual duties.

[10] Ross, *The Right and the Good,* pp. 41–42. Ross quotes Aristotle's *Nicomachean Ethics,* 1109 b 23, 1126 b 4, concerning perception.

[11] William K. Frankena, *Ethics,* 2d ed., Prentice-Hall, Englewood Cliffs, N.J., 1973, p. 47.

> . . . The principle of justice lays upon us the prima facie obligation
> of treating people equally . . . [that is], making the same relative
> contribution to the goodness of their lives . . . or asking the same
> relative sacrifice. . . .
>   . . . We can derive all of the things we may wish to recognize
> as duties from our two principles, either directly as the crow flies or
> indirectly as the rule-utilitarian does.[12]

Even though Frankena claims he has but two rules, it is easy to see
that the principle of beneficence contains four separate rules in it. The two
theories of Ross and Frankena are not as different as they might seem at
first. However, they do hold different theories of justice; and that, ul-
timately, would turn out to be a very important difference in choosing between them. In addition, Frankena wants his theory to be both a direct and
an indirect theory of obligation. The principle of beneficence is to be used
to derive other rules concerning injuries to others and liberty, for example.
However, these differences are less important to us now than the common
elements. Both theories are prima facie rule theories, and both recognize
the problem of the relative stringency of conflicting rules.

1. Noncategorical rules: a solution, a new problem   A prima facie
rule theory, as opposed to a categorical rule theory, allows rules to have ex-
ceptions; that is, the rule can apply and yet the person can avoid an actual
obligation to perform the action that falls under the rule. This is another
way of saying the obligation is not categorical, but the point is important
enough to make in a few different ways. Many people want to claim that
there are no absolute moral rules; what they mean is that there are no categorical moral rules. Adoption of a prima facie rule theory allows one to
maintain a rule theory of obligation and yet avoid a feature of some rule
theories that many people find objectionable—namely, rules that hold no
matter what. What are the problems with such theories?
One problem is what to do when two rules conflict.

> I see no way out of [the problem of conflict]. . . . It does seem to me
> that the two principles may come into conflict, both at the level of
> individual action and at that of social policy, and I know of no
> formula that will always tell us how to solve conflicts between their
> corollaries. . . . One can only hope that . . . we will . . . come to
> agree on ways of acting that are satisfactory to all concerned.[13]

Neither Ross nor Frankena supposes that there is a hierarchy of rules
such that one rule is always stronger than another. There are clear instances
in which the principle of justice overrides the principle of beneficence and

---

[12]*Ibid.,* pp. 47, 52. Remember that what Frankena calls *rule-utilitarianism* is
here called *indirect utilitarianism.*
[13]*Ibid.,* p. 53.

vice versa. For Ross the situation is more complex, since there are six rules; but the situation is essentially the same. There is no set order of the strength of the six prima facie duties. Frankena hopes that we shall all agree in time if we all come to have the "moral point of view." Ross supposes that at a certain point the issue is left up to "perception," that is, we just see in context which of the principles is stronger. I shall argue that neither of these responses is adequate; and, what is worse, they undermine the very theory the authors are trying to defend.

First, remember that both prima facie rule theorists hold that it is only via the rules that we are able to arrive at justified singular moral judgments. They hold that moral rules are *required* in order to arrive at singular justified moral judgments; without such rules we have no way of justifying our singular moral judgments. They hold, in short, that there is a set of moral rules that constitute our moral life—that there are moral constitutive rules. If there are ways of arriving at singular moral judgments without the rules the authors maintain are constitutive of morality (and there must be ways), then those rules are not constitutive of morality.[14] Furthermore, if it can be shown that the authors are committed to some such method, then they are shown thereby to give up the theory they claim they hold.

Suppose we take Ross and Frankena seriously when they say that in a given set of circumstances we can determine which of two competing prima facie rules and the corresponding obligations is more stringent, that is, which overrides which. Since the two rules of morality are not being used to determine which of the two conflicting rules of morality overrides the other, what basis do we have for making such a determination?[15] We could use some nonmoral basis, such as flipping a coin, but surely that is not acceptable to anyone who supposes that some moral judgments are justified and others are not. What we seem to use (and here it is open to the defender of prima facie rules to offer something else) is the knowledge that in this set of circumstances one of the proposed actions is obligatory and the other is not. However, if we can determine without the use of the prima facie rules that one action is obligatory and the other is not, then the rules cannot be the complete explanation of how to arrive at justified moral judgments. The basis of justified moral judgments cannot be the set of prima facie rules because we have at hand at least some justified moral judgments that are arrived at without the use of the rules. This conclusion, of course, is completely incompatible with a prima facie rule theory.

Let's catch our philosophical breath before we plunge on. You have been reminded that a rule theory requires that rules be used to arrive at justified singular moral judgments. When two prima facie rules conflict, this

[14] If this point has become vague, see again page 16 to refresh your memory concerning the nature of constitutive rules.

[15] You might be tempted to think that a third prima facie rule might settle the conflict, but this would not work. First, the prima facie rules are about actions, moral situations, and the like, not about rules. Second, the rule itself cannot state a fixed relationship of overridingness because on some occasions one rule overrides the other, but on other occasions this relation is reversed.

conflict is settled either with a rule or without a rule. It was shown above that the latter is not really a "live" option for the prima facie rule theorist. Well, if rules are to be used, are they constitutive rules or summary rules? If one maintains that we can arrive at justified singular moral judgments without the use of prima facie, or some other, constitutive rules,[16] one could maintain that the rules actually used are rules of thumb, inductive conclusions reached by having arrived at many singular moral judgments in just the manner described when there is a conflict between two prima facie rules. We can say that on the whole, in most cases, it is obligatory to try to make someone happier, but not always. This is good moral advice, a good rule of thumb, but it does require there be some means other than the rule of thumb to arrive at judgments that fall under that rule. The rule of thumb, if we put it in the familiar form, looks like this.

> If any person *a* can make person *b* happier, then it is likely that person *a* is obliged to do so.[17]

This kind of rule cannot serve as the basic method of determining what you are obliged to do. To see that, consider another rule of the same type.

> If any person *a* attends a university, then it is likely that person *a* can read.

This is a truth, but we arrived at it by observing that most persons attending universities can read. We performed, if you will, an induction in which we noticed two characteristics that tend to appear together—attending university and being able to read. Such an induction can be represented in the following way.

> Person *a* attends a university, and person *a* can read.
> Person *b* attends a university, and person *b* can read.
> Person *c* attends a university, and person *c* can read.
> Person *n* attends a university, and person *n* can read.
> _____
> Therefore,
> If any person *a* attends a university, then that person *a* can read.

Notice that the term 'likely' is not put in the conclusion of the argument. It is only added afterward, when we must remind the reader where the conclusion came from, that is, the kind of argument that supports it.

The conclusion, "If any person *a* attends a university then that person *a* can read," is drawn from premises that require us to know that someone can read without making use of that conclusion. We must be able to know

---

[16] The rules cannot be categorical, but this will be completely argued in the next section.

[17] It would make no difference for this context if we put the term 'likely' in front of the rule.

someone can read without making use of the general statement that we derive from knowing that some people can read and also attend a university. This is true of *summary rules,* rules drawn from inductive arguments like the one above; they presuppose some available method other than the inductive generalization to establish the truth of the premises. We can use the generalization, once we have arrived at it, to offer evidence that some given person can read. We do this kind of reasoning all the time without difficulty. However, we cannot say both that the generalization is the only way we can determine if someone can read and also that the generalization is an induction drawn from past instances, such as shown above.

Those who maintain that at least two prima facie moral rules are required to justify singular moral judgments cannot therefore also maintain that moral rules are summary rules. It cannot be maintained that sometimes we can determine which prima facie rule overrides another without the use of rules, for otherwise we undermine the whole basis of the claim that moral rules are required to arrive at singular moral judgments. So the attempt to provide summary rules as the means to settle the conflict between two prima facie moral rules fails.

2. A rule for determining stringency?   Suppose, then, that prima facie rule theorists do not claim to be able to determine which of two competing prima facie rules is more stringent without a rule. For, as we have just seen, this claim is incompatible with the theory. Well, then, they must claim that the conflict between two prima facie rules has to be settled by using a (constitutive) rule. What kind of rule? The rule that is to be used must be either itself a prima facie rule or a categorical rule. It is not, as Ross and Frankena both admit, a categorical rule, because in some circumstances the first prima facie rule overrides the second and in others the second rule overrides the first. There is no fixed hierarchy of prima facie rules.

If there is a rule that determines, in this set of circumstances, which prima facie rule overrides the other, then it must be a prima facie rule. If it is a prima facie rule, though, it cannot be a rule of the same set that contains the two that conflict; for those rules tell us which actions are obligatory and which are not, they do not tell us which rules to adopt. So the prima facie rule that tells us which of the two conflicting prima facie rules overrides the other in a situation must be an indirect or meta-moral rule.[18]

---

[18] Can a rule be both a direct and an indirect moral rule? Obviously the very same rule cannot, for one applies to actions and the other, as Frankena suggests, to rules. But one could use the same test, for example, maximizing utility, as the test for the moral worth of an action and the moral worth of a proposed direct moral rule. If one were to have both versions of utilitarianism, though, what would we do if there was a conflict between the direct and indirect rule in a given case? If we propose a given procedure to follow, for example, always let the direct rule override the indirect rule, then there will no doubt be counter-examples to this rule taken as a categorical rule. If it is a prima facie rule, then there would have to be another procedural rule, and the entire problem of the conflict of prima facie rules would arise at a different level.

If something is a prima facie indirect moral rule, though, there has to be at least one other such rule—for there is no such thing as one prima facie rule of anything. However, if there are at least two such indirect prima facie rules, then there will, again, be a situation in which there is a conflict of those two. And now the same problem arises that arose at the beginning: the conflict of the two indirect prima facie rules is either to be settled with the aid of a rule or without it. As we have seen, it is not possible for a prima facie rule theorist to allow the conflict to be settled without the aid of a rule. Therefore, the rule must be either a prima facie rule or a categorical rule. However, as we have already established it cannot be a categorical rule. Thus it must be a prima facie rule. However, it cannot be an indirect rule of the same type as the two that conflict, or else it could not settle the conflict.[19] If it is of a different level, then there is at least one other prima facie rule at that level with which *it* can conflict, and the conflict problem has not yet been resolved.

It would seem that this problem is not solvable by a prima facie rule theory. It does no good to talk about a moral point of view or what is known by perception, or the hope that in the future everyone will agree. None of these sentiments does away with actual conflicts that cannot be settled by a prima facie rule theory.

The above argument is more technical than any presented thus far. So a short summary revealing the structure of the argument more clearly is in order. In any system of prima facie rules, there are at least two such rules, PF-1 and PF-2. There are, in fact, situations in which PF-1 and PF-2 conflict. Such a conflict must be settled either with the use of a rule or without the use of a rule. It is not compatible with a prima facie rule theory that the conflict be settled without the use of a rule, for otherwise we would have to admit that we sometimes do not need rules at all to arrive at justified singular moral judgments. The rule that is used to settle the conflict must be either a categorical rule or a prima facie rule. It is not a categorical rule, for there is no set "weight" of PF-1 and PF-2; in some circumstances PF-1 overrides PF-2 and vice versa.[20] The rule is, then, a prima facie rule. However, the rule is not a rule of the same type, but an indirect rule, or a rule of a "higher" type. Let us call it IPF-1, for indirect prima facie rule 1. Since there are always at least two prima facie rules within a system of such rules, we know that there is a IPF-2. Since prima facie rules are designed to allow for conflicts that do, in fact, arise, a conflict situation will arise with respect to IPF-1 and IPF-2. At this point

---

[19] You might think that you could claim that the rules are of the same type if the indirect rules are of the same type, "If prima facie rules 1 and 2 conflict, then rule 1 overrides rule 2." However, the rule would then be something like "If indirect prima facie rules 1 and 2 conflict, then rule 1 overrides rule 2." This rule, though, is one of at least two that are about indirect prima facie rules 1 and 2; so the same kind of conflict situation with respect to it and the original can arise, and the same problem of a conflict situation has arisen at this indirect rule level.

[20] This is just another way of saying that there are effective counter-examples to the categorical rule.

we are back at the beginning of the argument, which starts with a conflict of two prima facie rules. Thus we see that the conflict situation leads forever to other conflict situations—something philosophers call a *vicious infinite regress*.

3. Counter-examples   In addition to the main argument against prima facie rules, there are some counter-examples that may be effective.[21] These are the type that show that there are instances of prima facie rules in which the action is not even prima facie obligatory. Recall, from our discussion of utilitarianism, that some actions (for example, scratching someone else's itch) bring about a small amount of benefit but are not thereby right or obligatory. If those counter-examples hold up, we can't even conclude that actions that fall under one of the purported prima facie rules are prima facie right or obligatory. The counter-examples concerning beneficence are to be found in the previous chapter on utilitarianism.[22] Perhaps the same kind of counter-example, concerning a principle of justice will round out the case against prima facie theories.

Ross and Frankena hold different theories of justice, so if we can construct counter-examples that don't depend on one specific principle of justice we'll be better able to do the job. Suppose the general principle of justice is as follows:

If any person *a* performs an action that consists of distributing some things of value in manner J, then that action is right (just).

If we consider the same kind of underwhelming value situation described above we can reach our counter-example. Suppose you have one M&M candy left in your bag on Halloween and ten children appear at your door. Can we say you have performed a just action if you carefully cut the candy into ten pieces? It hardly seems so. What about the man passing out free gum samples to anyone who wants one—regardless of race, religion, national origin, or sex? He does distribute something of some small benefit or value to people, but the action appears to have no positive moral worth. Again, you are asked to join in and construct examples from your own experience.

So we have one complicated criticism of prima facie rule theories and one criticism of the usual type with a twist. If these criticisms are effective, then there are apparently good reasons for rejecting prima facie rule theories. At this point, perhaps a word of sympathy is in order. Sooner or later, you are going to reach a state of intellectual fatigue and shock with respect to theories. As the next one comes up for consideration, the

[21] The main argument against prima facie rule theories is the immediately preceding one. I do not have nearly as much confidence in the argument that follows, for whether that argument is effective or not depends on the truth of certain things in theory of value.

[22] See pages 98 and 99.

thought arises, "I wonder what will be wrong with this theory?" It is easy to become cynical and skeptical about the possibility of reaching a correct theory because of the emphasis on critical comments. However, if you have been careful, you will also realize that the criticisms are becoming more complicated, because the theories are getting better; they are harder to criticize. If, for example, you read through this book and are inclined to pick a prima facie rule theory to defend, you can read Ross, Frankena, or any of the other authors listed in the bibliography to see what the complete theory looks like. You may yourself be able to construct a viable way to respond to the criticism. This is, after all, a book that shows you the main theories; it does not purport to give you the last word. So be of good cheer as you proceed.

Exercises: Prima facie rules

1. State the theory of egoistic utilitarianism as a direct rule prima facie theory with two rules, and then offer an evaluation of it.
2. Evaluate the Ten Commandments theory as a direct prima facie rule theory.
3. Suppose we take egoistic utilitarianism to be a two-rule prima facie theory, with the egoistic principle as a direct rule and the utilitarian principle as an indirect rule. Critically evaluate that theory.
4. Explain very clearly why we should not equate summary rule with prima facie rule.

D. Single categorical rule theories

Egoism and utilitarianism, both the direct and the indirect versions, are single categorical rule theories. They are teleological theories, though, and the views we are about to consider are deontological theories of obligation. That is, the single rule proposed is not concerned only with the consequences of actions. The multiple prima facie rule theories examined above did, in part, bring in consequences, for one of the rules made obligation or rightness a partial function of consequences. However, these single rule deontological theories do not make obligation a function of consequences at all. It is for this reason that such views are sometimes called *formalistic*.

1. Agapism   Let us begin with a brief look at a view Frankena calls *agapism*. There is both a direct and an indirect rule version of this theory of obligation. The basis of the view comes from such biblical passages as the following:

> Thou shalt love the Lord thy God with all thy heart, and with all thy soul, and with all thy mind. This is the first and great commandment. And the second is like unto it, Thou shalt love thy neighbor as thyself. On these two commandments hang all the law and the prophets.   (Matt. 22:37–40)

For now, let us not consider God but rather translate into the appropriate form only the requirement to love our fellow humans.

Direct agapism
If any person *a* performs an action out of love, then that action is right.

Indirect agapism
If any person *a* acts on a moral rule that is likely to increase the amount of love in the world, then that is a direct moral rule.

The indirect version talks about increasing the amount of love in the world; and since it does, the most plausible interpretation of this is via the notion of consequences. The rule directs us to pick those rules to act from which have as a consequence an increase in the amount of love in the world. If we take a standard utilitarian view, such as was discussed in the last chapter, and interpret the things of value as limited to love of fellow humans, then we have indirect agapism. Insofar as this is so, we don't have a different view at all, but simply one version of utilitarian theory. Therefore, all the criticism of any other indirect utilitarian views also applies to this version; we do not need to consider it separately.

In direct agapism it is not clear how obligation should be handled. In the indirect version we can make the same moves as we did for utilitarianism; the action that brings about the most love possible from the alternatives is the obligatory one. We could say that the action done from the greatest love is the obligatory one, but that is highly artificial. Since there are other problems with direct agapism, though, let us not worry about how obligation would be explained.

One could interpret direct agapism, as we did with indirect agapism, as a form of direct utilitarianism. Once again, this results in a view that has already been discussed. So let's try to interpret it as a view that is different from any presented thus far. To do this, we simply state that there is only one source of rightness—love. If someone performs an action out of love, then it is right regardless of the consequences.

This view, set out this baldly, is quite deficient. There are many sources of right that have nothing to do with love. For example, someone who rescues a drowning person often does not feel any love toward that person. In fact, a rescuer may save someone toward whom he feels no such love; he may even feel the opposite, whether this is said to be hate or a feeling that the person is not a good person, or whatever. It does seem that this is frequently done. If so, then there is a large class of right actions that are not covered by the moral rule concerning love.

You may be tempted to say that we should simply add another moral rule, whatever it is, to supplement the law of love. However, the view that would result would not be a single rule theory. Further, and more important, the rule added would have to be either a categorical or a prima facie rule. And as has been shown, there are apparently great difficulties with both these kinds of views. So this temptation should be guarded against.

In addition to the class of right actions not covered by direct agapism, there are some actions that fall within the rule that are apparently not right. For example, suppose it is out of a sense of love toward your neighbor that you smile at her in the morning and say hello. This hardly seems to transform the action into one that has positive moral worth, one that is morally right. It is polite to do so, the neighborly thing to do, but it is not morally right. Suppose that out of a sense of love you torture someone so that he will recant what you take to be a heresy. An action such as this, frequently performed in the history of humankind, especially by Christians, apparently not right.[23] Such counter-examples are abundant; you can no doubt construct others of the same type from your own experience.

2. Kantianism   Since the procedure for criticizing theories is so well known by now, no more will be done with agapism. You can follow up any interest you have in the subject by consulting the bibliography at the end of this chapter. Let us now take up the most influential single rule deontological theory, kantianism, named for its author. Immanuel Kant constructed a very complicated, subtle, and elaborate theory of obligation, so the following discussion does not purport to capture it fully. The intention is to give you an idea of the kind of theory he held and to indicate the kinds of criticisms that have traditionally been directed against it. To see the difficulty in interpreting Kant, let's examine a few passages from him.

> An action done from duty has its moral worth, *not in the purpose* to be attained by it, but in the maxim in accordance with which it is decided upon; it depends therefore, not on the realization of the object of the action, but solely on the *principle of volition* in accordance with which, irrespective of all objects of the faculty of desire, the action has been performed. That the purposes we may have in our actions, and also their effects considered as ends and motives of the will, can give to actions no unconditioned and moral worth is clear from what has gone before. Where then can this worth be found if we are not to find it in the will's relation to the effect hoped for from the action? It can be found nowhere but *in the principle of the will,* irrespective of the ends which can be brought about by such an action. . . .
>
> But which kind of law can this be the thought of which, even without regard to the results expected from it, has to determine the

---

[23] Here you may want to invoke the distinction between an action being right and a person being a good person. The action is wrong, you may want to say, but the agent is a good person for doing what he believes is right. This can be said, but it does not save the moral theory, for it concerns actions that people perform on the basis of certain evidence. The person is, so to speak, already built into the rule.

will if this is to be called good absolutely and without qualifications? Since I have robbed the will of every inducement that might arise for it as a consequence of obeying any particular law, nothing is left but the conformity of actions to universal law as such, and this alone must serve the will as its principle. That is to say, I ought never to act except in such a way *that I can also will that my maxim should become a universal law.* Here bare conformity to universal law as such (without having as its base any law prescribing particular actions) is what serves the will as its principle, and must so serve it if duty is not to be everywhere an empty delusion and a chimerical concept. The ordinary reason of mankind also agrees with this completely in its practical judgments and always has the aforesaid principle before its eyes.[24]

In order, Kant espouses the following views:

1. Consequences (purposes attained by the action) are not the determinants of moral obligation.
2. The moral worth of an action (that it is right or the fulfillment of an obligation) is a function of the rule (principle of volition) from which the action is performed.
3. The rule chosen must be chosen independently of any desire to achieve an end, or even from any desire regarding the rule itself.
4. The indirect moral rule that allows us to choose the direct moral rules from which to act morally cannot have any particular actions or moral rules contained within it.
5. The form of such an indirect moral rule is, as stated by Kant, "I ought never to act except in such a way that I can also will that my maxim [direct moral rule in this case] should become a universal law."

Maybe we can shed more light on these claims by translating them into our usual general form. The rule, an indirect moral rule that Kant calls the *categorical imperative,* would be written as follows:

If any person *a* performs an action from a rule R where R (1) is willed by person *a* and (2) can be willed to be a universal law of nature, then R is a rule of moral obligation.

The rule is categorical, in roughly the sense introduced above, but it does not apply directly to actions, only to moral rules.

[24]*The Moral Law: Kant's Groundwork of the Metaphysics of Morals,* translated and analyzed by H. J. Paton, Hutchinson University Library, London, 1948, pp. 66–70.

We have seen the words Kant uses to state one version of the categorical imperative, and we have translated that imperative into a rule of the form familiar to us all, but as yet we have no real understanding of how the indirect rule works in selecting direct moral rules. Kant attempts to help us once again, but I fear the help will not be as great as we might like.

> Suppose I seek, however, to learn in the quickest way and yet unerringly how to solve the problem 'Does a lying promise accord with duty?' I have then to ask myself 'Should I really be content that my maxim (the maxim of getting out of a difficulty by a false promise) should hold as a universal law (one valid both for myself and others)? And could I really say to myself that everyone may make a false promise if he finds himself in a difficulty from which he can extricate himself in no other way?' I then become aware at once that I can indeed will to lie, but I can by no means will a universal law of lying; for by such a law there could properly be no promises at all, since it would be futile to profess a will for future action to others who would not believe my profession or who, if they did so over-hastily would pay me back in like coin; and consequently my maxim, as soon as it was made a universal law would be bound to annul itself.
>
> Thus I need no far-reaching ingenuity to find out what I have to do in order to possess a good will. Inexperienced in the course of world affairs and incapable of being prepared for all the chances that happen in it, I ask myself only 'Can you also will that your maxim should become a universal law?' Where you cannot, it is to be rejected, and that not because of a prospective loss to you or even to others but because it cannot fit as a principle into a possible enactment of universal law.[25]

Here Kant attempts to give us an example of how his indirect rule works. He has chosen an easy enough case to understand, where we can get out of some trouble or solve a problem by promising to do something with no intention of fulfilling that promise. For example, I need money to pay off my gambling debts, so I lie to my friend when I borrow money, saying that I will pay it back next week when I know I can't. The moral rule (maxim) from which I act could be stated in the following way:

> If any person a performs an action of lying with respect to a promise that enables him to get out of a difficulty then person a has a right to perform the action (he has no obligation not to perform it).

This is clearly a recognizable direct moral rule and, in conjunction with the appropriate second statement (This person a peforms . . .), allows us to derive a singular moral judgment (The person has a right to perform the action). Kant supposes that the categorical imperative, the indirect moral rule, shows that this proposed direct moral rule is not acceptable as such. It is not acceptable, Kant says, because such a moral rule could not be willed to be a universal law; it does not pass the test of the indirect moral rule that he calls the categorical imperative. Why does he think this? Alas, I can't really say because I don't see how the indirect rule works. However, I can say how it is *not* intended to work.

Kant does not mean to say that if everyone told lies when they were in trouble and promised to do things that they had no intention of doing, confidence in other people would erode and soon no one would accept any promises made. If he took this approach, he would be offering a utilitarian defense of the direct moral rule; that would make the categorical imperative a version of the principle of utility. In fact, this is just the criticism Mill offers of Kant. So this is *not* how to interpret Kant.

Kant seems to think that there is something *logically* deficient about a direct rule concerning lying. He and many of his followers suggest that there is a contradiction in logic in willing such a rule. However, I see no logical difficulty in adopting the direct moral rule about lying, or in agreeing to allow anyone else in those circumstances to lie also. Even if I should be inconsistent and not allow anyone else to lie to solve a problem, this does not seem to generate a logical difficulty, a contradiction. If there really is no contradiction, then the test of the indirect rule does not seem to work, as the kantian requires.

In addition, there are times when the conditions for a moral rule laid down by the indirect moral rule are met and yet the resulting action from the direct rule is not morally right at all. The proposed direct rule "If any person *a* performs an action that enables him to scratch an itch on his head with his hand, then that person has performed a morally right action" is something that can pass the test of the indirect rule or categorical imperative. However, no such action has positive moral worth, and one can generate such rules indefinitely.

Someone might suggest that the rule should read that the person has a right to scratch his head, and not that the action is right. This would be a way to escape the counter-examples, but it raises another question of how the indirect rule works. Supposedly, any proposed direct moral rule that passes the test of the indirect moral rule gives us a source of obligation. Now, to save the theory, we are told that this is not so, that the rule generates *right to do,* not *right* or *obligation.* How then shall we account for such notions? Recall that a theory that can only account for *right to* cannot thereby account for *right.* In addition, the more or less mechanical way of generating out obligations from not having the right not to seems not to be open here because, as the first kinds of counter-examples appeared to show, there is almost no action we don't have a right not to perform. That is, the indirect rule appears to "pass" proposed direct moral rules that allow almost any action to be one we have a right to do. See the immediately preceding counter-examples for evidence of this.

Other counter-examples the kantian apparently can't handle are what we might call "pseudo-generalizations." Suppose someone wills a moral rule of the following sort: "If any person *a* whose fingerprints are such and such a type performs an action of so and so, then that action is right (obligatory)." You could demonstrate that this proposed moral rule passes the indirect rule, for since you are the only one with those fingerprints, there can be no conflict with any other willing and no contradiction with other direct rules. You may say this is cheating, but there is nothing in the indirect rule that makes this procedure illegitimate.

These are some of the standard problems philosophers have found with kantianism. However, to remind you, the actual view is much more complicated than I have indicated here. For this reason, some of you may wish to pursue Kant's ethical theory further, and this is, of course, what you should do. However, in our brief survey of single categorical rule theories we shall now proceed to a very popular view, relativism.

3. Ethical and cultural relativism   Relativism is a view held by many students and sociologists. As is true with most popular views, it is difficult to get a clear grasp of what the view actually is. Those who hold the view feel very strongly about absolutes; they deny the existence of any such things. However, as we have seen, except for those who claim that categorical direct moral rules exist, and perhaps those who claim that indirect categorical moral rules exist, no view so far examined claims that there are absolutes. Relativists maintain that the knowledge in the possession of the people performing actions should have a bearing on whether the actions are right or wrong. But again, this is something that almost all the ethical theories we have examined agree to and can easily account for. Instead of trying to discover what is distinctive about relativism only by citing what those who hold the view say about it, let us use the usual procedure and state the view in the general scheme. As a moral theory, the view appears first as a direct moral rule theory and then as an indirect moral rule theory.

If any person *a* of culture C performs an action that is believed by the people of C to be right (or obligatory), then that action is right (obligatory).

If any proposed direct moral rule R is believed by the people of C to be a direct moral rule, then R is a direct moral rule.

As usual, some of these notions need further explanation. What is meant by 'the people of C' is any people who have been raised in culture C and have been taught all the things that someone normally would be taught in that culture. For example, someone might have been raised in India but taught in American schools in that country, resided in a neighborhood that had only Americans, and then returned to the United States.

That person would be someone who, for a time, is *in* culture C but not *of* that culture. That person would be a person of the American culture.[26]

It does not happen, with the possible exception of extremely small populations, that every person in a culture agrees that an action of a certain sort is right or that a proposed moral rule is indeed a moral rule. So we must interpret the claim that the people of C believe the rule to be a moral rule or the action to be right as meaning that a *majority* of people in that culture do so. How much of a majority there must be before the rule is taken as a moral rule is difficult to say, but once again we should be able to arrive at some agreement about the (rough) percentage who must hold the belief.

Many of those who defend this kind of ethical theory use the expression 'true for' in both of the above statements. There is a sense of 'true for', as was mentioned in the first chapter, that means the same as 'believes' or 'accepts'. There is nothing wrong with using this expression, but there is the danger that those who use it will suppose it to mean the same thing as 'true', or that there is no use for 'true' but only a use for 'true for'. Both these claims are false, as has been shown in the first chapter. So we shall not use 'true for', but it is useful to see how it has been used by those who are fond of it.

The notion of *true for* often comes up in connection with the denial of something called an absolute. We shall discuss the problem of absolutes in this section, but once again it will be argued that whatever points one wants to make in this regard are best made using some other expressions.

Now we have before us the statements of relativism and an explanation of what those statements mean. Why would anyone hold this view? Most frequently, one finds an empirical view being put forward as a defense of the ethical theory. The empirical view is that anthropologists have discovered that moral opinions vary from culture to culture. The Eskimos, we are told, think it is right to put an aged parent on an ice floe and push it out to sea, but we do not. In some cultures they think it is alright to eat other human beings, and in other cultures they do not. This is the kind of exciting information all of us are aware of from television, if from no other source. This position, like psychological egoism, is clearly based on observation; thus it is called an empirical view. Philosophers call this view *cultural relativism,* to distinguish it from the ethical theories that we shall call *ethical relativism.* The ethical theories, you may note, allow the derivation of singular moral judgments, but the empirical theory does not. The ethical theory acts as an aid in arriving at moral judgments, whereas the empirical view only records the fact that moral judgments were arrived at. The

---

[26] You may think there is some precise set of items that indicate or define one culture rather than another. This does not seem to be so, or at least it is very difficult to pick out such items. All that is necessary to distinguish cultures is some set of items, however vague it might be, that most anthropologists or sociologists can pick out.

empirical view is one that almost all people agree to, for the evidence is very strong indeed. The ethical theory is much more controversial, and most people do not accept it. However, if the empirical view does support the ethical theory, and the empirical view is correct, then we have good grounds for accepting the ethical theory. First, though, let us have a more precise statement of cultural relativism, so we can see if it supports ethical relativism.

> If any person *a* of culture C makes a moral judgment (adopts a moral rule), then that judgment (adoption of the rule) is a result (causal) of person *a's* being of culture C.

Once again, a few parts of this statement of cultural relativism need clarification. The statement points up something that seems harmless enough—namely, that when we learn moral rules, for example, we learn them from our parents or in school or church. These are people or institutions that "reflect" a certain culture, and it is natural for them to teach children a certain point of view. As we all know, children are very much influenced by their teachers, and they wind up, on the whole, maintaining very nearly the same views as those espoused by their teachers and institutions. This relation is a kind of causal relation; the child is caused to come to hold certain views by cultural and societal pressures.

However, we must not say that the causal pressures are always effective. If you throw a ball with a certain force against a pane of glass that has a certain tensile strength, the glass always breaks. If you dip a naked human being in molten steel for 30 seconds, he always dies. If you push the same naked human being off a cliff, he always falls. These are invariant causal relations, for the causal forces are, we might say, very strong. This is not the case with cultural pressures. They are difficult to resist, but many persons do resist, holding views that are different and often inconsistent with those expressed by their culture. This is one reason we must talk about the majority of people rather than all of them, for many persons resist the pressures and adopt views different from those around them.

So now we have two kinds of views before us; one kind is an ethical theory, and the other is an anthropological observation about differences between cultures. What connection is there between the two views? Certainly the ethical theory doesn't follow directly from the anthropological view, although some persons seem to argue that it does. They argue as follows:

> The members of tribe x judge (believe) that action B is morally right. The members of tribe y judge (believe) that action B is not morally right.
>
> ―――――――――――――――――――――――――――――――――――
>
> Therefore,
> Action B is right in tribe x and not right in tribe y.

If we take this to be a deductive argument, it is clearly invalid, for the conclusion simply does not follow from the premises. To show that a deductive argument is not valid, remember, we need only show that another argument of the same form goes clearly from true premises to a false conclusion. We do not have to choose another argument that is about the same subject matter, for the subject matter or content is irrelevant to an illustration of the validity of an argument. Thus, to show that the preceding argument is invalid, all we need do is present another argument of the same type that clearly has true premises and a false conclusion. This is easy enough.

Tribe x judges (believes) that burning incense cures measles.
Tribe y judges (believes) that burning incense does not cure measeles.

Therefore,
Burning incense cures measles in tribe x and does not cure measles in tribe y.

It is easy to see that the premises of this argument are true, for there are tribes that believe this sort of thing, and yet the conclusion is false. It does no good to complain that the subject matter of the two arguments is not the same, for the subject matter is irrelevant to whether or not the argument is invalid.[27] You may not like the particular example chosen. Choose your own favorite if you want. For example, there are still some who believe that the earth is flat, that diseases are caused by evil spirits, that Richard Nixon is the illegitimate son of Warren Harding, and so on. Any of these, or anything else you choose that is a false belief, as we say, will do.

These counter-examples show that the argument attempting to go from cultural relativism to ethical relativism, if it is interpreted as a deductive argument, is invalid. These counter-examples neither presuppose that moral judgments are objectively true nor that they are not. They do not require the existence of moral absolutes, nor do they deny their existence; they are entirely silent on the matter.

Can there be some kind of inductive connection between cultural and ethical relativism? There is no inductive argument of the usual sort, at any rate, that allows ethical relativism to be drawn from cultural relativism.

One very clear kind of induction that may help us is *enumeration*.[28] In this kind of inductive argument, you establish that two different kinds of phenomena always or very frequently occur together, and conclude that one is the cause of the other, or that they will go together always or frequently

[27] You may wish to refresh your memory on this point by reviewing pages 19–21.
[28] See pages 21 and 22.

in the future. For example, drinking 6 ounces of alcohol within an hour goes together with a certain feeling. If we call the drinking AL and the feeling that results within an hour E, for euphoria, we can construct the following argument:

$$\text{AL}a \ \& \ \text{E}a$$
$$\text{AL}b \ \& \ \text{E}b$$
$$\text{AL}c \ \& \ \text{E}c$$

.

.

.

$$\underline{\text{AL}n \ \& \ \text{E}n}$$

Therefore,
For any person n, if $\text{AL}n$, then $\text{E}n$ $[(n) \ (\text{AL}n \rightarrow \text{E}n)]$.

In simple English, the argument is that we have observed enough instances of the two phenomena going together to conclude that whenever the one occurs, it causes the other. Drinking alcohol causes drunkenness.

In terms of this model, the argument connecting cultural relativism to ethical relativism would require that we have a series of statements conjoined; the first conjunct would be a statement of cultural relativism, and the second, ethical relativism. An instance of such a statement would be as follows: "If Jones of the United States judges that Richard Nixon did the right thing in resigning, then Jones's judgment is a causal result of being of U.S. culture." Supposing that Jones did make this judgment, we can then, by using affirming the antecedent, claim that Jones did make the judgment and that the judgment is a causal result of Jones's being of the U.S. culture.[29]

The corresponding statement of ethical relativism would be "If Richard Nixon of the United States performed the action of resigning the presidency, which is believed obligatory by the people of the United States, then resigning the presidency is obligatory." Once again, since we can assert the antecedent, we can claim that the action was believed to be obligatory; and given the correctness of ethical relativism, it also was obligatory.

To illustrate an induction, let us symbolize the cultural relativism statement as CRrn and the ethical relativism statement as ERrn. The statements can be read either in their "if . . . , then . . ." form or in the form resulting when we affirm the antecedent and subsequently conjoin the antecedent and the consequent. Either way, we will arrive at a series of statements that would appear as follows:

[29] About two-thirds of the people in the United States held this view when Nixon resigned.

CRrn & ERrn
CRcp & ERcp
CRa & ERa
.
.
.
CRn & ERn

Therefore,
If any action is believed by the people of the United States to be obligatory, then that action is obligatory.

In the preceding scheme, 'rn' refers to the Richard Nixon example; 'cp' is to be read as 'capital punishment is morally permissible', and 'a' as 'abortion is morally permissible'. I think that these are fairly representative issues and that the attitudes of the people of the United States are as described. If you prefer other examples, use whatever you wish.

The problem with this kind of argument is that since it requires the establishment of the correctness of ethical relativism, it cannot be used to establish the correctness of that ethical theory. Notice that the premises consist of two independent statements, one an instance of cultural relativism and the other an instance of ethical relativism. We have agreed that cultural relativism is a correct view, so we are justified in asserting instances of it. However, ethical relativism is the very theory now under examination; we cannot therefore assume its correctness in the middle of an attempt to determine if it is correct or not. Thus the right-hand conjuncts of each of the lines are illegitimate. This is not to say that they are false; that has not yet been determined. However, since we have yet to determine the acceptability of ethical relativism, we cannot assume that theory's correctness either. So this kind of argument cannot be used to establish the correctness of ethical relativism.

Someone might say that ethical relativism is the theory that best explains the phenomena brought to our attention by the correctness of cultural relativism. Ethical relativism is, they say, the best theory concerning the phenomena of cultural relativism. However, whether that is so or not is just the question we are attempting to answer. Very likely, we will be able to say in a short time whether this is so or not, but certainly we can't answer the question before we begin the examination.

So the most obvious kind of inductive argument cannot help, and the kind of argument that is most likely to be the best one is not quite ready for use yet.

Another defender of ethical relativism might suggest that it is the best explanation of the fact that there is a higher degree of intracultural agreement on moral matters than intercultural agreement. Let us examine this claim. First, the fact that cultural relativism is correct does not support the above claim about differences in cultural agreement and dis-agreement. In fact, there is an enormous amount of cross-cultural agree-ment (the bibliography at the end of this chapter contains a few relevant items on this). Frequently, what appears to be a cross-cultural disagreement about a moral matter is really much closer to a more basic agreement than you might think. For example, the Eskimo who puts his aged parent on the ice floe agrees with us that parents ought not to be killed. Eskimos also hold that if there is a choice between allowing a small child to die and an aged parent who is no longer contributing to the society to die, then it is better for the aged parent to die. This is a difficult view to maintain, but notice that to get to it we traversed at least two moral agreements. The moral opinion last expressed may also be one that most people agree to. However, we shall examine moral agreement and disagreement more closely in the next chapter.

The claim that ethical relativism is the best explanation of intracul-tural agreement and intercultural disagreement is, then, somewhat dubious because it is not all that clear that there is more disagreement of the one type than the other. However, let's continue our examination to see if other ethical theories can account for the same phenomenon equally well. Let us consider utilitarianism as a rival, for it has the advantage of being a pretty clear theory. The utilitarian can account for the different moral judgments, supposing for a moment that they are different, in the following way. First, people may disagree about the calculation of what is to their benefit. A per-son in a culture that believes that incense cures measles agrees that getting rid of the disease is a good thing; but this person thinks that one course of action does it and we suppose another does it. Do we have a moral disagree-ment? Yes, in the sense that we disagree about what is the cause and cure for measles. We both agree that good health, say, is a benefit. If we espouse an indirect version of utilitarianism, we can say that we agree on the principle of utility as the indirect moral rule, but we disagree about which of the direct moral rules is picked out by the indirect moral rule. This allows moral disagreement cross-culturally and, as a bonus, seems to account for some of the underlying cross-cultural agreement; yet it does not embrace ethical relativism.

If the above reasoning is acceptable, then we cannot say that the best hypothesis to explain intracultural agreement and intercultural disagree-ment is ethical relativism, for utilitarianism apparently does as good a job. In addition, there are other phenomena that utilitarianism accounts for that ethical relativism apparently does not. For example, utilitarians can account for why people change their mind about moral matters—they realize that more or less benefit results from the action. The relativist has no such ex-planatory mechanism. More will be said on this point in a short time.

The conclusion is that there is no obvious way in which cultural rela-tivism supports ethical relativism. This is not to say that someone will not come up with some way of showing support, but none appears to be avail-able now. Thus we must consider ethical relativism by itself, without any supposed support from cultural relativism, to see how it fares as an ethical theory.[30]

As has been noted, there are moral disagreements within cultures. This is a fact that ethical relativists have a very difficult time explaining. They could say that subcultures exist within a culture and that each subculture has its own set of moral opinions. However, there are historical instances in which whole cultures have changed moral opinions without any significant outside influence. This is true of the change in moral attitude toward slavery in England and the United States in the early and late nineteenth century respectively. People within the culture argued that the action of keeping slaves was morally wrong, and they carried the day. If ethical relativism were correct, this kind of argumentation could not occur. Imagine, if you can, Harriet Beecher Stowe on an antislavery lecture tour of Mississippi in 1850. She delivers, we'll suppose, her standard lecture on the evils of slavery, and at the end asks for questions. Someone in the audience rises and points out that the majority of people in that subculture believe that slavery is morally acceptable. If ethical relativism was a correct ethical theory, the only thing Mrs. Stowe could do would be to apologize for having made such a stupid mistake.

The point can be generalized: if ethical relativism is correct, then anyone who attempts to bring about moral reform is doing something incredibly silly. Those who argued that the U.S. involvement in Indochina was morally wrong, supposing ethical relativism to be correct, would have been making a simple error about public opinion. At that time, in the middle and late '60s, the vast majority of Americans believed the war to be morally justified. Later on, this opinion changed as a result, in part, of the arguments of those who were against the war.

So change in moral opinion and argumentation are phenomena that ethical relativism does not seem to be able to account for adequately. In addition, the standard kind of counter-examples could be presented. What we want to find are kinds of actions that are apparently right or wrong independent of cultures, or actions that have been thought to be right in a culture but are clear instances of wrong actions. For the latter, consider the actions of the Nazis in taking away the civil rights of the Jews. For the former, consider the action of keeping slaves. By this time, you should be

---

[30] It is interesting to compare the relationship between psychological and ethical egoism with the relationship between cultural and ethical relativism. In the former, the empirical view was found to be false, although we could see some connection between the ethical theory and the empirical theory. Here, in the latter, we find that the empirical theory is correct, but it seems not to offer any support for ethical relativism.

True	If PE, then EE.	False	If CR, then ER.
False	PE.	True	CR.
	Therefore,		Therefore,
	EE.		ER.

aware that counter-examples are not magic; everyone should join in to find the counter-examples that seem most effective.

As an ethical theory, then, ethical relativism does not have much to recommend it. It does not compare favorably with other ethical theories; there are no reasons to accept it; and there are serious criticisms of it.

E.   A look back; a look ahead

In summary, the deontological single categorical rule theories suffer from the same counter-example difficulties as did their teleological counterparts. The counter-examples are not the same, but the results appear to be the same. Since there are no single prima facie rule theories, we have exhausted the theories to be considered in this chapter. In the next chapter we shall finish our survey of the major theories of obligation with an examination of act theories. At that time I will indicate my choice of the best theory among all the ones examined and argue in its favor. However, this fact should not be taken as earthshaking. Everyone should finally pick a theory to defend, for this is not only necessary for our moral life but is the best way to come to decide which theory is best. It is in defending a theory that one comes to understand its strengths and weaknesses. Hopefully you will do this and will understand the spirit in which I defend the view I think is best.

Exercises: Evaluating various deontological theories
1. Joseph Fletcher is associated with a position called *situationism*. That view has not been discussed directly, but you can get an idea of it from the following two passages.

> In this moral strategy the governing consideration is the situation, with all of its contingencies and exigencies. The situationist enters into every decision-making situation armed with principles, just as the legalist does. But the all-important difference is that his moral principles are *maxims* of general or frequent validity; their validity always depends upon the situation. The situationist is prepared in any concrete case to suspend, ignore or violate any principle if by doing so he can effect more good than by following it.

> . . . Nothing is inherently good or evil, except love (personal concern) and its opposite, indifference or actual malice. Anything else, no matter what it is, may be good or evil, right or wrong, according to the situation.

(The quotations are from Joseph Fletcher, "Love is the Only Measure," *Commonweal,* January 14, 1966, reprinted in *Situationism and the New Morality,* ed. Robert L. Cunningham, Appleton-Century-Crofts, New York, 1970, pp. 57, 61–62.) Is this view best understood as an instance of agapism or a form of utilitarianism? Is it best understood as some third view?
2. Some philosophers and theologians have said that kantianism is just an elaboration of the Golden Rule ("Do unto others as you would have others do unto you").

What are the similarities and differences between kantianism and the ethical theory that would result if you assumed the Golden Rule to be a single rule theory? Do you have to suppose it to be an indirect rule or a direct rule? Which is more plausible?

3. Show how your favorite form of utilitarianism, kantianism, and relativism would explain the moral phenomenon that a mother (usually) has an obligation to feed her own infant but does not have an obligation to feed the infant of the family down the street. Which of these theories does a better job in explaining this phenomenon?

4. Explain, as best you can, what you think most people have in mind when they deny the existence of moral absolutes. Given the sense of your explanation, show which of the theories examined so far suppose the existence of moral absolutes and which do not.

Recommended reading

Fletcher, Joseph. *Situation Ethics: The New Morality.* Westminster Press, Philadelphia, 1966. You might think this is a kind of utilitarian view or a form of agapism.

Frankena, William K. *Ethics,* 2d ed. Prentice-Hall, Englewood Cliffs, N.J., 1973. The view examined is discussed in chapter 3.

Kant, Immanuel. *Groundwork of the Metaphysics of Morals,* trans. H. J. Paton. Hutchinson University Library, London, 1948.

Ladd, John. *Ethical Relativism.* Wadsworth, Belmont, Calif., 1973. This is a collection of essays representing many different positions.

Ross, William David. *The Right and the Good.* Clarendon Press, Oxford, England, 1930.

Five

Chapter five

Act theories

All the theories examined so far are *rule theories,* that is, theories that explain justified singular moral judgments by means of rules. Rules are required to arrive at singular moral judgments. If you do not use a moral rule, judgment is just a matter of guessing which alternative is justified. *Act theories,* in contrast, claim that moral rules are not required to arrive at justified singular moral judgments. Such theories offer a method, of course, for arriving at singular moral judgments, but it does not include the requirement of a rule. In order to understand these claims and be in a position to evaluate act theories, it is necessary now to explain at much greater length than in chapter 1 the difference between rule and act theories. This leads us to begin with the distinction between summary rules and constitutive rules.

In this chapter the following topics will be taken up:
A. Summary and constitutive rules
B. The claims of the act theorist
C. Basic units
D. The method of the act theorist
E. Act theories evaluated
F. Comparison of theories of obligation: a summary

A. Summary and constitutive rules

We shall distinguish two kinds of rule, summary and constitutive. *Summary rules* are inductions from individual instances, as exemplified by what in chapter 1 is called induction by enumeration. Such rules are often summaries, we say quite naturally, of past singular justified judgments of that type. Such summary rules presuppose a method of arriving at singular justified judgments that is quite independent of the summary rule. When we put the summary in the form of premise 1 of the general scheme, we can add some statement of probability so that it looks like the following:

If any x is F, then probably x is M.
or
Probably, if any x is F, then x is M.

We do not usually put in such terms, for the way the statement is justified tells us what kind it is.

Suppose, for example, we wish to determine how many people in a class wear or carry watches. One way to do that is to take a sample of all the people in the class—perhaps all the people in the first two rows. If we discover that 75 percent of them wear watches, we can conclude, using induction by enumeration, that 75 percent of all the members of the class wear or carry watches. The argument, put in more formal attire, would appear as follows:

75 percent of all the observed members of the class wear or carry watches.

Therefore,
75 percent of all the members of the class wear or carry watches.

Recall that we need not put in a probability term before '75 percent', for the form and nature of the argument tell us that. However, we could put in some such term to remind ourselves. We could rewrite the statement in its equivalent form as "If any person is a member of this class, then the probability is .75 that the person wears or carries a watch." If we rephrase the conclusion in this way, it helps us to understand better the nature of the statement.

In order to arrive at the conclusion that 75 percent of the members of the class wear watches, we must have some method other than the conclusion itself to determine that individual members of our sample wore or carried a watch. To make this clearer, consider the corresponding statistical syllogism.

75 percent of all the members of the class wear or carry watches.
Person *a* is a member of the class.

Therefore,
Person *a* wears or carries a watch.

Notice, again, that we do not include a probability term, or even the degree of probability in the conclusion—although we can if we wish. In both arguments, of course, something may have gone wrong; there may have been a bad sample, or person *a* may be a peculiar subject. For example, person *a* may have taken a vow never to carry a watch to show his or her belief that time is unreal.

If a conclusion is general and is the result of an inductive argument, it is a summary rule. An individual judgment falling under it—for example, that person *a* wears a watch—need not be justified by reference to the rule that 75 percent of all the members of the class wear or carry watches. In fact, the opposite is true, for the general statement depends on some method of determining that individual people wear or carry watches that is independent of the general statement. In this instance, we look at a person's wrist, examine his or her pockets, or perform some other such operation. The justification of the general statement depends on the singular judgments rather than the justification of the singular judgments depending on the general rule.

The above is quite compatible with the view that sometimes the only justification available to someone for a singular judgment is the general judgment. If we are at home and the person in question is not before us to examine or question, then we can do no better than to use the general rule. However, it is clear that the basic method is the one we use to determine whether an individual wears or carries a watch—and that method is not the use of the general statement to justify the singular judgment that falls under it.

However, not all general statements or rules are summaries. The other type of general statement we are interested in is a constitutive rule. *Constitutive rules* define a practice; they bring an activity into existence by their existence. Sports are a good example. The game of baseball started with a simple game for which there were already rules; then, so we are told, Abner Doubleday codified the rules. He added a good number of new rules and thereby brought the game of baseball into existence. The game has changed through the years in a number of ways: the uniforms and equipment are quite different; and the training methods, strategy, and economics are far different now from what they were in Abner Doubleday's time. However, another kind of change involves the game more intimately. When it was decided that a walk no longer would be counted as a time at bat, this was a rule that all scorers had to follow, whether they thought this was the best way to score a game or not. When a "spitter" was no longer allowed, no matter how much a pitcher's record would be improved, he could not legally use it.

The set of rules that tell us what a game is and the rules that cannot be changed without a change in the game are the ones that define it. These are the rules that are changed only by some person or group of people who have authority to do so. When they change the rules of the game, the game has changed. (We should, of course, still call it baseball unless the change was very radical and occurred within a short period of time. If the game evolves, though, as did baseball and basketball, the chances are that we will go on using the same name, even though the game has changed substantially.)

Two kinds of constitutive rules of games should be distinguished, those calling for punishment and those which simply are not a "move" in the game. For example, if a pitcher balks, then any runner on base is allowed to advance one base. The penalty is assessed, and the pitcher continues. The same is true of those pitchers who throw a spit ball. However, if the catcher sprays mace in the eyes of the batter, he is not allowed to continue. Sometimes, something happens that is not even mentioned in the rules but that the umpire, as interpreter of the rules, can clearly disallow *because* the rules don't allow for it or *because* he or she judges it contrary to the rules of the game. If a pitcher shoots a base runner to prevent him from reaching first, the umpire will not allow the pitcher to continue this kind of activity, nor will he allow the batter to be ruled out—if he is still alive. One kind of constitutive rule calls for a punishment, for the violation is recognized within the rules. The other kind calls for a judgment that the person is no longer even playing the game when that rule is violated.

This point becomes clearer in such a game as chess. One can be penalized a pawn if the pawn is moved past a piece that could have taken it. However, if someone moves a king two spaces to avoid checkmate, this is not a permissible move. It is not that the person is penalized a pawn, or even the queen, for moving the king two spaces; rather, it is just not any kind of move in the game of chess at all. Of the two kinds of rules, we shall be most concerned with the kind for which there is no provision in the rule for violation. However, both kinds of rules share one feature that makes them constitutive—they must be used to justify any decision falling within their "jurisdiction."

Constitutive rules are required to justify individual or singular judgments that fall under them—namely, statements of the form of the third statement of the general scheme. No consequent of the first statement can be asserted without first having the appropriate whole first statement and then asserting the antecedent of it.

Suppose that player *a,* in a basketball game, hits another player *b.* The referee is authorized (by the appropriate league to be a referee, and) by the rule to eject player *a.* If one of the coaches questions the decision, the referee justifies it by citing the appropriate rule (the "one punch" rule). It would do no good for the coach of player *a* to argue that since he was on his home court and the fans had come to see their team win that player *a* should not be thrown out. The rules prevail, for the game is what the rules say it is.

Not only are constitutive rules required to justify singular judgments falling under them, but (to make this more explicit; this requirement indicates that there is no other method to justify such judgments. Perhaps a contrast with a *strategy rule,* which is a kind of summary rule, will make this clearer: "If you are playing a team that 'presses', then use at least three men to bring the ball down court." This is a basketball rule that, when followed, will increase the likelihood of winning. At the very least, if you do not follow it, you are much more likely to lose. The very fact that you can lose, though, shows that you don't have to fulfill the rule in order to play the game. However, you must fulfill the rule that forbids one player from lifting another up to reach the basket.

One additional consequence of a rule being constitutive is that there is no possibility of arriving at a singular moral or nonmoral judgment that is inconsistent with it. The rules are what make the singular judgment justified; there can be no singular justified judgment (of that type) that is inconsistent with the rule.[1] If you do find a singular judgment that is justified and is inconsistent with a rule, then you know that the rule is not a constitutive rule in that area. It is a purported constitutive rule, but it is *not* a constitutive rule. In brief, constitutive rules can have no counter-examples.

All the ethical theories we have considered so far claim that one or more constitutive rules of morality exist. What we have been doing, in part, by presenting counter-examples, is showing that such purported constitutive rules are not constitutive. The counter-examples come from the phenomena. The theorist who proposes such a rule must be able to show, in some way that is neither ad hoc nor question begging, that the proposed counter-examples fail to be effective.

Exercises: Constitutive and summary rules
1. Classify each of the following rules as either constitutive or summary. Present reasons for the classification.
    a. The Big Ten team playing in the Rose Bowl next year will be either Michigan or Ohio State.
    b. A barking dog does not bite.
    c. A pass across two lines in hockey is not allowed.
    d. If you want to pick a rose without being pricked by a thorn, wear gloves.
    e. If you can vote in the United States, then you are at least eighteen years old.
2. Are all categorical rules constitutive? Are all prima facie rules constitutive?
3. Present a constitutive rule of some activity and a summary rule within that same activity. Present what would be a counter-example to the summary rule if it were taken as a constitutive rule. Explain why you continue to hold to the summary rule in spite of the counter-example.

B.   The claims of the act theorist

The preceding clarification and explanation of the distinction between summary and constitutive rules allows us to state the nature of act theories very briefly. Such theories claim:

1. There are no moral constitutive rules.
2. There is a describable and usable method for arriving at justified singular moral judgments.

[1] If the rules of the "game" are inconsistent, there is no correct or incorrect way to play—or, if you like, every way is correct. In either case, no game is described, or no *playable* game is described.

These claims have not yet been argued for, but the first is clear enough by this time. The second has not been discussed at all, so a brief description of the method should be given.

Roughly, act theorists claim three conditions must be met in order for singular moral judgments to be arrived at:

1. You must know the relevant facts.
2. You must check to make sure that you are not abnormal.
3. You must not use any rule theories to derive the singular moral judgments.[2]

These conditions have to be explained before the theory can be defended and argued for.

The first claim is very much like any standard requirement of knowledge. Recall, for example, the requirement the utilitarian sets for us: roughly to know all the consequences that are important and relevant to the action. Of course, no one can know all the facts in a given situation, and there are always occasions when you will be mistaken. This is, though, a truth about any ethical theory that does not require us to have infallible knowledge. A theory requiring infallible knowledge would have a more serious defect; we could never apply it since we cannot have infallible knowledge about the world and our relation to it. So, whatever the criteria any proposed ethical theory sets up to determine what knowledge is relevant and how much knowledge is needed, the act theorist can use those criteria.

The requirement of non-abnormality is more important to the act theorist than, say, to the utilitarian—or so it seems at first. For example, no one who has such brain damage that no distinction can be made between a person performing an action and the person on whom the action is performed is able to make moral judgments about the people in such a relation. The same comments apply to those under the influence of drugs (for frequently such people are in no position to make judgments about anything, let alone moral matters). However, the description of what is normal and what is abnormal must contain no moral notions. It would not do to sneak a moral judgment or notion into a description of how we are to arrive at singular moral judgments.

"How are we to arrive at singular moral judgments?"

"Simply make sure that you haven't any disabilities."

"What kind of disability?"

"Oh, the kind that prevents you from making justified singular moral judgments."

---

[2] Alternatively, this could be put as a requirement not to use any mistaken theories to arrive at singular moral judgments. It is not, though, the requirement to use an act theory.

Such an answer is not enlightening, to say the least. You must, instead, give a morally neutral description of what a normal or an abnormal person is. The one that seems most workable is the one given by those psychologists who are not at that time using any moral notions: A normal person is one who is able to pass the tests for normalcy for knowledge of nonmoral matters.[3]

The third requirement is clear enough: don't use any of the rule theories. However, about this time you are probably getting very impatient with the act theorist. You want to know exactly how you do arrive at singular moral judgments. Do act theorists have a special faculty? Is morality like the smell of flowers? What is going on? Answering these questions requires more than just an explanation of the claims of the act theorist, which is what we have been doing. It requires a greater examination of the underlying structure of all the theories we have been considering so far. We must now try to explain how any theory, whether act or rule, justifies the basic unit within it, and how anyone can explain how to arrive at those justified basic units.

C. Basic units

Basic predicates are those used to explain (analyze, define) other predicates within an area but which are not themselves explained (analyzed, defined). *Point* is a basic predicate in Euclidean geometry; *red* or *triangle* is one in visual discrimination. In every area, some set of predicates is taken as basic, although it may be that one set may do as well as another as the basic one.

Not only are some predicates basic within some area, but some are basic among all areas. A predicate may, we all recognize, be basic within one area and yet not be basic within another. For example, *number* is taken as a basic predicate within arithmetic but not in set theory or logic. Many suppose the same kind of thing with respect to the basic predicates of chemistry and physics.

So far we have been talking only about knowledge (epistemology of morals) and not about the nature of the "things" that are known (metaphysics of morals). We shall discuss the metaphysics of morals in a short time, but for now, let's stay with the epistemology of morals.

If the basic unit of our justified moral judgments is a singular judgment, as the act deontologist claims, then (by definition of 'basic') no further moral evidence is required (or available). We must, of course, know what kind of action we are examining, and this means that we must be

[3] Was Hitler a normal observer in this sense? There is evidence that he was, at least at the beginning of his regime. The problem of what to do about disagreement will be handled shortly; however, the problem cases are no doubt beginning to disturb many of you now.

aware of the relevant values of F. Once we have all that, if act deontology is correct, we have done all we need to do. The rule theorist claims that something further is *required* for our justified singular moral judgments— namely, a moral rule or set of such rules. The act theorist's criticism of this kind of theory will be presented shortly.

In spite of the lack of availability of any further required *evidence* to justify our singular moral judgments, we have to see if the act theorist can offer advice on how to be in a proper position for coming to have justified singular moral judgments and, as we are about to see, if he or she can propose a method for being able to resolve moral disagreements.

However, to digress a little before going on, it is actually somewhat misleading to say the act theorist's basic unit of justified judgment is a sin- gular moral judgment. Some act theorists (for example, H. A. Prichard) do maintain that position, but there is some evidence that even Prichard did not clearly hold that position, and probably no one except Plato and G. E. Moore actually held such a view. Let us distinguish between someone who maintains that it is the singular moral judgment itself that is the basic moral unit and those who claim that it is the moral judgment as related to the relevant factual judgment that is the basic unit.

The two views can be represented schematically as follows:

Ma
Fa → Ma

In the first view, there is no way to understand how factual claims could be at all relevant, nor how evidence could ever be brought to bear. All one does is directly apprehend the moral "property." In such a situation, it is difficult to understand how one could argue rationally or settle disagree- ments reasonably. For this reason, the act theorist's position will be taken to be the second one. We shall assume that the basic unit of justified moral judgment is the moral judgment standing in a certain relation to the rele- vant factual judgment.

You will want to know how we know when the relation holds, and the act theorist does give you position rules. You will also want to know what the relation is. Is it a causal relation, a logical relation, or what? The simple answer is that it is a *moral relation,* the relation of being sufficient moral evidence. This is the kind of unenlightening answer we give when we tell someone that something is causally sufficient for something else. We usually don't explain the nature of causality, or even feel any need to do so. However, philosophy being the kind of discipline it is, there will be, in the last chapter, an attempt to say something more about the nature of the connection between the nonmoral evidence and the moral judgment.

So, in the rest of this chapter, 'singular moral judgment' will mean the moral judgment as supported by its nonmoral evidence. To arrive at the singular moral judgment unconnected with its nonmoral evidence, all you need do is confirm the nonmoral evidence. The situation would then be as follows:

If Fa, then Ma.
Fa.
_____

Therefore,
Ma.

This allows us to see similarities and differences between the act and rule theories. The act theorist can provide us with a general scheme also, but it contains no general statements. The difference may seem small at first, but the difference in the two first statements makes all the difference in the world.

D. The method of the act theorist

All disagreement is traceable, according to the act theorist, to some disagreement about F, to some problem about being in a position to come to have correct singular moral judgments, or, more rarely, to some theoretical disagreement about the nature of philosophical theories themselves.

Let us start with the F's and see how such disagreement is explained. The best way to see how this kind of view works is to consider instances of moral disagreement. The form of all such disagreements, when they are analyzed (and if the act theorist is correct) will be hypothetical. In fact, if the act theorist is correct, such a conditional disagreement is more accurately called conditional agreement. Let us first use this method on a somewhat artificial situation.

Person *a:* "Slavery is morally wrong because it doesn't allow some people to develop fully as human beings, to realize all their potential."

Person *b:* "Slavery is not wrong because it consists of taking care of those who really have no potential of the same sort that you and I do."

Person *a:* "Can we agree that if those slaves have the same potential that you and I do, then slavery is wrong?"

Person *b:* "Yes, for that is my reason for claiming that it is not wrong. However, if slaves are not really people, as you and I are, and your reason for claiming that slavery is wrong is that they are people, then you would have to admit that slavery is not wrong."

Person *a:* "Yes indeed, and now the question is whether these beings have the same kinds of characteristics as you and I do."

The question of whether or not slaves have the same potential as the rest of us is not a moral question (per se). It is a question that can be answered by using established methods of the social and behavioral sciences. There is now moral agreement, if only conditionally.

However, you will say, what good does conditional agreement do if we are not in a position to affirm one of the two antecedents on which we have reached agreement? At least now, however, a clear and definite procedure exists that can be carried out to settle the disagreement. This enables us to work toward a settlement of our moral disagreement not only on a hypothetical level but on every level.

Furthermore, the same problem, if it is a problem, besets the rule theorists. They begin with a rule of the form "If any x is F, then x is M," and then they must affirm the antecedent in order to generate out the justified singular moral judgment. If there is a disagreement about whether x is F, about the antecedent, then there is no way to arrive at the justified claim that x is M. Since both act and rule theories have this same problem, it cannot be an effective criticism of an act theory. However, it should be remembered that there are many times when we can agree on the antecedent or (when these are not the same) at least justify an antecedent.

The test of such a method, as mentioned earlier, is in practice. Let us now practice with yet another case, this one developed by students in a course.

In a class on social and political philosophy, the question of the moral justification of the marijuana laws came up, and we attempted to use the act theorist's method of hypothetical agreement to settle the dispute. At the time, act deontology was not introduced as an ethical theory, for that would not have been to the point. We merely attempted to arrive at two statements, however complicated, that everyone in the class would agree were justified or true. Some of the terms in the statements, such as 'moderate', were discussed at great length before we felt comfortable with them. (In that case, it was decided that 'moderate' was to be understood on the model of 'moderate use of alcohol'.) The question marks after some of the statements indicate uncertainty as to whether assertion of the statement was necessary for the consequent to be supported by the antecedent. Since, as it turned out, it didn't matter, the statements were included—but with a question mark.

Statement A (pro)
If the moderate use of marijuana

1. leads to no harm for anyone other than the user[4]
2. leads to no more harm than alcohol
3. doesn't lead to the use of "hard" drugs

---

[4] All the conditions are conjoined—that is, all of them together are thought to be sufficient for the consequent. A person might think that one or more are not needed, but then you can probably agree that they are redundant. *If* all the conditions were fulfilled, then the consequent would be established. You do not have to agree with the truth of any one item in the consequent to agree with that claim. When one makes progress in moral negotiation, often some items drop off the list included in the antecedent because all the parties agree to their irrelevance. However, anyone could agree to inclusion of irrelevant items, as long as they are not "red herrings."

4. is not addictive
5. when illegal, leads to control of its trade by criminal elements who would otherwise not gain further influence over the users
6. when illegal and widespread, leads to disrespect for the law and impractical and arbitrary enforcement of the law

then the marijuana laws are not morally justified.

Statement B (con)
If the moderate use of marijuana

not-1, not-2, not-3, not-4, not-5(?), not-6(?)
7. leads to crime (perhaps identical with not-5)
8. leads to a significantly large number of people harming others while under the influence of the drug (as a result of the lowering of physical and psychological sharpness), for example, automobile accidents caused by people driving while under the influence of marijuana
9. leads to a significantly large number of people escaping from reality
10. is significantly more harmful to the user than alcohol or tobacco (partially identical with not-2)
11. leads to possibly dangerous consequences (where the force of 'possibly' is that other drugs, for example, thalidomide, have turned out to have very bad side effects, and we do not yet know enough about the effects of marijuana to be sure that it has no such bad side effects)
12. is the result of a communist conspiracy

then the marijuana laws are morally justified.

This is just one issue and is not by itself strong evidence of anything. What you must do is try the method out yourself.

How do we know these moral matters? Many of you will still remain puzzled by all this, no matter how successful you are. Here, you say, is a nonmoral characteristic or set of such characteristics F and a moral characteristic M; somehow we can get people to agree that given some specific F, some M also holds. But how are we able to make the "move" from the F to the M? In terms of knowledge or justification, how does F justify M?

It has been claimed that conditional singular moral judgments are basic units of knowledge or justified judgment. If this is so, then there is no knowledge or justified judgment more basic that justifies it. When we have knowledge or justified judgments of this type, we can be said to know them or be justified directly. The rule theorist claims to know a rule or set of rules directly (to be justified in claiming that this is the rule or set of rules directly). At the end of the chain of justification, that which is claimed to be justified, and yet not justified by something further, is justified directly.

In a sentence such as "Today is Monday," the meaning of the whole sentence is a function of the meaning of the component words. The words, however, are not meaningful because the letters are meaningful (at least in the same sense of 'meaning'). The simplest unit of meaning is a single word.[5] It is not, however, the simplest unit that can and has to be recognized in order to come to know the meaning of the word. It is necessary for someone to know the individual letters in order to come to know the meaning of a word, even though the individual letters are not units of meaning. The meaning of 'today' is not inferred from other knowledge of meaning, as is done for the meaning of a whole sentence. We can say the knowledge of the meaning of a simple term is basic with respect to meaning, although the knowledge of a whole sentence is not.

The above discussion relates to justification in the following way. There are some units within an area that do not require further justification. However, in order to understand this, it was necessary to explain the sense of 'basic unit' so that we could have a more firm grasp of that claim. *Meaning* was chosen as an example to help explain the notion of basic unit, but no analogy with morality is claimed. However, once it is established that the basic unit of justified judgment within the area of morality is the singular moral judgment as attached to the corresponding factual judgment (Fa→ Ma), then we realize the demand for further justification within the area of morality is not legitimate.

The same kind of claim, as will be seen later, can be made concerning the basic unit of any rule theory. The form of such units is "If any x is F, then x is M" {(x) (Fx→ Mx)}. One can ask for the justification of this unit. It certainly seems to make sense to do so. However, if one such unit is indeed the basic unit of justified judgment within the area of morality, then it is not legitimate to require justification within the area of morality for that unit. One establishes that it is the basic unit within the area of morality by establishing a theory as the best in the area. One performs that task, in turn, by doing the kinds of things that we have been doing for the past hundred pages or so.

Exercises: Basic units of morality

1. Write down the basic unit of morality according to the utilitarian of your choice, and next to it write the basic unit of morality according to the act theory discussed here. Describe the differences and the similarities.
2. Show how the act theorist either can or cannot take the utilitarian basic unit to be a summary rule. Are there counter-examples to the rule taken as a summary rule?
3. Find one of the constitutive rules of chess in a book of rules, and write it down. Can that rule be justified within the game of chess by further rules? Can it be justified in some other way?
4. Choose some topic involving a moral judgment on which there is widespread

---

[5] Many philosophers claim that a sentence, or perhaps even some longer unit, is the simplest unit of meaning. If this were so, a slightly different kind of example would be used.

disagreement. Attempt to effect a conditional agreement among those who disagree. (If you are alone on a desert island, construct various characters who disagree.)

E.   Act theories evaluated

Various criticisms of specific rule theories have been presented. At this time, those criticisms can be summarized very briefly for the sake of an overview of what has been done.

It was claimed that moral rules are either categorical or prima facie, and rule theories contain one or both kinds. A categorical rule, whether direct or indirect, has effective counter-examples; this conclusion is justified by the examination of egoism, utilitarianism, the Ten Commandments theory, agapism, kantianism, and ethical relativism. (These are not the only such theories, but it is a good sampling, and many of the criticisms are general ones.) A prima facie rule theory, whether it is Ross's, Frankena's, or anyone else's, has difficulty, to say the least, in accounting for a situation in which two or more of the prima facie rules conflict. Furthermore, counter-examples exist, of the underwhelming value sort, for each of the prima facie rules. If a theory is a combination of categorical and prima facie rules, then the above criticisms would also seem to apply. The failure of the rule theories gives one more confidence in asserting an act theory as correct, supposing (and this is a big supposition) that it can survive the critical onslaught directed against all ethical theories. Let us now examine some of the arguments rule theorists use against act theorists, as well as the latter's responses.

1. **The problem of disagreement**   One of the chief arguments concerns disagreement. Rule theorists point out that if act theorists are correct, then either there is no way to settle moral disagreements involving singular moral judgments or there are no such moral disagreements. Why this dichotomy? The first part—there is no way to settle such disagreements—is justified, say the rule theorists, because, according to act theorists, singular moral judgments are the basic units. So there can be no further evidence within the area of morality to justify the judgments, and thus, no evidence to settle disputes. Still, say the rule theorists, the act theorist has the other side of the dichotomy available as a choice: the act theorist might claim that moral disagreements do not occur. But this flies in the face of abundant evidence from the phenomena that there is such disagreement.

Act theorists can respond in two different ways.[6] First, there is an unclarity, they would say, about the claim that no moral disagreements

---

[6] Notice that, after a long time, I am defending a view I think is correct. However, to remind you, this is no big thing; everyone thinks some view or other is correct.

occur. Act theorists can admit to moral disagreement, but according to their theory, it is based on some kind of factual disagreement, some kind of ethical theory disagreement, or on the abnormalcy of at least one of the disputants. As we saw earlier, disagreements of this sort can be accounted for by act theorists. Furthermore, there is another kind of disagreement—namely, hypothetical disagreement—that act theorists use to explain at least many cases of what look like disagreements about singular moral judgments. There are many cases of what start out as disagreements about singular moral judgments that turn out to be instances of conditional disagreement/agreement only, not disagreements about the singular moral judgment at all.

However, someone might persist, couldn't disagreement about the singular moral judgment exist even after we have closed off all three of the sources of disagreement mentioned above? Act theorists can give two different responses to this question. They can say, first, that of course it is always logically possible for there to be disagreement about any matter. It is never a contradiction to describe a situation in which there are two people who assert the opposite sides of an issue, no matter what the issue. We can always find someone, perhaps in a mental institution, who will sincerely assert that $2 + 2 \neq 4$ or that he, the person speaking, is dead. However, such occurrences are extremely rare. Furthermore, when they do occur, there is something further we can do, even when the subject matter about which the judgments are made is basic.[7] Let us consider a simple example to help us over this rough area. Color predicates are most likely basic within the area of perceptual discrimination. Of course, it is true that color is physically dependent on all manner of things, such as pigment, molecular structure, and so on. It is also true that we would not see unless our eyes had a certain structure, light struck our eye, and so on. However, we do not have to be aware of, or know about, these things in order to be able to know that a ribbon is yellow. (We can know that something or other is yellow without even knowing what it is that is yellow.) Suppose someone insists the ribbon is green, and we find the person is sincere. Could it also be that the person doesn't hold an odd theory about ribbons, such as "Ribbons that look yellow are always really green," that she's perfectly normal, and that we agree about all the conditions of observation (including the use of 'yellow' in other instances)? It is logically possible, of course, just as the moral disagreement was logically possible. But it is extremely unlikely.[8] Nevertheless, suppose it did occur. Well, we would ask other people what color they see. We wouldn't do this because we suppose they see better than we do, but rather because consensus offers some evidence of correctness. The greater the consensus, the greater is the confidence.

[7] Later we will discuss the difference between predicates that are not only basic within an area but are also basic among all areas, but we aren't doing that now.
[8] Some philosophers have argued that it is impossible to have such a disagreement. Some might wish to argue that such a disagreement would show that the person does not understand the color terms involved. It will be assumed that this line is not effective, though no reason will be given here for that assumption.

Such a procedure does not *prove* the person to be incorrect, and subsequently we may all discover that she was correct. However, the lack of certainty does not seem difficult to accept—we bear it in almost every other area without any problems. There is no certainty about any matter of fact; and if the act theorist is correct, there is no certainty about any singular moral judgment. This does not prevent us from successfully dealing with the world and matters of fact, and it should not prevent us from successfully dealing with moral matters.

The second kind of response, apparently given by some act theorists,[9] is that there couldn't be any disagreement once the sources of disagreement have been covered. This response is not one I am sympathetic with, but it has been influential in the philosophical world. If you wish to follow up this response, look to the bibliography at the end of the chapter.

Thus, to the part of the criticism claiming that act theorists are committed to the view that no moral disagreement is possible, the above responses can be given. Now we shall consider the response that can be given to the first part of the criticism—namely, that there is no way to resolve moral disagreement. Act theorists would have to admit, of course, that no further *moral* evidence is available to resolve diagreements. Someone who holds a prima facie rule theory, for example, could always bring in another moral rule. This, of course, is not open to the act theorist, except for summary rules, which are useful but not essential. However, act theorists can do something further to bring about a resolution of disagreements. Lots more evidence can be brought in, as we have seen in the few sample disputes outlined above. This is not only compatible with the act theorist's view, but it is the very way it is supposed to work. At this point, it might be relevant to examine some other theories in relation to act theory. Suppose one of the disputants maintains that ethical egoism is the correct theory of obligation, uses that theory to arrive at the singular moral judgment, and thereby arrives at a judgment different from ours. We can show that person that the egoist theory of obligation is deficient, and that it is only his or her acceptance of that theory that stands in the way of agreement.[10] Finally, we may notice something wrong about the person, for example, that he or she is wearing a straight jacket, which leads us to think he or she may not be normal. This is also one of the sources of disagreement.

In short summary, then, act theorists can make a variety of responses to the claim that act theory cannot account for disagreement. There are

[9] See, for example, H. A. Prichard, *Moral Obligation,* Oxford University Press, New York, 1950.

[10] It should be noticed that we don't have to assume the correctness of an act theory in order to criticize ethical egoism. We didn't do that in chapter 2, and there is no reason now, or ever, to do so. If our opponent asks us to present our own theory of obligation so that he can consider it and whether it is acceptable or not, then we should be prepared to do so. If you have not made up your mind, you can always say that you don't know which theory is correct, but that you do know that ethical egoism is not.

ways both to resolve disagreement and to account for it when it occurs. Therefore, the available evidence indicates that this criticism is not effective.

2. The problem of justification: categorical principles   Act theorists must meet an argument set forth by rule theorists that purports to show that a rule must justify every singular moral judgment. If this argument is successful, then some rule theory or other is correct and any act theory is incorrect. We may not know which rule theory is correct, if the argument is a good one, but we can be sure that some one rule theory, perhaps one not as yet known, is correct. This argument, then, must be successfully countered by act theorists.[11]

R. M. Hare lists three reasons for needing principles.

> The first reason applies to anyone, even a man with complete insight into the future, who decides to choose something because it is of a certain character. The second reason applies to us because we do not in fact have complete knowledge of the future, and because such knowledge as we do have involves principles. To these reasons a third must now be added. Without principles, most kinds of teaching are impossible, for what is taught is in most cases a principle.[12]

Let us begin by examining the use of principles in teaching. Act theorists can admit that what is taught in most cases is a principle, but we may need only summary principles in teaching morality. One way to teach color terms to children who can count to two is to say "Start at the top of the American flag and count the first stripe *one* and the second one *two*. Number one stripe is red and number two stripe is white." The rule, while it could be used by someone who can count, is not required to justify the specific judgment that this stripe is red. The child may not know that there is another way to arrive at the justified judgment that the stripe is red, but we know there is.[13]

We often use principles to teach. Most of the time, however, we use summary rules; these are not constitutive rules, rules that are required for justifying judgments. For example, when we teach American history, we

---

[11] The counter-arguments presented on pages 165–175 are found, in very much the same form, in Bernard Rosen, "Rules and Justified Moral Judgments," *Philosophy and Phenomenological Research,* 30, No. 3 (March 1970), pp. 436–443; and in Bernard Rosen, "Promulgations and Presuppositions," *The Journal of Value Inquiry,* 5, No. 1 (Winter 1970), pp. 54–56.

[12] R. M. Hare, *The Language of Morals,* Clarendon Press, Oxford, 1952, p. 60. All quotations from *The Language of Morals* that appear in this chapter are reprinted by permission of the Oxford University Press.

[13] If the children are color blind or totally blind, there is probably no other way for them to justify color judgments than to use this rule or one like it. But effectiveness of the rule depends upon its having been established by sighted people who did not use the rule.

can use the rule "In a nonpresidential election year, the party out of office gains power." Or, for another type of example, "If an argument has two existential premises and an existential conclusion, then it is invalid." But for some subjects, such as arithmetic, we use constitutive rules to teach students how to justify judgments that fall under those rules. Since this is so, we cannot say that all teaching is done with summary rules (although it may be possible to get along with only such rules), nor can we say that all teaching makes use of constitutive rules. What we must do, then, is determine which kind of rule is used in teaching morality.

The rules used in teaching morality appear to be such rules as, "Do not lie," "Lying is wrong," or "Never tell a lie." As we know, there are effective counter-examples to such rules. For example, if one's wife asks "Do I look all right this evening?" one has at least a right to lie if she looks terrible. This is sufficient to show that the general statements are not unchallengeable, and that sometimes, when they clash with specific judgments, the specific judgments are accepted. Thus we do not always need constitutive rules for moral teaching. Furthermore, we have revealed no real need for constitutive rules. When Hare claims that rules are required for teaching, he is right, but summary rules seem to be sufficient.[14]

Hare's first reason for the necessity of principles is that we "choose something because it is of a certain character." He gives as an example, "If I decide not to say something, because it is false, I am acting on a principle, 'Never (or never under certain conditions) say what is false', and I must know that this, which I am wondering whether to say, is false."[15]

When we decide to do something, it would seem that Hare believes our justification (and our reasoning) has the following familiar form:

1. If any x is F, then x is M.
2. This x is F.

Therefore,
3. This x is M.

For F, one can put in the appropriate nonmoral expression (such as 'is an instance of saying what is false'); and for M, one can put in the appropriate moral term (such as 'wrong'). We must obviously suppose that premise 1 is a statement of a constitutive rule. If it is a summary rule, then, as we have seen, the effective use of the rule requires that such rules are not needed to arrive at justified moral judgments.

[14] Someone might say that the use of the counter-example involves a constitutive rule, and it is only because of such a rule that the individual judgment can be used as a counter-example. However, we do not seem to require a rule to justify the individual judgment that is the counter-example. Furthermore, no trouble-free constitutive rule can be found. As soon as we fix up the rule, or state a new one, it meets with the same difficulty. This is a point that will become clearer later.

[15] Hare, *The Language of Morals,* p. 56.

First, counter-examples are appropriate to instances of premise 1, such as "If any action is an instance of lying, then it is wrong." It is morally permissible to lie in many circumstances, this is something we all know. From this it follows that the principle is not a constitutive principle with respect to such judgments as "John Smith's act of lying is wrong."

The defender of the need for constitutive principles would probably now add conditions to the principle. It would be claimed that the unrestricted principle is subject to counter-examples, but the restricted one (for example, "If any action is an instance of lying to a friend, then it is wrong") is not. However, we are seldom given a restricted principle, nor are we told how to construct one. Furthermore, restrict the principle as you like, and as past experience with such principles shows, counter-examples will still be found. If no counter-example-free principles are discovered, then we have good evidence that we do not need constitutive rules to arrive at justified judgments of that sort.[16]

This same sort of argument can be presented in a variety of ways, so let's examine one more instance to gain confidence.

> Moral and value judgments imply reasons, and reasons cannot apply in a particular case only. If they apply in one case, they apply in all similar cases. Moreover, in order to give a reason in a particular case, one must presuppose a general proposition. If Jones answers your question "Why?" by saying "Because you promised to" or "Because it gives pleasure," he presupposes that it is right to keep promises or that what gives pleasure is good.[17]

[16] One could trivialize the principle completely and make it something like "Any action of lying that is such that its conditions make it wrong to lie is wrong." Now the principle is not subject to counter-examples, but it is no longer required to jusify the specific judgment. If we use it in an argument of the form presented, the second promise will be "This is an action of lying that is such that its conditions make it wrong to lie." This premise is all that is contained in the conclusion, so we do not need the first premise to arrive at the conclusion. Thus, even trivializing the principle in this way does not show that a constitutive rule is required to justify the specific judgment.

We might also restrict the rule in such a way that it uniquely describes the specific act of lying. If this were done, then we could provide no counter-examples of the sort that have been presented. Notice, though, that counter-examples could not be provided because we have described the principle so that it only applies to this one case. We did that because we knew that lying was morally permissible in this case; and if we could only restrict the application of the principle to this case, then it would be safe from counter-examples. Now, however, the knowledge that it is morally permissible to lie in this case precedes the knowledge represented by the principle. It precedes it not only temporally, but in every other sense. If the knowledge that lying in this case is morally permissible is prior to the knowledge of the principle, then the knowledge of the principle is not required to justify the specific judgment, and the principle is not, with respect to that judgment, a constitutive rule.

[17] William K. Frankena, *Ethics,* 2d ed., Prentice-Hall, Englewood Cliffs, N.J., 1973, p. 25.

In this passage, William Frankena seems to be presenting the same kind of argument as we just examined. One new notion is introduced by Frankena—that one *presupposes* a rule or a principle when one makes a specific judgment. According to Frankena, a person *a* who makes a moral judgment such as "x is M" usually or always presents reasons to support that judgment. Person *a* justifies the judgment by saying "x is M because x is F." If there is a y that is F, then person *a* is committed to judge that y is M also. In short, to look back to the general scheme, if person *a* asserts the third statement and gives the second as the reason, then he is presupposing the first. If he denies the first, then he cannot consistently give the second as the reason for the conclusion. Once statement 1 is accepted, then person *a* has accepted a moral principle. Therefore, Frankena concludes, any specific judgment presupposes a principle.

The preceding line of reasoning may be perfectly acceptable, but it does not establish that constitutive principles are required to justify singular moral judgments. This can be shown by presenting another argument of the same form that fails to establish anything about constitutive rules. Suppose person *a* gives as his reason for the claim that a stripe of the American flag is red that it is the top stripe. He says "x is red" (third statement), and gives as his reason "x is the top stripe of the American flag" (second statement). If person *a* denies that any similar stripe is red, he is, suppose for the moment, being inconsistent. He cannot give statement 2 as his reason for the conclusion and yet deny statement 1—namely, "Any top stripe of the American flag is red."

If the ethical argument Frankena presents allows us to conclude that principles are required to justify individual moral judgments, then we can equally conclude that principles are required to justify individual color judgments. Since the latter claim is apparently false, the former is not established by the argument presented.

In an attempt to show a difference between the two arguments, someone might be tempted to claim that any principle concerning colors, such as "If any x is the top stripe of the American flag, then x is red," is false, and so the two kinds of argument cannot be compared. However, any moral principle of the form "If any x is F, then x is M" is just as unacceptable. We say the color principle is false because the top stripe of flags is sometimes dyed, or factories make mistakes, or something else happens. We have seen the various difficulties different kinds of moral principles fall prey to.

Other people might be tempted to say that we do not require color principles because we have other ways of determining the color of objects, but we do require moral principles to justify our specific moral judgments. To make this claim, however, is to beg the question. Act theorists claim that moral principles are not required to justify singular moral judgments, so the contrary assumption is not at this point allowable. It is a claim that must be argued for.

We can all admit that perhaps there is some relation of *presupposition* between making a specific judgment and a general principle. However, as has just been shown, the relation of presupposition does not demonstrate that constitutive rules are required to justify specific moral judgments.

3. The problem of justification: prima facie principles   All the principles examined so far are supposed to have been categorical principles. As we saw in chapter 4, the same kind of counter-examples cannot be raised against prima facie principles. Let us consider a prima facie principle in W. D. Ross's sense, one that confers an actual duty if no other principle conflicts with it. Now Frankena's claim concerning rules can be put another way. Whenever anyone makes a singular moral judgment, a number of prima facie principles apply, and, depending on whether they apply negatively or positively, the judgment is justified.

Recall that some philosophers maintain that Ross's prima facie principles are themselves subject to counter-examples.[18] The counter-examples will not consist merely of actions that are, say, instances of promise-keeping that are nevertheless wrong actions, for Ross can account for this by pointing out that the action is of another morally relevant type, perhaps pleasure-producing. In this instance, the obligation to bring about the pleasure overrides the obligation to keep the promise. So the counter-example will have to consist of actions that are wrong *because* they are instances of that kind of action. R. B. Brandt presents criticisms of this type.

> Consider promises, for instance. Is it really the case that *every* promise creates *some* obligation to fulfill it? Well, consider promises made under duress, or promises made on the basis of a deliberate misrepresentation of the facts by the person to whom the promise has been made. Obviously such promises create no obligation. Take enjoyment as another example. Is every kind of enjoyment good-making? Is sadistic pleasure so? This is at least debatable. Or, take knowledge. It is often said that a state of knowledge is good-making. But is this true of *every* kind of knowledge? Is it good-making to know the intimate details of the lives of others? Or, are there no facts so insignificant that knowing them is not good-making at all?[19]

If Brandt's criticisms are effective, then we have a somewhat different kind of counter-example, but one that plays the same role with respect to prima facie principles as did our other counter-examples with respect to categorical principles. The principle "If any x is an instance of pleasure-producing, then x is prima facie right, or obligatory" has sadistic pleasure as its counter-example. Once again, the ability to produce counter-examples is evidence that the principle is not a constitutive rule.

[18] The main criticisms of prima facie rule theories appear in chapter 4. Most of this section is just a reminder.

[19] R. B. Brandt, *Ethical Theory,* Prentice-Hall, Englewood Cliffs, N.J., 1959, pp. 199–200.

The criticism of prima facie principles presented in chapter 4, in summary, is that there is no procedure for determining the stringency of the applicable principles. Since the principles often conflict, we must choose the more stringent one without the use of the principles. In so doing, we have evidence that the principles are not required to justify individual judgments, since we apparently sometimes use our knowledge of the right course of action to justify the selection of the principle. At the least, we can say that in part the selection procedure resulting in the choice of the right act involves something that is not a constitutive rule.

4. The problem of justification: knowledge   Variations of Hare's first reason for the necessity of principles seem not to be successful, so we conclude that none of them shows that constitutive rules are needed to justify singular moral judgments. There are other variations of that argument, but they do not seem to be any different. Supposing that such is the case, let's move on to the last reason, "we do not in fact have complete knowledge of the future, and because such knowledge as we do have involves principles." Let's examine Hare's elaboration of this.

> The kind of knowledge that we have of the future—unless we are clairvoyant—is based upon principles of prediction which we are taught, or form for ourselves. Principles of prediction are one kind of principle of action; for to predict is to act in a certain way. Thus, although there is nothing logically to prevent someone doing entirely without principles, and making all his choices in the arbitrary manner exhibited in the first kind of answer, this never in fact occurs. Moreover, our knowledge of the future is fragmentary and only probable; and therefore in many cases the principles which we are taught or form for ourselves say, not 'Choose this kind of effect rather than that,' but 'You do not know for certain what will be the effects; but do this rather than that, and the effects are most likely to be such as you would have chosen, if you had known them.' It is important to remember, in this connexion, that 'likely' and 'probable' are value-words; in many contexts 'It is probable (or likely) that P' is adequately rendered by 'There is *good* reason (or evidence) for holding that P.'[20]

To what sort of principles of prediction can Hare be referring? The most likely candidates are principles such as "Do not lie to a student who has failed your course, even though lying will at the time cause less pain, because in the long run it will bring about a worse situation." It is not necessary to go through the complete critical procedure again, but we should point out that the principle is open to effective counter-examples. Furthermore, in this instance, the principle seems to be a summary based on past

[20] Hare, *The Language of Morals,* pp. 59–60.

happenings. If this is so, then the principle requires that we have garnered individual justified judgments of that sort; thus it is not a constitutive rule.

In the previously cited passage, Hare points out that our knowledge of the future is fragmentary and only probable. This is true, and this is precisely why we do well to rely on summary rules constructed from our past experience. Summary rules seem to fulfill all our needs for principles. Furthermore, we often abandon the general principle when the evidence of the specific situation seems to warrant it. Since we are sometimes justified in doing this, that is good evidence that the principle used is not a constitutive rule.

Finally, we can admit that 'It is probable that P' in most contexts is to be rendered as 'There is good reason for holding that P'. One can say the good reason for holding the P that is a moral principle is that more often than not, acting on P is not contrary to what we would decide in the specific case without the principle. This is just what the act theorist says! Now that we have come this far, this last bold claim is not to be taken as simply a claim, but as being supported by the failure of the rule theory arguments and the apparent fact that all the moral phenomena that involve rules can be accounted for by the use of summary rules.

If the preceding distinctions are acceptable, and there are no other *kinds* of arguments to examine, then there are no good reasons to suppose that constitutive rules are required to justify singular moral judgments. Since there are reasons to suppose that such rules are not needed,[21] and the need for rules seems to be fulfilled by summary rules, we can conclude that rules play only a secondary role in justifying singular moral judgments.

5. Promulgation   One part of the preceding argument in favor of rule theories deserves additional attention. When the rule theorist claims that rules are required to justify singular moral judgments, and that singular moral judgments presuppose moral rules, we should ask in what sense anyone actually does promulgate rules.

In the clearest sense, a rule is that which someone lays down—that such and such is to be the case or is to be done. Many people suppose that in a like manner someone laid down the moral law. God has been the most popular candidate for the role of lawmaker. But some philosophers have supposed that human beings collectively legislate (Rousseau); and some have supposed that individual people legislate for all people (Hegel). What is relevant here is that some people suppose that when a person wills for himself, he is somehow, by virtue of some principles of logic or reasoning, willing for everyone (this is something like the view of Kant and Hare).

The traditional problems with God as a promulgator are sufficiently difficult that we need not add them to the discussion. At this time, neither the metaphysics of Hegel nor Rousseau's notion of the *general will* requires close attention. There are many, though, who support what is often called

---

[21] As indicated by the success of the act theorists' methods described earlier.

the "generalization argument." Sometimes this seems to be a kind of pro-mulgator view and sometimes it doesn't. Let us consider it as a promulga-tor view to determine if it fares better in that guise.

The generalization argument, by this interpretation, is an attempt to support the claim that each person is a promulgator for all people. The au-thority for the promulgation is, in some sense, reason or logic. However, we run into a problem right away, for examples of such general moral state-ments are not of the form of statement 1 of the general scheme. They do not connect nonmoral and moral characteristics or terms.

> (U4) If A is good, then anything similar in all non-moral but morally relevant respects is also good.[22]

> It is true that the generalization argument involves an inference from "not everyone has the right" to "no one has the right," from "it would not be right for everyone" to "it would not be right for anyone." This inference, however, is mediated, and therefore qualified by the princi-ple that what is right (or wrong) for one person must be right (or wrong) for any similar person in similar circumstances. For obvious reasons I shall refer to this principle as "the generalization principle," even though it has traditionally been known as the principle of fairness or justice or impartiality.[23]

> The fact is that when one makes a moral judgment in a particular sit-uation, one implicitly commits oneself to making the same judgment in any similar situation, even if the second situation occurs at a dif-ferent time or place, or involves another agent. Moral and value pred-icates are such that if they belong to an action or object, they also belong to any other action or object which has the same properties. If I say I ought to serve my country I imply that everyone ought to serve his country.[24]

> If I call a thing red, I am committed to calling anything else like it red. And if I call a thing a good X, I am committed to calling any X like it good.[25]

These are representative contemporary interpretations of the claim that all moral judgments somehow presuppose a general statement. How-ever, they clearly are not instances of statement 1 of the general scheme.

[22] Andrew Oldenquist, "Universalizability and Nondescriptivism," *The Journal of Philosophy,* 65, No. 3 (1968), 59.
[23] Marcus G. Singer, *Generalization in Ethics,* Knopf, New York, 1961, p. 5.
[24] Frankena, *Ethics,* p.25.
[25] R. M. Hare, *Freedom and Reasom,* Oxford University Press, New York, 1956, p. 15.

They cannot, in conjunction with a corresponding statement 2, allow the derivation of a singular moral judgment. Here is the general scheme that results when we replace statement 1 with a general statement like those described by the quoted authors.

1'. If any x is M, then any y that is like x in respect R is M.
2'. This x is M.

Therefore,
3'. Any y that is like x in respect R is M.

It is to be noted that statement 3' is not a singular moral judgment but is another general statement—perhaps a kind of moral rule. Thus statement 1' allows only a general statement to be derived, whereas statement 1 allows a particular statement (the singular moral judgment that this x is M) to be derived. Therefore, this scheme cannot by itself support a statement of the form 'y is M'. However, since statement 3' is an instance of premise 1, the rule theorist might suggest it can be rewritten to derive 'y is M'.

3'. [Rewritten] If any y is like x in respect R, then y is M.
4. This y is like x in respect R.

Therefore,
5. This y is M.

Here, says the rule theorist, is an instance of statement 3 of the original scheme derived by making use of a general statement that is, we shall assume, promulgated by an individual.

However, the picture is clouded by the fact that statement 2' ('This x is M') is required to get statement 3'. Statement 2' is also an instance of statement 3 of the general scheme (a singular moral judgment); and if we can arrive at statement 2' without making use of statements 3' and 4, then statements 3' and 4 are not required to arrive at instances of statement 3. In other words, this kind of scheme presupposes that we are able to arrive at singular moral judgments without the need for any moral rules. Regardless of the correctness of the generalization argument as interpreted here, it can apparently shed no light on the original general scheme and the justification of singular moral judgments. It is certainly of no help to the rule theorist.

Furthermore, there is a problem with statement 1' ("If any x is M, then any y that is like x in respect R is M"). Either x and y have *some* similar nonmoral characteristics or they are alike in *all* such respects. An example of the former is when both x and y are instances of truth-telling, although they differ in other respects. "If any action x is right, then any action y that is like x in being an instance of truth-telling is right" is the general statement. This interpretation, however, runs afoul of effective counter-examples. No matter what characteristic or group of characteristics you suggest, there are instances of things having those characteristics that are not M. It would seem that there are many instances of truth-telling that are not right (as well as instances of lying that are right). You are not likely to have difficulty in finding such cases, for they are abundant.[26]

It might be claimed that the general statement is true only when x and y have *all* their nonmoral characteristics in common. The statement would then look something like the following: "If any action x is right, then any action y that has all its nonmoral properties in common with x is right." Notice, though, that we now need to say nothing about truth-telling and have arrived at something very much like Oldenquist's statement (U4). If we add that the rightness of an action is a function of other characteristics, then this statement is quite safe; it is necessarily true.[27] Unfortunately, the use to which such a statement can be put is limited. It cannot, as has been argued, shed any light on the general scheme with which we began, since its use requires the very statement we wish to derive. However, enough of such speculation, those who believe that it has an important role should tell us what that role is.

6. Moral education and moral maturity

One further reason in support of act theories will be mentioned briefly here. It has to do with moral education and moral maturity—what they are and what they are not. Parents

[26] When someone asks whether the water is safe to drink, in most circumstances telling the truth is the right thing. However, if someone performs the like action of telling the truth to our familiar maniac when he asks if his intended victim is hiding under the bed (when that is indeed where the victim is), then that person is not doing the right thing.

[27] This may seem like a very fancy claim, but in actuality it is not all that complicated. Suppose that figure *a* is a triangle by virtue of being a three-sided (F) plane figure (G) that is enclosed (H) by straight lines (I). All and only those four properties determine that a figure is a triangle. Suppose this is true, and suppose we find that figure *b* has all the properties that figure *a* has that are relevant to something's being a triangle. It would be necessarily true to assert, "If figure *a* is a triangle solely by virtue of having F, G, H, and I, and if these are all and the only properties determining triangularity, and if figure *b* has F, G, H, and I, then figure *b* is a triangle." It would be a contradiction to assert that figure *a* is a triangle solely by virtue of having F, G, H, and I, that these are all and the only properties determining a triangle, that figure *b* has F, G, H, and I, and that figure *b* is not a triangle.

The problem is that this statement, which is necessarily true, and whose negation is a contradiction, does not offer any help in finding new instances of triangles until we establish that all parts of it are true. Is it true, we would ask in this instance, that something is a triangle on all and only those occasions in which it has those four properties? If the answer is "yes," then we have found a rule, no doubt a constitutive rule, of geometry. Now the similar question in morality is whether there is some set of F's (plus G's, H's, and so on) that result in a similarly true or correct statement. The fact that we have found counter-examples to all the proposed statements of this type, and that there are other kinds of troubles as described in chapter 4 and in this chapter, indicates that there is no such set of F's.

Once again, then, the argument that was to establish that there is such a set of F's, and thus that there is some constitutive moral rule, fails.

teach their children moral rules, as was noted earlier, and the children usually take these rules to be constitutive. When a parent teaches a child not to lie because it is wrong, the child does not distinguish between the rule as a summary and the rule as constitutive. The parents, however, if asked, would certainly say you should lie if a maniac asks where his enemy is hiding. If the enemy asks where your family is hiding, you have a right to lie. The parents know this, and insofar as they do, they know that the moral rules are not constitutive. Of course, the parents probably don't know the fancy terms 'constitutive' and 'summary', and most would be hard pressed to follow the complicated discussions in this work. However, in their actions and in their responses it is not difficult to elicit the fact that they take the rules to be summaries. Thus, moral education, as given by the parents, indicates that summary rules are taught, even though the children take them to be constitutive.

Interestingly enough, though, at a certain age children do recognize that moral rules are not constitutive. Without proposing a study now as to when that time comes, it does come. Instead of applying rules as if they were constitutive, they come to understand that moral rules may sometimes be broken. Not only do we break them when we are not acting morally or in the proper way, but we may also break them occasionally *in order to* act in the morally proper way. When a person knows how to do this with sensitivity and insight, we say the person is wise. The ability to know when to abandon a rule and to act in some other manner is something that almost all human beings come to have—it signals the onset of moral maturity.

This ends the long section presenting reasons in favor of act theories. The arguments are by far the most complicated we have examined, and the discussion has opened up yet new problems. However, if you review the arguments, your efforts will be rewarded with greater understanding. Philosophy is not easy, and the area you are now in is not an easy area in philosophy, but it is one that has practical importance for every human being.

Exercises: Act versus rule theories

1. Now that you have examined the main rival normative theories of obligation, you may wish to ask yourself which of them does the best job in accounting for the moral phenomena. Turn to page 26 to refresh your memory concerning the moral phenomena discussed at the beginning of this investigation. You may wish to add some other items and should feel free to do so (as long as they are not theories that compete with the ones already examined). Present your reasons for claiming that one theory does a better job than its rivals in explaining the moral phenomena.
2. Suppose someone attempts to save a rule theory by including an "all things being equal" clause in the following way:

If any x is an instance of F, then, all things being equal, x is M.

When we propose a criticism in the form of a counter-example, the person says, "Aha! This is an instance in which not all things were equal, so that case is already covered in the rule." What is wrong with this response?
3. Present the strongest reasons you can give for or against the following claim:

"Whenever you offer justification for a claim within an area, there are going to be other claims within that area that are not justified."

4. Most decisions concerning travel from one point to another are made without a map, most decisions about food are made without a theory of nutrition before us, and most moral decisions are made without having a normative theory of obligation before us. What are some functions for such theories? Argue either that such functions are important or that they are not.

5. The citation below indicates that the author holds some kind of act theory. Attempt to indicate what sort it is, and if you cannot tell, indicate why.

> If the exercise of moral judgement, the holding of moral views, is to be the reasonable affair which it is surely ideally supposed to be, there should not occur any simplifying, undiscriminating, rather child-like acceptance of rules; for there is nothing to make such acceptance really reasonable. Rather, there should occur the constantly repeated attempt to achieve the best judgement on the full concrete merits of each individual case. One should thus consider what there is reason to do or not do, or what view there is reason to take, rather than, less discriminatingly, what is required by some rule, or permitted or ruled out by some rule.

(The quotation is from G. J. Warnock, *The Object of Morality*, Methuen, London, 1971, p. 67.)

F.   Comparison of theories of obligation: A summary

In chapter 1, the various theories of obligation were laid out on a chart. You may now want to review that chart (see page 16) so as to see where we have been and better understand what has been done. In chapters 2 and 3, the two main kinds of teleological theories were examined—namely, egoism and utilitarianism. We concluded in that chapter that egoism is a weak view because the psychological theory used as its main support is not itself supportable. Even if that psychological theory were correct, the resulting ethical theory does not cover all the moral phenomena. The version of ethical egoism that derives support from psychological egoism is the "right to" version, and one cannot, in any obvious way at least, derive actions that are right from ones that we have a right to do. There are problems with other people, counter-examples of various types, and also difficulties in accounting for moral disagreement. Utilitarianism does a better job in accounting for the moral phenomena concerning other persons and disagreement. On these grounds, therefore, it was concluded that some form of utilitarianism, most likely the indirect version, is the best of the teleological theories. This is not to say that that theory is free of difficulties. The primary difficulties involved various counter-examples and the problem of justice.

In chapter 4, a variety of deontological theories of obligation were examined. It was argued that a multiple categorical rule theory was most difficult to defend because of the problem of the conflict of rules. Such conflicts would lead to the conclusion that we have incompatible actual obligations—an unacceptable conclusion. The two views that seemed best were the indirect single categorical rule view and the prima facie rule view. The most prestigious of the former is some form of kantianism, one instance of which was examined. The views of W. D. Ross and W. F. Frankena were also examined briefly, although it would be misleading to think that their views are all that different. Some interesting types of variations, for example, a theory that holds that some prima facie rules are direct and others are indirect or that claims that sometimes the prima facie rules are to be taken as direct rules and sometimes as indirect rules, were not examined. From my point of view, no differences in kind in the criticisms are really required. So we can say that the three views that appear best among the rule theories are indirect utilitarianism, kantianism, and prima facie rule theory. I have argued that a variety of ills afflict each of these, and that a certain version of an act theory, the one just dealt with, is a better theory of obligation. The arguments for this claim are to be found primarily in this chapter, although the arguments against the other theories are to be found in the chapters in which those theories are examined.

Those who suggest that one of the theories mentioned is better than the act theory that I defend are (intellectually) obliged to respond to the issues raised in the criticisms, as well as to show some deficiencies in the act theory presented. This does not have to be done immediately; there is no great hurry about choosing theories or in constructing arguments. However, it would seem that you must at least acknowledge the problems that your theory faces and begin to think about the most defensible one. You cannot simply ignore the views of others and hold your own position regardless of the criticisms outstanding.

Finally, some of you may want to wait until you have examined the theories of value before you make a decision about a theory of obligation. You will recall that for the first statement of the general scheme the teleologists replaced F with some value term (for example, "If any action of person *a* maximizes the greatest good for the greatest number, then person *a* is obliged to perform that action"). The value terms were all the most general ones, for example, 'good', and we deliberately did not attempt to specify them further. The other half of normative ethics is theory of value, and we shall turn to that next. It may be that a general theory with a somewhat defective theory of obligation fits best with a theory of value that is itself the best theory in that area. Given this, you would then opt for a theory of obligation that, if there were no such area as theory of value, you would reject. Furthermore, some theory of value may exist that will allow a specification of the value terms in teleological theories of obligation in such a way as to escape the criticisms offered so far. It does not seem to me that this will happen, but these are the kinds of claims that philosophers have made, and we should take them seriously. With all of these considerations in mind, then, let us turn to theory of value.

Recommended reading

Carritt, E. F. *The Theory of Morals.* Oxford University Press, London, 1952. Carritt presents an act theory, though not the one defended in this chapter.

Hare, R. M. *The Language of Morals.* Clarendon Press, Oxford, 1952.

Prichard, H. A. *Moral Obligation.* Oxford University Press, New York, 1950. Prichard is an act theorist who defends an act theory modeled on our knowledge of mathematics.

Singer, Marcus. *Generalization in Ethics.* Knopf, New York, 1961. Singer argues for a rule theory via what is called the "generalization argument." This argument is not taken up directly in this chapter, though it is the subject of the next item in this bibliography.

Sobel, J. Howard, "Generalization Arguments," *Theoria,* 31 (1965), 32–60. Reprinted in *Readings in Ethical Theory,* eds. Wilfrid Sellars and John Hospers, Appleton-Century-Crofts, New York, 1970.

Six

Chapter six
Value

Normative ethics includes theories of obligation and theories of value. We have examined the main theories of obligation in chapters 2 through 5 and, hopefully, presented the main tools required to evaluate those theories. Using the familiar "if . . . , then . . ." statement, we can exhibit the general form of a statement of obligation by making 'MO' stand for any term of moral obligation such as 'right' or 'obligation'.

If any person *a* performs an action that is F, then that action is MO.

In partial English the statement tells us that if someone does something of a certain sort, then it is obligatory, right, or something similar. 'F', recall, stands for the appropriate nonobligation predicate. One of the substitution instances of F, especially for teleological theories of obligation, was some value predicate. The utilitarians, for example, specify F as 'increases the amount of benefit or value for the greatest number'. In the discussion of utilitarianism, and all the other theories of obligation, when a value term was used, it was said that no specific theory of value would be presupposed because we had yet to examine such theories. It was further claimed that some people believe pleasure alone is of value, while others believe pleasure plus love, friendship, knowledge, and many other things are of value. Well, now it is time to investigate those theories of value, just as we investigated all the theories of obligation. Our task will be made much easier by the fact that we have looked at many theories of obligation and know how to evaluate them. Furthermore, most of the tools and arguments we shall use in this chapter have been introduced before.

The sections of this chapter are the following:

A. Intrinsic value
B. An outline of theories of value
C. Categorical direct rule theories
D. The problem with single categorical direct rule theories: a summary
E. A single categorical indirect rule theory: relativism
F. Multiple rule theories—prima facie and categorical
G. Act theory
H. Taking a stand; looking ahead

A. Intrinsic value

The key notion in this chapter will be *intrinsic value*. Although the following definition tells us what intrinsic value is, it will require further explanation before it is clear.

> x has intrinsic value =df 1. x has value.
> 2. The value of x is not exhausted by the value of what it leads to.

In this definition we find the term 'value', which is another value term. So if you thought the definition was going to define 'intrinsic value' via non-value notions, you are no doubt disappointed. However, in every area, some term is taken to be basic and is assumed to be understood without definition in that area. This was done in theory of obligation, and there seemed to be no difficulty. The notions in theory of obligation were more closely specified by the individual theories of obligation, and in the same way, the notion of value will be more closely specified by theories of value. However, some further explanation of the notion of value is possible.

There is a close connection between what we take to be valuable and goals we voluntarily pursue. If my brother chooses to go to the Pumpkin Festival in Circleville, Ohio, then this is at least partially explained by showing that there is something there he values. Perhaps he likes pumpkins, or is fond of small towns, or enjoys a ride in the country. These are all goals or ends my brother may be seeking, and we suppose they must be goals he finds valuable. We can say, generally, that people seek ends voluntarily because they believe the ends have value.

The goals we seek are almost never isolated from other goals. For example, if you choose voluntarily to go to college, this leads to the goals of a degree, greater knowledge, and increased mobility. This set of goals, when achieved, in turn leads to such goals as having friends of a certain sort, obtaining a job of a certain type, living in a certain city, and so on. Some of these goals are thought valuable only because they lead to other goals, and some are not. For example, you may not ever choose pain by itself, so to speak, but you do choose voluntarily to go to the dentist and subject yourself to considerable pain. This is chosen, though, to achieve the end of health and perhaps freedom from other pain. You choose to suffer pain, then, not for its own value, but only for the value it is essential for. Freedom from pain, in contrast, is likely to be chosen not only because it leads to other things of value, but because it has some value in addition to, or independent of, the value of what it leads to. For example, the freedom from pain may lead to enjoying an evening with friends that otherwise would not have been possible. However, even if that evening had not come about, the freedom from pain would have had some value. This is not so of the suffering in the dentist's chair. Had the dentist been a poor one, so that at the end of a great deal of suffering the original problem remained, or even became worse, we would say the experience of being in the dentist's chair was of no value at all. When an experience (or relation, or institution, or character trait, or any other large number of things) has value, and its value is not totally exhausted by the value of other things to which it leads, then it has *intrinsic* value.

In the sense used here, something can not only have intrinsic value but can lead to other things of intrinsic value. Something might have a small amount of intrinsic value and be very valuable because it leads to other things with great amounts of intrinsic value. This can be made clearer if we contrast the notion of intrinsic value with that of beneficial value.

x has beneficial value =df 1. x has value.
                             2. x leads to an intrinsically
                             valuable y.

The painful experience was beneficially valuable for the absence from pain; its value is a result of just the fact that it leads to something else. However, something can be both beneficially and intrinsically valuable. The absence of pain is apparently valuable whether it leads to anything else of value or not. When it leads to enjoying an evening with friends, which is assumed to have some intrinsic value, the freedom from pain is also beneficially valuable. So something can easily be both beneficially and intrinsically valuable. In fact, given the interconnections among our experiences, it would be very rare that something would be intrinsically valuable and not also beneficially valuable. In contrast, however, there are many things, foremost among them is pain, that are sometimes of beneficial value but never of intrinsic value. We could make up a special term for things that are beneficially valuable but not intrinsically valuable (for example, 'extrinsically valuable'), but that doesn't really seem necessary. We can say of such a thing that it is beneficially valuable only, or that it has only beneficial value.

1. Intrinsic disvalue   We shall have some small need for a notion of intrinsic disvalue as well. There is certainly a difference between an absence of intrinsic value and the presence of something that makes itself felt but is disvaluable. If one drinks water when thirsty, the resulting experience is pleasurable. If further drinks are taken, the experience is neutral with respect to value. But if you continue to drink, the experience is not neutral; it is positively disvaluable. The pain that is experienced is something whose disvalue is not exhausted by the disvalue it leads to. We could construct formal definitions of disvalue notions on the model of the definitions of the value notions.

x has intrinsic disvalue =df 1. x has disvalue.
                              2. The disvalue of x is not exhausted
                              by the disvalue x leads to.

x has maleficent value   =df   1. x has disvalue.
2. x leads to an intrinsically disvaluable y.

Pain is a clear instance of something that has intrinsic disvalue. It has been proposed that slavery is another instance, but it is perhaps a clearer instance of something with maleficent value. It leads to pain, ignorance, loss of dignity, and many other things that appear to have intrinsic disvalue.

Some things have only maleficent value, for example, having put the wrong answer down on a test; they are not intrinsically disvaluable things, but they lead, more often than not, to things that are intrinsically disvaluable, for example, pain and humiliation.

In some discussions it might be useful to have the notion of intrinsic disvalue, and so we now can say that we have added it to our arsenal.

2. The notion of leads to   Having added to our arsenal of terms, let us continue to explain the rest of the key notions in the definition of *intrinsic value* (as well as the notion of *intrinsic disvalue*). The term 'leads' is deliberately vague because it is intended to include a variety of different relations. For example, one kind of leading to is a kind of causal relation, as when breathing deeply causes the smell of fresh air to be conveyed to us. There are other kinds of causal relations, as when we study all night to pass an examination. The studying is not as good a guarantee of passing as breathing deeply is of smelling the fresh air, but they are both kinds of causal relations. Sometimes, the relation is part to whole, as when there is a total experience (for example, enjoying the outdoors) and one part of it (say, smelling) is necessary for the total experience. It may well be that the smelling, all by itself, would have little or no intrinsic value without the activation of the other senses. Suppose, for a moment, that a certain melody has intrinsic value. One note that is essential to the melody does not seem to have any intrinsic value, but it, along with many others in a relation, comprise the melody.

3. Moral and nonmoral value   The justification for making *beneficial value* so broad is that it allows us to keep the terminology to a minimum and to carry out the examination of theories with a minimum of verbiage. However, a few more clarificatory remarks are necessary.

Philosophers sometimes distinguish between moral and nonmoral senses of 'value' on the same model they use to distinguish moral and nonmoral senses of, say, 'right'. In the expression 'The right way to build a house is to start with the basement', the term 'right' is used in a nonmoral sense. There are legal obligations that are seldom confused with moral obligations, and there are legal rights that are not the same as moral rights. Are there moral and nonmoral senses of 'value', 'intrinsic value', and the other terms of value? At any rate, something very much like that exists, which we shall call the distinction between the efficiency and the value sense of value terms.

When we say that this is a good knife or a good car, or that a person does something well, it is usually a statement about efficiency in carrying out a task. A knife cuts meat without great difficulty, a car carries passengers without discomfort and at a reasonable cost, or a runner can run at a certain pace for a certain distance. There is usually an implicit comparison with others of the same kind, so that the standard of what is efficiently good may change. Many of the items in the list of efficiently good things can equally well be called instrumentally valuable, or valuable for carrying out a certain purpose. The knife is good for cutting, and the car for transportation. However, the notion of *efficient value* seems broader and appears to include the notion of *instrumental value*. At any rate, when we discussed *intrinsic value* and *value,* it was not in either of these senses. It is important to distinguish other senses only to make clear that they are not the concern of this chapter. They cannot explain why we carry out tasks and seek certain ends. If we ask the murderer why he carried out his deed, we do not find it acceptable as an answer if he says he had a knife and everyone knows that a knife is good for cutting throats. So remember, when we talk about value, we are concerned about the value sense and not the efficiency sense.

4. The value sense of 'value'   The value sense can be made somewhat clearer when we understand it applies primarily to people and to things true of people. Consider, for example, this list of things many people find to be valuable—perhaps intrinsically valuable:

1. People ("Socrates was a good man.")
2. Character traits of people ("His most valuable assets were his courage and integrity.")
3. Relations among people ("Friendship is valuable." "Slavery is evil.")
4. Experiences ("Pleasure is good, pain is not.")
5. Institutions ("Slavery is evil." "The best government is a democracy.")

It would help us if we could relate some of these things to each other to reduce them to a more manageable number. The claim made here is that people are good or not depending on the character traits they have. If the character traits turn out to be good ones, such as honesty, intelligence, loyalty, wisdom, and the like, then the person is a good person. The same can be said about institutions; they are good if they foster certain character traits in people and allow for certain experiences. At the very least, then, we can cut the list down to the middle three things. Whether the list can be pared down to fewer basic things of value or not will be seen shortly.

The question of whether or not there is actually anything of intrinsic value can be firmly settled only after we have chosen the best theory of value, given the evidence available. However, what can now be shown is that given the phenomena, we can argue that there are things of intrinsic value. It was part of the phenomena of theories of obligation that some actions are obligatory, and some are not. In theory of obligation, no one term was taken as basic and the rest defined via it; so the tendency was to appeal to the phenomena directly when discussing such different notions as *obligation* and *right action*. In theory of value, though, one notion (*value*) has been taken as basic, and others defined via it. So if we are to say that something is intrinsically valuable, since it is a defined notion and is not found in ordinary discourse in the clear sense presented here, we must provide some additional evidence for this claim. The following evidence will come from the phenomena, but, as you will see shortly, in an indirect manner.

Even though the notion of *intrinsic value* is not an ordinary notion, it is not difficult to show people that they use it, or something very close to it, in ordinary situations. The primary way to show that someone accepts something as having intrinsic value is via the notion of rational choice. Suppose someone chooses to do something, almost anything, rather than do nothing or not make a choice. For example, suppose someone reading this book decides to turn the page and read the next page—where the decision is a rational and conscious one. We can ask the person why she continues to read on rather than stop (and perhaps do something else). A common answer would be that the person wants to see how the paragraph ends, or, more likely, that it is part of an assignment. However, we can reasonably ask why the assignment is fulfilled. If the person is patient and continues, we shall perhaps learn she made a decision to try to pass the course. When we pursue the question *why,* we would find a sequence of answers such as the following: I choose to pass the course so as to get credit; the credit is needed to secure a degree; the degree is required to get a certain kind of job; the job is sought because it brings other things. By this point the answers would become more diverse; some readers would answer that they want a certain job because it is interesting or it brings security, fulfillment, freedom from worry, prestige, and so on. These are all ends that, even though they may lead to other things that have value, seem not to have their value exhausted by the value of what they lead to. In the dialogue we seemed to have reached something the person supposes is of intrinsic value; and having reached this kind of goal, we are somewhat satisfied.[1] We shall probe further and inquire as to whether beliefs in these matters are justified or not. This is part of the subject matter of theories of value.

Contrast the above kind of dialogue with one that is very difficult to understand.

"Why did you go to the dentist?"

"To have holes drilled in my teeth."

"Why did you want to have holes drilled in your teeth?"

---

[1] People understand the notion of *intrinsic value* and can use it to describe phenomena concerning themselves and others, even though they would not have been able to construct the notion themselves and may require help in its application. The application to situations, people, institutions, character traits, and such generates the phenomena for our investigation.

"So they could be filled with a silver amalgam."

"Why would you want to do that, though?"

"Because of the pain and discomfort one gets from such visits and operations."

If the person does not value pain independently of what it leads to, as most of us do not, this kind of dialogue is very difficult to understand. Unless there is some recognizable goal being sought that contains something that person or we would call intrinsically valuable, it would be difficult to understand why the visit to the dentist occurred. The person could say he wanted to have healthy teeth, or avoid the pain of tooth decay, or have an attractive smile. However, unless we suppose some such answer, we would begin to suspect the person had not acted rationally. It appears that we understand rational choice among goals in terms of what things a person finds intrinsically valuable; the person has given a justification of working to attain a goal, if we understand the goal (or something it leads to in fairly short order) to represent something of intrinsic value. Unless there is something a person takes to be of intrinsic value, it is difficult to explain rational action. Thus the fact that rational choice among alternatives of action occurs is evidence that the person takes something to be of intrinsic value.

The limiting case of this kind of reasoning concerns death. Each of you reading this now has decided to continue to live or at least did not decide not to live. The explanation of why someone would do something rather than either do nothing or commit suicide almost always has to do with weighing the positive and negative values of the alternatives. Most of us have thought about committing suicide and have decided not to do so. In terms of this model, the explanation is that there is more of intrinsic value to be gained by staying alive than not. (This is not to say that living, or life itself, is intrinsically valuable, only that there is something or some group of things of intrinsic value that can be had only when you are alive.) You may not have an understanding of what intrinsically valuable things are gained only in life, and it is not part of the claim here that you do. However, it can be assumed that something has intrinsic value to you, and this best explains your decision (or lack of decision) concerning life and death. This, then, is the second piece of evidence of the existence of something intrinsically valuable in the phenomena. Again, one of the main purposes of a theory of value is to help us find those things which are of intrinsic value, if anything is.

There is a third way to establish things of intrinsic value as being in the phenomena. Consider the distinctions drawn so far: the notion of *value* as undefined, and the defined notions of *intrinsic value* and *beneficial value*. If we admit that something has intrinsic value, then we have accepted it as part of the phenomena that something or other has intrinsic value. This is also true if a person admits that something has beneficial value, for it is something that leads to something that has intrinsic value. It could not lead to something of intrinsic value if that thing of intrinsic value did not exist. (This is true in all the uses of 'leads to', the causal sense and the part/whole sense.) The other sense of *value* discussed—the sense in which things merely have utility—was seen as not relevant to theory of value and its questions. *Value* itself is a notion that appears to require further specification in terms of *intrinsic* or *beneficial* and at any rate cannot bear the burden of explaining the topics discussed above. So it would seem, once again, that when we accept any of the phenomena concerned with value, the explanation seems to involve something of intrinsic value. However, this is not to assume that this or that theory of value is correct; it may turn out that nothing at all is actually of intrinsic value.

5. Value and obligation   As a last topic in this first section, let's contrast the views of those who think that value predicates are explained in some way by, or are reduced to, obligation predicates with the views of those who think it goes the other way. This topic will be discussed in chapter 7, but simply consider, so that you can see what such people have in mind, the following definitions.[2]

> x is intrinsically valuable =df Any person *a* in a position to bring x into existence is obliged to do so.
>
> *a* is obliged to do action B =df B brings more intrinsic value into existence than any other available action.

While both definitions are probably compatible with the definition of intrinsic value, for that is an analysis of the notion itself as contrasted with what it depends upon or is reduced to, they represent opposite and conflicting positions about what is the more basic notion within moral philosophy. The discussion of theory of value will not attempt to settle that question, but will instead concern itself with an examination of different theories of value, just as we concerned ourselves with different theories of obligation without concern for theories of value.

Exercises: The various value notions
1. Now that you have a better understanding of the notion of *intrinsic value,* but before you have examined particular theories of value, examine the value questionnaire you filled out at the beginning of the book. Make any changes that now occur to you in light of your understanding of intrinsic value. Describe what kinds of changes, if any, you made, and explain why they were made.

---

[2] I do not present these definitions as my own. They are only contrasting specimen views. One character trait that is apparently valuable is the tendency to fulfill obligations. Some people may be called good simply because they do almost always, in spite of temptations and difficulties, fulfill their obligations. In this case, this valuable character trait requires a theory of obligation for a complete understanding of what it is. But this is not necessarily a bad thing.

2. Give examples of things that are:
   a. intrinsically valuable and beneficially valuable
   b. intrinsically valuable and maleficently valuable
   c. beneficially valuable and maleficently valuable
   d. intrinsically disvaluable and beneficially valuable
   e. intrinsically disvaluable and maleficently valuable

3. List two or three kinds of things (experiences, institutions, character traits, or whatever) that a friend of yours supposes are intrinsically valuable. What led you to think your friend supposed those items to have intrinsic value? Now do the same thing for two or three kinds of things a friend of yours supposes are intrinsically disvaluable.

B.   An outline of theories of value

The general scheme used to explain the common and different elements in theory of obligation can be used in a similar way in theory of value.

   If anything x has F, then x is IV.[3]

   F will be replaced by some appropriate nonvalue notion such as *pleasure, friendship, democracy,* or whatever. In the consequent will be placed the appropriate term of value, almost always 'intrinsic value'. The method of distinguishing theories of value will be the same as was used for theories of obligation; theories are either rule theories or act theories. If they are rule theories, they are either categorical or prima facie rules. If they are categorical rule theories, they are either of the direct or the indirect variety. Within a categorical rule theory, there is either one or more than one such rule. Among the single categorical rule theories we shall examine are hedonism (the sole replacement for F is pleasure), happiness theories, and value relativism. We shall examine Ross's prima facie rule theory of value and attempt to apply the results there to any prima facie rule theory. Finally, there will be an examination of the act theory that is the corresponding theory of value to an act theory of obligation. We shall begin with the categorical rule theories.

C.   Categorical direct rule theories

In chapter 4 it was shown, it will be supposed, that a multiple categorical rule theory, one that maintains the existence of many categorical rules of obligation or value, has insuperable difficulties. One problem is the

---

   [3] IV, of course, will be translated as 'intrinsic value'. 'Thing' is to be taken in a wide enough sense so that it includes experiences, character traits, relations, and the other items on the list in the preceding section.

inconsistency that results when two of the rules apply and give different results. So such a theory will not be examined here. All the categorical rule theories will propose only one rule, whether the rule is direct, that is, applies directly to the things, or indirect, that is, picks out the rules of intrinsic value that apply directly to the things.

1. **Hedonism**   The first view to be examined will be *hedonism*, whose single categorical rule is as follows:

> If any x is an instance of pleasure, then it is IV (intrinsically valuable).

The hedonist will want to account for intrinsic disvalue, just as the egoist will want to account for wrong actions as well as right actions. We will suppose that for each of these theories of value there is an obvious way to generate out the rule concerning intrinsic disvalue by making use of the polar opposite characteristic of the one connected to intrinsic value.

> If any x is an instance of pain, then it is IDV (intrinsically disvaluable).

There have been views that claim that while pain is intrinsically disvaluable, it is only the absence of pain that is intrinsically valuable. They claim that the pleasures we have are either not really intrinsically valuable or, since they always lead to more pain than the pleasure, not worth pursuing. However, we shall suppose that this is not always so and will consider the version of hedonism that has it that pleasure, and not just the absence of pain, has intrinsic value.

Those of you who have read what precedes in this book should understand what a categorical rule is: such a rule holds no matter what else is true of the thing to which it applies.[4] The rule works to get out singular value judgments by adding a statement that affirms the antecedent, thus allowing us to derive the singular judgment that this particular x is intrinsically valuable. The first and second statements, along with the singular value judgment, appear as follows.

> If any x is an instance of pleasure, then it is IV.
> This x is an instance of pleasure.
> _____
> Therefore,
> This x is IV.

The notion of *pleasure* is thought by most to be clear, but some people have doubts about it. At the very least we must distinguish *pleasure* from *happiness*, the former being a short-run experience and the latter being a relatively long-run state. For example, suppose you hike the whole of a hot afternoon under a fierce sun on a dusty plain. At the end of that time you are

[4] See pages 115 and 121.

very thirsty, and when you come to the waters of a stream just down from the mountains, you take a drink. Imagine the feeling you have when you drink the water—that is a pleasurable experience. Suppose again, you like to have your back rubbed, as most of us do, and now someone is expertly doing it. You are having an experience that is pleasurable. It is hard to imagine a human being who does not know what we are talking about when we mention pleasurable experiences.[5]

Contrast the experience of drinking cool water when you are thirsty with being happy with your job. The former is something that occurs within a short time span; you have the pleasure and then, a short time later, it is gone. You can have it again with another drink, but you may have to wait a bit. In contrast, being happy with your job is not an experience you have one day while working, it is something true of you over a fairly long span of time. It may come to you suddenly while at work or on your way home that you are happy with your job, but the happiness itself is not something that occurs on the way home or while working. Other terms that have a weaker force than 'happiness' but are of the same type are 'satisfaction', 'contentment', and 'fulfillment'. The hedonist, as the position is interpreted here, claims that pleasure is the only thing of intrinsic value, not that happiness is the only thing of intrinsic value.[6]

To the suggestion that another thing has value, the hedonist's response is that the thing has only beneficial value, no intrinsic value, unless it too is an instance of pleasure. If someone claims, for example, that love has intrinsic value, the hedonist will respond, whether correctly or not remains to be seen, that love has value only because it gives the people involved some pleasure. That is, the value of love is just its beneficial value in leading to pleasure. The same claim will be made by the hedonist whenever any other proposed intrinsically valuable thing is mentioned. Is this, though, a correct claim? This move is similar to the one made by the utilitarian, for example, when we propose sources of obligation other than those involving the maximization of happiness for the greatest number. The utilitarian will attempt to show that such other actions are obligatory only because they do maximize the happiness of the greatest number. As you will recall, though, the mere claim that this is the sole source of obligation is not enough, there must be some plausibility to the claim and hopefully some positive reasons for supposing the claim to be true. If these conditions are not met, and if there is another theory that can do a better job of

---

[5] There are those (for example, G. Ryle in *The Concept of Mind* and other places) who insist that pleasure is not an experience of the sort pain is. There are pleasurable experiences, they insist, but no experience of pleasure. I think the former is probably all the hedonist needs, but it does also seem to me that there are not only pleasurable experiences but something identifiable in those experiences that is itself an experience. Drinking water is an experience that causes or includes a pleasurable experience (under certain circumstances). However, you should decide for yourself.

[6] Some hedonists, recall, have identified pleasure with the absence of pain, but this will not be the main view considered here.

explaining obligation, one that can respond to objections without employing ad hoc devices and has some other reasons in its favor independently of
the statement of the theory, then that theory is preferable to utilitarianism.
Similarly, we must now examine hedonism to determine its acceptability.[7]

2. Hedonism as a theory of motivation: an evaluation   As was true of
ethical egoism, the main support of hedonism presented by most defenders
is a psychological theory of motivation. Fortunately, we have already examined that theory in its most general form and so will not have to spend
much time on one specific instance of it. In its general form, which we
called psychological egoism, it looked like this:

> If any person *a* performs a voluntary action, then person *a*'s sole mo-
> tive for performing that action is to benefit himself.

In the specific version we are now considering, psychological hedonism, the term 'benefit' is replaced with 'pleasure'.

> If any person *a* performs a voluntary action, then person *a*'s sole mo-
> tive for performing that action is to increase his pleasure.

If the criticisms of the general theory of psychological egoism in
chapter 2 are effective, then they are effective against psychological hedonism. Please review those arguments and, in reading, replace 'benefit' with
'pleasure' throughout.

It will be supposed that those arguments against the general position
are effective whether we are considering the view as a more strictly scientific theory of motivation or as a common-sense theory of motivation. The
very same evidence cited to show that psychological egoism is not acceptable as a more strictly scientific theory of motivation shows that psychological hedonism, taken in the same way, is not an acceptable theory of
motivation. A bit more will have to be said about the theory when taken as
a common-sense view of motivation.

You will recall that we constructed a theory, called *psychological altruism,* that contended that our only motive was to bring about good for
others. Further, it was argued that since psychological altruism was very
low on the scale of acceptability of theories, and that the two theories were
equally acceptable, psychological egoism was also low on the scale of acceptability of such theories. The same argument can be used against psychological hedonism, but just as we specified *benefit* or *good* as pleasure we
now must specify it this way for psychological altruism. Very briefly, then,
according to the more specific version of psychological altruism, our only
motive is to bring about pleasure for others. In the more familiar form,

> If any person *a* performs a voluntary action, then person *a*'s sole mo-
> tive for performing that action is to increase others' pleasure.

[7] You may wish to review the criteria of acceptability discussed on page 24.

When people present purported counter-examples to this view, on the common-sense level, the defender of psychological altruism makes use of ad hoc devices in "explaining" why the counter-examples are not acceptable. Suppose the purported counter-example is drinking a glass of water when I am thirsty for, as I think, the pleasure I get when I take the drink. The psychological altruist would suggest that if I did not drink the water, then I would become irritable, thus disturbing others, and finally would become nonproductive with respect to the pleasure of others. The psychological altruist concludes (mistakenly) that the motive in drinking the water was to increase the pleasure of others. This kind of explanation is not very good, as we all recognize, yet it is apparently just the kind of explanation psychological hedonists give when they "defend" their view. If this is the only kind of defense for that view, then we would be justified in ranking psychological altruism specified with respect to pleasure and psychological hedonism at about the same level on the scale of acceptability of theories—in a very low place.

Given the examination of psychological egoism in chapter 2 and the apparent effectiveness of the criticisms of that view against psychological hedonism (which is merely a specific version of the former view), we are seemingly justified in rejecting psychological hedonism.

In chapter 2 an argument was constructed showing how one could support a "right to" version of ethical egoism on the basis of psychological egoism. It was then argued that this did the ethical egoist little good because he could not then defend psychological egoism. However, there is no similar argument that can be used to support hedonism by presenting psychological hedonism. The situation can be represented in the following way:

Ethical egoism

True	If PE, then EE.[8]
False	PE.

False	EE.

Hedonism

Not true	If PH, then H.
False	PH.

False	H.

Arguments have been presented to show that the second premise in each argument, the psychological theory of motivation, is not true. In addition, there is apparently no way in which the antecedent of the first premise of the second argument supports the consequent. This results, at least in part, because humans often fail to value what is valuable. So from the supposition that people can only value pleasure, it would not yet

[8] This is true only when we restrict the ethical theory to notions of *right to*.

follow that only pleasure is valuable. We might be able to conclude that people have a right to value only pleasure, but that is not the claim of hedonism. That claim is that only pleasure is (intrinsically) valuable. Since there is no argument to establish the absence of a connection between psychological hedonism and hedonism, we don't want to say that the premise is false—but we can conclude that there is no evidence to suppose that it is true.

The conclusions of the two arguments, which represent the theory of obligation and theory of value respectively, must find some support other than the previously presented arguments. It was argued in chapter 2 that ethical egoism was not a very good theory; there are competitors, such as utilitarianism, that do a better job as theories of obligation. It is now time to examine hedonism as a theory of value.

There seems to be little question that pleasure is *one* goal that humans seek not just for what it leads to. We often do things, drink certain wines, sing certain songs, and carry on with members of the opposite sex, not only for the more remote goals (euphoria, stardom, parenthood) those activities bring into existence but also for the pleasure. To the question "Why did you put yourself in that state?" a sufficient answer often is "Because I find being in that state pleasurable." So, as J. S. Mill points out, it is some evidence that pleasure is the only thing of intrinsic value that it is at least one of the things of intrinsic value. We shall take it to be a part of the phenomena that pleasure is one of the things of intrinsic value. Our final decision may be that pleasure has no intrinsic value at all, but that is a conclusion we should reach only after we have completed our inquiry into theory of value.

3. **Hedonism as a theory of value: an evaluation**   It is much more difficult to establish that pleasure is the only thing of intrinsic value, but the hedonist makes a strong claim. A variety of apparently ineffective arguments have been used to attempt to establish this claim, some of which we shall examine in the course of criticizing the theory.

There are two main types of criticisms of single categorical rule theories of value, hereafter called *monist* views for short. First, there are counter-examples—instances of, for example, pleasure that are not intrinsically valuable. Second, there are additional kinds of things that are of intrinsic value. The first type is the easiest to consider, so let's start there.

Some philosophers indicate that there are instances of pleasure that have intrinsic disvalue. For example, the pleasure that a sadist experiences when torturing a victim is thought by some to be positively disvaluable. However, it does seem that the hedonist can reasonably claim the pleasure the torturer has is intrinsically valuable, but the pain the victim has is intrinsically disvaluable. We may all admit that the total situation that consists of the pain of the victim plus the pleasure of the torturer contains more pain than pleasure, and thus the total experience is one that does not have positive intrinsic value. However, this is compatible with the pleasure of the torturer having intrinsic value. This is not the clearest kind of case, and if we can find more clearcut examples, then we are well advised to do so.

You will recall that in the discussions of counter-examples to egoism and utilitarianism we used some counter-examples of the "underwhelming" value type. An action was described that would increase a person's good or the good of the greatest number, but the amount of good was so small that it did not impart an obligation to realize it. It may be that scratching an itch, a very mild itch, brings some benefit for oneself, but the act does not seem thereby to be obligatory. Similar considerations were raised with respect to utilitarianism.[9] The notion of benefit in those examples was usually instanced by pleasure, so they can be used as counter-examples to the claim that if anything is an instance of pleasure, then it is intrinsically valuable. For example, that very same small sensation of pleasure we get from scratching an itch is an instance of pleasure but it does not appear to have any intrinsic value. We may indeed get a great deal of pleasure from drinking a glass of water when we are quite thirsty, but suppose we take a drink when we are not thirsty at all. The successive sensations of pleasure that we derive from drinking successive glasses of water decrease until there is no pleasure at all, and finally pain results. Consider the smallest amount of discernible pleasure one would get from drinking one of those glasses of water; it is an instance of pleasure, but it hardly seems to be something of intrinsic value.

All examples of this type, as well as all counter-examples, are drawn from the phenomena with which we began. It is open to any theorist to show that something appearing to be a counter-example is not actually a counter-example at all. However, the burden of proof is on such a person to show we are mistaken. In addition, as usual, you are invited to construct your own counter-examples—ones that strike you as most reasonable.

The main type of criticism leveled against hedonism, and against all monists (single categorical rule theories), is that additional things of intrinsic value do exist. Accordingly, the argument to establish this is called the *addition test*. According to this test, if it can be shown that a thing, say, pleasure, has intrinsic value, and it also can be shown that there is an instance of another thing that, when added to pleasure, say, happiness, results in a total amount of intrinsic value greater than the intrinsic value of the pleasure alone, then the happiness added has some intrinsic value in addition to the pleasure with which we began. Schematically, this appears as follows:

1. IVx.
2. IV(x + y) > IVx.

Therefore,

3. IVy.

[9] See pages 98 and 99.

The first premise says that something, x, has intrinsic value. It might be the claim that an instance of pleasure has intrinsic value. The second premise says that when we add some y, say, an instance of happiness or love, to the pleasure, the resulting whole has more intrinsic value than the pleasure alone. This entitles us to conclude that the thing added has some amount of intrinsic value itself.

This argument does not commit one to the view that value is quantifiable in a strict sense. It will be supposed that in a rough sense values can be compared in quantity and added. If hedonism were correct, perhaps some strictly quantifiable manner of talking about intrinsic value would be possible, but whether hedonism is correct or not remains to be seen.

The "addition principle" is widely accepted by philosophers, though there is another widely accepted principle that appears to be inconsistent with it. The "principle of organic unities" tells us that in some contexts intrinsic value is not additive. Supposing that pleasure has intrinsic value and that humiliation has intrinsic disvalue, it does seem that the humiliation of wetting your pants added to the pleasure that your arch enemy has in witnessing it has more intrinsic disvalue than the humiliation itself. This should not be if we used the addition test, for then we would subtract the intrinsic value of the pleasure from the intrinsic disvalue of the displeasure to arrive at the total of intrinsic value (or disvalue) of the situation. For this situation we can say, in defense of the addition test, that the intrinsic disvalue increased because human beings usually feel more humiliation when they are in such a predicament *and* it is noticed by their enemies.

No argument has been presented to indicate that this kind of response can be made generally for supposed instances drawn from the principle of organic unities.[10] However, with that warning and an indication of the kind of response that would be made, we can move on. We can say that the argument presented is not without its critics. However, the critics question the truth of the second premise, for there is little question that the argument form is valid, but what we must show is that there actually are such y's.

Let us consider first *happiness* and *pleasure. Happiness* is, you will recall, a relatively long-run state, and *pleasure* is a relatively short-run state. There appear to be many times in each of our lives in which we have an adequate amount of pleasure but are short on happiness. Films, such as *La Dolce Vita,* are made about this state. However, we do not have to take the most dramatic cases, since many moments in each of our lives appear to contain the same ingredients. Consider such moments in your own life, and

[10] The principle of organic unities is stated clearly by G. E. Moore: "It is certain that two bad things or a bad thing and an indifferent thing may form a whole much worse than the sum of badness of its parts. . . . *The value of a whole must not be assumed to be the same as the sum of values of its parts*" (G. E. Moore, *Principia Ethica,* Cambridge University Press, London, 1959, p. 28). *Principia Ethica* was published in 1903, when the principle of organic unities was widely accepted. Whether it is now I cannot say.

if there are such moments, then you admit thereby that happiness has some intrinsic value.

The same kind of reasoning can be applied to *love* and *pleasure.* Which is more valuable, a life that contains only pleasure or one that contains both pleasure and love? If it is the latter, then you have thereby admitted that love has some intrinsic value. If you feel more comfortable considering *freedom, security, friendship, motherhood,* or any other number of candidates, then, of course, feel free to use those things.

When the addition test is used, the monist attempts to show that any additional intrinsic value results from just more of whatever he maintains is the only thing of intrinsic value. For example, the hedonist will claim the explanation of why the addition of happiness or love makes pleasure more valuable is that each of those leads to more pleasure; that is, they are valuable only because they are beneficially valuable. How are such claims evaluated?

First, it would be an error to conclude that whatever some experience, relation, state of affairs, or whatever leads to is the *value* explanation of why that thing is sought. Suppose someone seeks happiness in addition to pleasure—hedonists claim that happiness is sought for the pleasure it leads to. Their evidence, if any evidence is presented, is that pleasure results from happiness. However, this kind of argument is "too strong," as philosophers are fond of saying. If this were a good argument we could establish, contrary to the claim of hedonists, that pleasure is not intrinsically valuable at all. Almost all pleasure leads to a loss of energy, and sometimes to a state of pain. This is certainly true of such pleasures as sex and food. Shall we say that the thing of value sought from sexual relations is fatigue? Shall we say, finally, that what we seek from everything we do is death? After all, in the course of our experiences we all die sooner or later.

Eating food leads to defecation. It would be a mistake, though, to conclude that the purpose of eating is to defecate and the end we seek when we eat is to increase the amount of fecal matter in the universe. None of us accepts this defense of fecal monism as plausible in any way, and yet it appears to be as good as the hedonist's defense of his view. The conclusion is that this kind of defense, just by itself, cannot be used to support hedonism.

Even if happiness did lead to pleasure, one could not so conclude that happiness was only beneficially valuable. Furthermore, there are times when apparently happiness does not lead to more pleasure but is nevertheless apparently intrinsically valuable. This is the claim J. S. Mill makes when he suggests that it is better to be a Socrates dissatisfied than a pig satisfied. All of us have completed tasks such as building a model airplane when not finishing it would have resulted in more pleasure. However, we do such things for something we can call satisfaction or happiness. Again, a person may pass up sexual pleasure to achieve other goals, such as fidelity or happiness.

It is open for the hedonist to claim that the person actually pursues pleasure, but then again, it is open for anyone to say anything. When we question people, and here it is best if I talk about myself, it seems that on

many occasions the goal sought is not pleasure but something else. Sometimes, the other additional goal sought is happiness. When we asked earlier
how to evaluate the claim that pleasure is always sought when we seem to
seek other things, surely one part of an answer is to discover what the person who is pursuing the goals believes. If that person supposes that it is
some goal other than pleasure that is sought, we then have some evidence
of goals other than pleasure that have intrinsic value. The person could turn
out to be mistaken, for not all the things we suppose to have intrinsic value
do indeed have intrinsic value. However, when hedonists make the claim
that it is a mistake to think that happiness has intrinsic value, they must
present some reasons.

Anyone can maintain that y, whatever it is, is the only intrinsically
valuable thing, and then provide us with ad hoc explanations of why, even
though other things seem to have intrinsic value, they do not. For example, someone could maintain that only knowledge has intrinsic value.
Suppose we say that pleasure in addition to knowledge has intrinsic value
and use the addition test for our evidence. An instance of knowledge plus
an instance of pleasure has more intrinsic value than the instance of knowledge by itself. The person can always say that the pleasure is just beneficially valuable for more knowledge. After all, we do know that pleasure is
one of the elements that leads to knowledge—as in stimulus-response models of learning. The same kind of "defense" can be provided for any theory.
If this defense were any good, all the competing and inconsistent theories
would be the best theory. This is obviously not possible, for it is not possible that pleasure, knowledge, freedom, love and so on are each the only intrinsically valuable thing. This is a situation exactly similar to the kinds of
suggestions in chapter 2 when we discussed pyschological and ethical
egoism. You may want to look again at that discussion to refresh your
memory.

Summary of hedonism   To summarize this section, there is apparently
no way to establish the correctness of hedonism as a theory of value on the
basis of psychological hedonism. That is, 'If PH, then H' appears not to be
true. In addition, PH is not true—for all the evidence adduced against psychological egoism applies against it. Finally, when we consider hedonism as
a theory of value, it appears not to fare very well. There are apparent
counter-examples of the underwhelming value sort, and the addition test
seems to show that once we establish that at least one thing of value exists,
we can show that others exist. As usual, though, no one should make a
final decision to reject hedonism until we see a comparison of it with other
theories.

4. A theory of happiness   In this section we are examining monistic
theories of value, those which maintain that one and only one kind of thing
has intrinsic value. The most popular candidate among nonphilosophers for
that one thing is pleasure, but among philosophers happiness probably
ranks first. In distinguishing *pleasure* from *happiness* for the discussion of

hedonism, we also described *happiness* sufficiently for our purposes. It is a relatively long-run state in contrast with the relatively short-run state of pleasure. It goes under other names, such as 'satisfaction', 'fulfillment', and 'contentment', but we all understand fairly well what it is. Presented as a single categorical rule of intrinsic value, the view appears as follows:

If anything is an instance of happiness, then it is IV.

This statement works, as do all the others, with an appropriate second statement to the effect that a particular thing is an instance of happiness to derive the judgment that this particular thing has intrinsic value.[11] If the rule is the only one, then the claim is that it and only it is required to justify singular intrinsic value judgments.

The evidence in favor of happiness theories is of the same type as is presented by the hedonist in favor of that theory. There is some evidence that happiness is intrinsically valuable, we can conclude this from an examination of the phenomena and use of the addition test. Furthermore, on at least some occasions, other things are beneficially valuable for happiness. For example, we might take a lower paying job not because we want to have less earning power but because of the happiness we suppose we shall get. We abstain from certain sexual relations with, for example, sheep and seek relations with human beings not because we suppose human beings are intrinsically better than sheep or (we'll suppose) because there is more pleasure, but because there is usually more satisfaction from sexual relations with other human beings.

In addition to this kind of evidence, some have presented a happiness version of psychological egoism—namely, that the only motive one has is to increase one's own happiness. This is done most notably by J. S. Mill.

> There is in reality nothing desired except happiness. Whatever is desired otherwise than as a means to some end beyond itself, and ultimately to happiness, is desired as itself a part of happiness, and is not desired for itself until it has become so.[12]

Since this view in various forms has been examined at great length in chapter 2 and in the immediately preceding sections, there is little reason to discuss it once again. Recall, though, that there is apparently no way to go from this kind of psychological theory of motivation, even if it were true, to the corresponding theory of value.[13] However, this fact is less important than the fact that the psychological theory is apparently mistaken.

The evaluation of the happiness theory is made easier because much of

---

[11] More clearly, when we talk about happiness, we are concerned with states of people, and not character traits or relations between people.

[12] Mill, *Utilitarianism,* p. 48.

[13] In chapter 4 of *Utilitarianism,* Mill's attempt to do just that is to be found.

what was said about pleasure applies to happiness. For example, the counter-examples of the underwhelming value sort also seem available to apply against happiness as the only intrinsically valuable thing. Supposing that contentment is one part of happiness (or another name for it), there are some degrees of contentment so slight that they seem not to have any intrinsic value at all. One may get happiness from a job well done, but the happiness one gets from properly drying a plate does not usually appear to have any intrinsic value. Again, self-improvement may be a part of happiness, but improving your vocabulary by one word does not appear to be intrinsically valuable. As usual, you are invited to supply your own examples of this type.

The addition test against hedonism made use of happiness and love as the two proposed additional items of intrinsic value. We can use the same trio in the examination of the happiness theory. Imagine a life that has a certain degree of happiness, and add to it a degree of pleasure. If the resulting complex of happiness and pleasure has a greater amount of intrinsic value than does the happiness alone, then there is something—namely, the pleasure—in addition to happiness that has intrinsic value. This application of the addition test is certainly easy enough to suppose, for it seems that all of us are familiar with both happiness and pleasure. The specifics of any example, though, will be left to you. Having gotten this far, you must realize that you must take an active part in this enterprise.

The same type of counter-moves are open to the happiness theorist as were open to the hedonist, but the same type of counter-counter-moves are available. It could be claimed that the pleasure is only beneficially valuable, that is, it is only valuable insofar as it leads to more happiness. However, the evidence from the phenomena does not indicate this. All the remarks made concerning pleasure can now be carried into this discussion with only a substitution of 'happiness' for 'pleasure'.

5. Other candidates   An examination such as this, the presentation of counter-examples of the underwhelming value type, and the use of the addition test lead to the conclusion that there are serious difficulties with the happiness view. These difficulties are of the same type as those of hedonism; and furthermore, one finds the same difficulties with all single categorical rule theories. Given this, it does not seem necessary to examine each such view at length. Below you will find a list of candidates thought by some to be the only rule of intrinsic value. At the end of the chapter you will find a bibliographic entry for each one so that you may investigate any interest you have.

1. If anything is an instance of love, then it is IV. (value agapism)
2. If anything is an instance of freedom, then it is IV. (moksaism)
3. If anything is an instance of (having or exercising) power, then it is IV. (nietzscheanism)
4. If anything is an instance of health, then it is IV. (vitaminism)

5. If anything is God, then it is IV. (theologism)
6. If anything is an instance of a good will, then it is IV. (kant-ianism)

D. The problem with single categorical direct rule theories: A summary

Many things have been presented in this chapter in a very short space, so perhaps a quick review of what has been done is in order before we go on. The key notions, *intrinsic value* and *beneficial value,* were explained. Then it was argued that if someone made conscious, rational, voluntary choices, this was evidence that something was taken to be of value. Furthermore, if someone supposes that something has value, the best explanation of this includes the supposition that something does indeed have intrinsic value. Finally, the addition test shows that if you admit that one thing has intrinsic value, then we can show you that you admit that at least two things have intrinsic value. In a tabular form we have the following:

1. Something x has value.
2. If something x has value, then something y (x and y may be the same or different) has intrinsic value.
3. If one thing x has IV, then another thing y in addition to x has IV.[14]

What is indicated, then, is that single categorical direct rule theories are not correct. Let us take a very brief look at one single categorical indirect rule theory before we turn to the multiple rule theory views.

Exercises: Problems of intrinsic value
1. The addition test and the principle of organic unities can be compared directly if we put each in the form of a principle. One difficulty is that the addition test makes universal claims about all things and the organic unities principle deals with specific things. This is solved, in what follows, by using indication in the form of quantifiers.

Addition
$(x)\ (y)\ [(IDVx < IDV(x+y) \rightarrow IDVy)]$

Organic unities
$(\exists x)\ (\exists y)\ [(IDVx\ \&\ IVy)\ \&\ (IDV(x+y) > IDVx)]$

---

[14] This is not an unqualified statement that can be used to generate an infinite number of intrinsically valuable things. It does work for monist views and does appear to increase the kinds of intrinsically valuable things to a large, perhaps indefinitely large, number.

In English the first statement, one of the variations of the addition test, claims that if the intrinsic disvalue of any thing is less than the intrinsic disvalue of that thing plus another thing, then the second thing has intrinsic disvalue. The second statement, one of the variations of the organic unities principle, says that there are some things such that one of them has intrinsic disvalue, the other intrinsic value; and yet, when you add the two things together, you get a whole that has more intrinsic disvalue than the intrinsic disvalue of the one of the two that has intrinsic disvalue. Present considerations, perhaps in the form of an example not given in the text, in which the two principles give different results. Argue in favor of one of the principles and against the other—at least in this context. Can your argument be made general?

2. Obviously, we cannot say that whenever something x leads to something y, that y is what a person who pursued x actually wanted or sought. For example, taking one more picture of the Grand Canyon leads to your missing the tour bus, but you didn't take the picture so as to miss the bus. On the other hand, sometimes we seek x only because of its beneficial value. Try to give some guidelines on when we are justified in making the "leads to" claim and when we are not.

3. Suppose the form of hedonism is taken that views pain as the only intrinsically disvaluable thing and the absence of pain as the only intrinsically valuable thing. Critically evaluate that view, making clear which of the criticisms offered so far apply and which do not. Does this version of hedonism fare better than the one that assumes pleasure as the positive value?

E.   A single categorical indirect rule theory: Relativism

Value relativism is the value-theory analogue of the relativism discussed in chapter 4 as a theory of obligation. It is a single rule that does not itself select what is intrinsically valuable but chooses the rules that then directly select the things of value. The statement of the single rule is as follows:

> If any proposed direct value rule R is believed by the majority of people in culture C to be a direct value rule, then R is a direct value rule (in culture C).

A *direct value rule* is the kind represented by hedonism or value agapism. It is a rule that, in conjunction with the appropriate second premise, allows the derivation of singular value judgments. For example, one instance of R might be "If anything is an instance of freedom, then it is intrinsically valuable." This rule, along with the fact that not being owned by anyone is an exercise of freedom, would allow us to conclude that not being owned by anyone is intrinically valuable. In addition, though, there may be many other rules that are believed by the majority of persons in culture C to be direct value rules. They might suppose that satisfying the gods and bathing once a month are intrinsically valuable also.

One often hears people say that in our society success is valued, whereas in other societies it is not. The same sort of thing is said about aggressiveness and security. One can see how this kind of observation fits in with value relativism and might lead people to hold that view.

1. **Carryover from obligation relativism**   The same distinctions and problems we found in ethical relativism as a theory of obligation arise with value relativism. You will recall from chapter 4, that cultural relativism is the view that in different cultures different actions are thought obligatory and the cause of that, in part at least, is the fact that the people involved are in different cultures (see the section on cultural and ethical relativism, pages 138–146, for a fuller discussion of those views). This position can be extended to judgments of intrinsic value without any difficulty. The explanation, or part of the explanation, as to why freedom is more highly valued by people in India than it is by people in the United States is that the people live in different cultures.

Supposing that CR stands for cultural relativism, ER for ethical relativism (the view discussed in chapter 4), and VR for value relativism (the value theory described above), we can set out the relation among the theories in the following manner:

Ethical relativism
If CR, then ER.
CR.

Therefore,
ER.

Value relativism
If CR, then VR.
CR.

Therefore,
VR.

In chapter 4 it was pointed out that no argument is available to establish the truth of the first premise of the scheme representing ethical relativism. It was admitted that the second premise, the thesis of cultural relativism, is correct, but that without the truth of the first premise, the truth of that second premise is not enough to establish ethical relativism. The latter view was then examined as other theories of obligation were, and it was found wanting.

The two main arguments that purport to establish ER on the basis of CR were deficient for reasons that had nothing to do with the subject matter. In one case the argument was invalid, and in the other the inductive argument required the assumption of ER, the very view the argument was going to establish.[15] Are there any additional arguments that can be used to show that CR can support VR? There are none that I know of; usually the

[15] Look again at these arguments on pages 140–144.

very same bad arguments are presented. It is a mistake in logic to attempt to conclude that something is intrinsically valuable in one culture and not in another merely from the fact that the thing is valued differently in the two cultures. The bad argument would appear as follows:

In culture C1, x is believed to be F.
In culture C2, x is not believed to be F.

Therefore,
x is F in C1 and x is not in C2.

This argument can be shown to be an unacceptable deductive argument on the grounds that it is invalid. Validity, as you will recall, has nothing to do with the content of the arguments, but only with the form. If there are other instances of the argument form that go from clearly true premises to clearly false conclusions, then the argument is invalid. As was shown in chapter 4, this is quite easy to do with the above argument. The form of the argument is:

In culture C1, x is believed to be IV.
In culture C2, x is not believed to be IV.

Therefore,
x is IV in C1 and x is not IV in C2.

A clear argument of this form that goes from true premises to a false conclusion is as follows:

In the United States, disease (x) (of a certain type, say, measles) is believed to be caused by germs (F).
In some parts of New Guinea disease (x) is believed not to be caused by germs (but by evil spirits).

Therefore,
Disease is caused by germs in the United States and disease is not caused by germs in certain parts of New Guinea.

This argument form is clearly invalid. If you are tempted to say that judgments of value are not like judgments about disease, then you should turn back to chapter 4 and go over all those moves. The subject matter in the argument is not being compared at all, only the argument form is under consideration.

It does not seem necessary to go through the arguments concerning value relativism, for they would be exactly the same as those presented with respect to ethical relativism. You can, as an exercise, go through the arguments presented with respect to ethical relativism and translate them into the appropriate language concerning value. The outcome will be the same in each case since we concluded that the arguments to establish ethical relativism on the basis of cultural relativism fail. If they do, then so do the arguments to establish value relativism on the basis of cultural relativism. Thus we must examine value relativism as a theory of value without any support from cultural relativism.

2. Value relativism evaluated   Just as there were several problems with ethical relativism, there are several with value relativism. There are counter-examples, and there are the problems of disagreement and change of opinion within a culture. The Assyrians, more than 3000 years ago, valued heartlessness toward enemies and tortured them cruelly. In Nazi Germany, apparently, loyalty as a character trait was held to be very valuable—certainly among the highest of all the intrinsic values. Even if we suppose that loyalty is intrinsically valuable, we do not suppose it is at the level the Nazis thought. These are apparently instances in which something was valued in a culture and yet it is not valuable or not valuable to the degree they supposed. These elements from the phenomena represent counter-examples to value relativism.

The standard moves are open to the value relativist, but you must recall your philosophical obligations. It does no good to say that on the *supposition* that value relativism is correct, the purported counter-examples are not actually counter-examples. That is true of any theory and any set of purported counter-examples. If we assume the theory to be correct, then the purported counter-examples are never actually counter-examples. However, since the counter-examples are drawn from the phenomena, we must be given some reason for supposing that they are not actual counter-examples. Failing that, we are justified in treating them as effective until we can be shown otherwise.

In addition to counter-examples as a kind of problem, the value relativist has difficulty in explaining a change of mind of a person and the change of mind, so to speak, of a culture. Slavery as an institution was thought to be a good thing in the United States by the majority until about the nineteenth century. To present this first as a counter-example, we will say that anyone who asserted that slavery was a good institution was mistaken—regardless of what the majority of people in that culture said. However, the explanation, or at least part of the explanation, of why people changed their minds was that they came to believe that slavery was not a good institution and that slavery was not intrinsically valuable— perhaps beneficially disvaluable or intrinsically disvaluable. We say this change was based on considerations other than what the majority supposed was correct, or else the change could not have come about. The fact that such changes occur,[16] within every cultural group and subgroup, is something that weighs against value relativism.

The same kind of consideration can be put dramatically, as was done in chapter 4, by discussing an instance of change. When Harriet Beecher Stowe claimed that slavery as an institution was evil, intrinsically

---

[16] This is a purported fact, an empirical claim.

disvaluable, she could not be refuted, even in Mississippi, by being shown that a majority of people accepted it as being intrinsically valuable (or not intrinsically disvaluable).[17]

When you, as an individual, change your mind about the value of something, it is a very rare thing indeed when you do it on the basis of what the majority of people in your culture accept. This may be what is going on all the time; but if so, it is strange that we are not aware of it. This indicates that the phenomenon of changing opinions, both opinions of individuals and those of cultures, is not something that value relativism does a very good job in explaining. If other theories of value do not have these problems nor have difficulty doing a better job of accounting for the phenomena, then we shall not, of course, adopt value relativism as our theory of value.

It should be recalled that the rejection of value relativism and the adoption of another view, whatever it is, does not commit us to a doctrine of "absolutes." Hedonists and happiness theorists can account for much, if not all, of the phenomena in this area that can be accounted for by the value relativists. Certainly, what gives one person pleasure or leads one person to be happy is not always what gives another pleasure or leads another to be happy. In various cultures, for whatever reason, certain kinds of experiences are chosen for pleasure and other kinds are chosen to reach happiness. These are claims these two theories, and many others, can accept. So, if you wish to maintain the "subjectivity" of value judgments, you need not think that the only way is to maintain value relativism, for this is not true. We shall see why this is so in the next chapter.

Exercises: Value relativism

1. Critically evaluate the following claim: "No one can make something valuable for someone else, anything that a person thinks is valuable is valuable for that person. No one can impose values on someone else. Each society has its own values, and this is what value relativism claims. In order to deny this you must suppose that there are some things that all cultures suppose are valuable, but this is just what cultural relativism shows is not so."

2. Give an explanation consistent with value relativism for the phenomenon of people changing their minds and of whole societies doing the same thing. (Remember, any theory can be made consistent with any set of phenomena, although this is not to say that the theory thereby does a good job in explaining the phenomena.) Now offer a critical analysis of your explanation. Compare the explanation you have given with a happiness value theory.

3. Relativism consists of two views, as we have seen, a theory of value and a theory of obligation. If you think that one of these views is better—is a better theory in its area than the other—explain why you maintain that view.

[17] This should be cast in the indirect rule framework, but it is less obvious when so cast. It can be done, though. Mrs. Stowe claimed that a direct rule of value was "If anything is an instance of the institution of slavery, then it is intrinsically disvaluable." Her opponents made use of the indirect rule to show that it is not a direct rule in Mississippi because a majority of people in that subculture did not accept it as such.

F.   Multiple rule theories—prima facie and categorical

There is a difference between theory of obligation and theory of value concerning multiple categorical rules. The difficulty with the Ten Commandments taken as a categorical rule theory of obligation was that we could wind up with incompatible obligations (for example, to visit a parent and not to visit a parent). This problem was solved by interpreting each obligation as a prima facie obligation, so that although you had two different and conflicting prima facie obligations, there were not two conflicting and incompatible actual obligations. One of the prima facie obligations was said to override the other, and thus the conflict did not arise on the level of actual obligations. This same kind of problem cannot arise in theory of value as set up because of the way the notion *intrinsic value* is defined. A person can hold that happiness is always intrinsically valuable and also hold that pleasure in all of its instances is intrinsically valuable, as well as that there are times when you have to choose between the two of them in a given set of circumstances. For example, you may find that a succession of *La Dolce Vita*–type nights will be a succession of nights of great pleasure but of little happiness. On the other hand, you may find that a night (or a week) spent visiting close relatives will contain little pleasure but a great deal of happiness. Suppose you must choose between the two for a given period of time. There is no incompatibility of values as such, only the fact that one person cannot do two different kinds of action over the same time period. It was the very action of traveling to see your parents that violated the commandment to honor the Sabbath and fulfilled the one to honor your parents. This was a moral conflict, and there was no way to choose without violating an actual obligation. In the value case, you have a way to choose, even if you hold both rules to be categorical rules of intrinsic value. Choose the one that has the most intrinsic value. This phrase is almost the same as the one involving prima facie obligations—namely, choose the one that is strongest with respect to obligation. So it seems the very notion we have used as our basic working notion has the idea of prima facie built into it.[18]

So multiple rule theories in theory of value, in contrast with theories of obligation, will be of one type only. We shall interpret such theories as claiming that there are at least two rules of intrinsic value that pick out at least two different kinds of things of intrinsic value. The use of the addition test indicates that perhaps once we begin the addition of kinds of things as intrinsically valuable, we are not justified until we have added a large number. Certainly, all the rules, and thus the kinds of things, listed

---

[18] Some people may say that this is not a good thing because it destroys the parallel between theory of obligation and theory of value. There is some force to this complaint, but I think this points out the difference between the "action" orientation of theory of obligation and the "state of affairs" orientation of theory of value. This is, I think, a difference in the subject matter. If the subject matters were the same in every respect, we could treat them the same—but then we wouldn't have two subject matters, but only one.

at the end of section C seem to be good candidates. So, although it will seem like a rather vague way to state a theory, this manner of saying what is meant by a multiple rule theory of value appears to be adequate.

1. The counter-example problem   What are the problems with such a theory? The problems are the same ones that beset prima facie rule theories of obligation: all the counter-examples of the underwhelming value sort and the problem of a decision procedure when more than one value is available and we must choose between them. Let us begin with a mention of the counter-example problem.

In the examination of the monistic views, counter-examples were presented, for example, an amount of happiness that is so slight as not apparently to warrant a judgment of intrinsic value. It is contended that such counter-examples are available for each kind of thing claimed by our pluralist to have intrinsic value. This would constitute a powerful criticism of such a theory. In addition, there may be counter-examples for some of the rules that are of the same type as was presented with respect to rules of obligation, a thing that is an instance of the kind mentioned in the rule (say, pleasure) and is intrinsically disvaluable. As was mentioned, some philosophers think that an experience of pleasure derived from sadistic torture, say, is such an example. Although it does not strike me that this kind of criticism is effective, you should form your own opinion.

2. The decision-procedure problem   The most serious problem, though, with multiple rule theories of value is the decision-procedure problem. The rules are constitutive of value; they and only they are required to justify judgments of intrinsic value that fall under them. If we are justified in claiming that something has intrinsic value, it is only by virtue of standing in a certain relation to one of the rules—the relation expressed in the general scheme.

Let us consider a complex thing, something that falls under at least two rules, one of which applies positively and one negatively. A situation can be brought into existence that is high in pleasure, say, and low in happiness. Consider the situation of consuming a gourmet dinner where the food consumed is part of what is required for adequate nutrition of another group of persons. Perhaps you can create a society in which 90 percent are happy, but 10 percent are unhappy because they are the slaves of the majority. Construct for yourself a situation in which two of the things you suppose have intrinsic value seem to conflict, a situation in which one thing has a positive instance and the other a negative instance. In this situation, the two rules conflict; that is, if each were the only one that applied, the total situation would be intrinsically valuable and intrinsically disvaluable, respectively. The problem is to decide whether the total situation has a surplus of intrinsic value over intrinsic disvalue, or the other way around. Another way to state this is to ask if the total situation is one that is intrinsically valuable or one that is intrinsically disvaluable. The claim will be that the multiple rule theory offers no way of determining the answer to this question; thus some judgments of intrinsic value are made that the theory cannot adequately account for. Since this kind of situation is a common one, for often we must choose between competing values, this is a serious criticism of the theory.

The argument is exactly the same as the one presented in chapter 4 against prima facie rule theories.[19] The decision about which of the competing values is weightier, which of the rules overrides the other, is made with the use of a rule or it is made without the use of a rule. However, it is not compatible with the rule theory under consideration to allow the justified decision to be reached without the use of a rule. Thus it must be through the use of a rule. The rule used, however, cannot be one of the list that picks out the intrinsically valuable things, for those rules are about things that are intrinsically valuable and not about the application of rules about things that are intrinsically valuable. A rule used to rank values in terms of weight cannot make use of a fixed hierarchy, a categorical rule, for sometimes a situation in which happiness and pleasure conflict is one in which happiness is weightier and sometimes it is one in which pleasure is weightier. In the list of the rules that pick out the kinds of things that are intrinsically valuable, there is no kind, that is always more valuable in all its instances than another kind. That is, for any two things x and y that are intrinsically valuable and are in a conflict situation, there are times when the value of x overrides the value of y and other times in which the value of y overrides the value of x.

The rule to choose between the competing rules may be thought to be another set of prima facie rules. However, this new set of prima facie rules will also have conflict situations, and the problem begins anew. This complex argument is summarized here, but for the details please turn back to chapter 4.

The conclusion is that insuperable difficulties exist for a multiple rule theory of value of the same type that beset prima facie theories of obligation. If that is so, then let us try to state the last view to be considered, an act value theory.

G. Act theory

The claims of the act theorist with respect to value are of the same type as those made in theory of obligation.

1. There are no constitutive rules of value.
2. There is a describable and usable method for arriving at singular intrinsic value judgments.

[19] See pages 127–131 for the details.

	Resultant	Nonresultant
Obligation	Fa→ MOa	MOa
Value	Fa→ IVa	IVa

Figure 6-1   Resultant and nonresultant act theories

The justification of the first claim is the failure of the various rule theories of value and, if it can be supported, the contention of the act theorist of being able to account for the value phenomena. The method of the act theorist is also the same as described in chapter 5:[20]

1. Know the relevant facts.
2. Check to make sure you are not abnormal.
3. Don't use any of the rule theories to derive the singular intrinsic value judgments.

For the complete specification of these position rules you should see pages 155–156. It is important in the explanation of the notions that no value terms be used, for then the specifications are not descriptive of the position one has to hold to arrive at justified singular moral judgments unless one already knows how to arrive at such units.

1. **Basic units**   The basic units of act theory of value and act theory of obligation have the same form. Supposing that we represent the two main types of act theories that have been defended in the history of moral philosophy, and we call the view that has been defended here a *resultant view* and the Plato/Moore-type view a *nonresultant view,* we can picture these views as in Figure 6-1.

According to the resultant theory, the basic unit of morality within each area is a singular moral judgment as related to its appropriate nonobligation or nonvalue term. You will recall from the last chapter that every theory proposes some units within an area that are not justified within that area. This is true of rule theories, which propose that the basic unit is some rule, say, the principle of utility, as well as act theories. The two theories disagree, of course, on what the basic unit is. The examination of theories is in large part an attempt to determine which purported basic unit is best taken as the basic unit within the area of morality. In the course of the last four chapters it was argued that an act theory of obligation is best and that a resultant model of that theory was the best of the lot. We have deferred until chapter 7 the question of whether the basic unit within the area of morality is basic to all areas. We are getting close to that question now. However, first we are engaged in this one last task of normative ethics—the examination of theories of value.

[20] See section B of chapter 5, pages 158–161, for the details.

2. Justified moral judgments   Working from our model of an act theory of obligation, we have been able to generate the claims of the corresponding theory of value. The details explaining the key notions were presented in chapter 5. The reasons why a resultant model is preferred were spelled out earlier: a nonresultant model, we saw, cannot explain why the presence or absence of other characteristics is relevant, and it does a very poor job of explaining how reasons can be relevant if all we need to do is be aware of the value property itself. However, even though all the theoretical terms may be explained and all the arguments against the rule theories may be in, this does not show us in any concrete way how an act theory of value works to arrive at justified singular moral judgments.

The key element in adjudicating disputes, you will recall, was the method of hypothetical agreement. All disagreement about what things have the most intrinsic value is traceable to a disagreement about one of the relevant nonvalue F's, to some problem about being in a position to come to have a correct singular value judgment, or to some theoretical disagreement about a philosophical theory. However, we shall be working with a different framework in theory of value than in theory of obligation, for the basic notion chosen within the area of value, *intrinsic value,* has built into it, as it were, the notion of prima facie—or something equivalent to it. The disagreements will not be whether or not something has intrinsic value, but which of two or more things has greater intrinsic value. Let us try some examples, and then explain this further.

In the last chapter, we examined a constructed conversation concerning slavery. The dispute was whether or not one was doing something wrong if slaves were kept. The dispute can also be seen as a disagreement concerning the relative values of two different societies—a free society versus a slave society.

Person *a:* "When we agreed that slavery's interference with the development of a person's potential would be a reason for claiming that slavery is wrong, we seemed to be agreeing also that the development of human potential is intrinsically valuable."

Person *b:* "Yes, but we should say *if* slaves have human potential, *then* there is a reason for saying that slavery is wrong. However, there does seem to be agreement that developing the potential of certain kinds of creatures, of which I am a good example but blacks are not, results in the creation of something intrinsically valuable. You, though, must agree that if we have a situation in which blacks do not have the same potential and must be taken care of in order to prevent them from harming themselves, then we create the intrinsic value by taking care of the people, *not* by allowing them to go off on their own to try to develop a potential they do not actually have. It would perhaps even be intrinsically *dis*valuable to allow such creatures to attempt this kind of development. The institution of slavery has the characteristic of protecting limited humans, and it does not have the characteristic of preventing human development of the clearly valuable type."

Person *a*: "I can agree that the protection of those who are not capable of taking care of themselves is valuable, and can even admit that it is intrinsically valuable, although that is not a very clear case. You, I assume, will agree that the situation in which human beings are allowed to develop their potential is intrinsically valuable. Now we must determine the factual question about the potential of blacks, for that is all that remains in dispute."

Here we have a highly simplified disagreement, soon to be complicated, in which the two parties are disputing about only the presence or absence of intrinsic value. Suppose that $Fx = x$ consists of the protection of those who are not capable of taking care of themselves and $Gx = x$ consists of preventing those who are capable of developing as humans from doing so. Then we can represent the dispute concerning slavery (in the United States in the eighteenth century, say) x, as follows:

Person *a:* If Gx and not-Fx, then not-IVx.
Person *b:* If Fx and not-Gx, then IVx.

The above situation is too simple, for usually there is competition among recognized intrinsic values, as well as the kind of hypothetical agreement sketched. A more realistic dialogue would appear as follows.

Person *c:* "Blacks are more like whites than they are like cats or dogs—that is, they are a kind of human being. However, they are human beings with much less potential than whites. They are much less capable of taking care of themselves, of being creative, and so on. So, while some intrinsic disvalue is brought into existence as a result of the institution of slavery (for, being enslaved, they are deprived of some dignity, control over their own affairs, and so on), the amount of intrinsic value brought into existence is greater. The resulting whole situation that contains slavery and not the negative intrinsic value of people being taken advantage of by businessmen, of people receiving improper health care, and the like has more intrinsic value than a whole situation that does not have slavery but has all those other things. This is the argument in favor of slavery."

Person *d:* "The argument is somewhat more complex than the previous one, but it is still essentially the same. You suppose that blacks lack the degree of potential that whites have, and it is this lack that justifies you in thinking that slavery is right. If the potential of the races was the same, or very nearly the same—for after all, this is not a matter of exactness—then you would admit that your on-the-whole argument does not work."

If we are to represent this kind of argument as we did the first, we must have considerably more complicated predicates. Those predicates might appear as follows: $Fx = x$ (blacks) have significantly less potential than whites (for such things as taking care of their own affairs, education, culture, and so on); $Gy = y$ is a situation in which human beings are deprived (of a significant part) of the opportunity to live with dignity and to realize their own potential; and $Hx = x$ is a situation in which human beings are allowed to live freely (that is, to develop their own potential). Suppose that s equals 'institution of slavery', and b equals 'blacks'.

Person c: If not-Hs & Gs & not-Fbn, then not-IVs (or IDVs).
Person d: If Fb & not-Gs & not-Hs, then IVs.

Person d might even agree that slavery in the United States in the eighteenth century deprived human beings of a significant part of the opportunity to live with dignity and to realize their own potential. However, he would add, this is not so significant a deprivation as to create more intrinsic disvalue than the value created by slavery and the disvalue created if blacks attempt to run their own affairs when they are not capable of doing so.

Even this more complicated statement is not yet elaborate enough to say all that should be said, and does not allow us to capture what is perhaps the most important kind of value claim we make—namely, a comparative value claim. If in the preceding instance we wanted to replace the IVs and not-IVs predicates with comparative predicates, the statements of persons c and d would become:

Statement c′: If not-Hs & Gs and not-Fb, then not-IVs > IVs.
Statement d′: If Fb & not-Gs & not-Hs, then IVs > not-IVs.

The consequent in statement c′ would now say that the intrinsic value of not having slavery is greater than the intrinsic value of slavery. The consequent in statement d′ would claim the opposite, that the intrinsic value of slavery is greater than the intrinsic value of not having slavery. This statement, the capturing of the dispute in two conditionals that have comparative value judgments in the consequent, much better reveals the nature of value disputes.

One thing remains constant in the restatement of the conditionals: the normative disagreement appears to revolve around the factual questions of the potential of blacks. This question, although a socially sensitive one, is capable of being settled. Even if we accept as accurate the studies that show a very slight difference in IQ between the races, this is not the kind of difference that one would need to establish in order to support slavery. In addition, as is well known, the measurement of IQ is just one way to measure intelligence. Furthermore, even if IQ level and intelligence were the same, we are concerned about the development of human potential at all levels, not just the development of the potential of genius. It is this potential that is being shut off, and it is to this area that we trace most of the intrinsic disvalue.

Most of the disputes concerning intrinsic value, especially those concerning what course of action we should take to secure something of value, are about different things and the comparative value of them. So let us consider one case of that sort. Suppose someone is considering whether to pursue a career as a dentist or as an auto mechanic. With the following defined predicates and constants, we can represent one way of deciding schematically:

d = career as a dentist
m = career as an auto mechanic
Mxy = x will result in more money than y
Pxy = x will gain more prestige than y
Txy = x will result in more tension than y
Hxy = x will contain more happiness than y

If (Mdm & Pdm & Tdm & Hdm), then (IVd > IVm).
If (Mmd & Pdm & Tdm & Hmd), then (IVm > IVd).

In English, what the first statement says is that if dentistry as a career results in more money than a career as a mechanic and also contains more prestige and happiness, and even granted that being a dentist will bring about more tension than being a mechanic, it is better to be a dentist than a mechanic. The second statement claims that if the money earned as a mechanic is greater than that earned as a dentist (or perhaps about the same) and granting that you will have more prestige as a dentist than as a mechanic, but holding fast to the view that dentistry carries more tension and that being a mechanic will result in greater happiness, then being a mechanic is better than being a dentist.

If this were a self-dialogue, the person would have to find out the facts about himself or herself in order to determine which of the two antecedents was more likely to be true. It would be very difficult to make the decision, for evidence about such matters is difficult to come by. However, once again, the truth of the matter is something that is not, as such, a value concern. Later on in life, after you have made your decision, you may decide that you made a mistake. However, people must decide without the best evidence quite frequently. This method will not make the evidence any better, but it will enable you to see more clearly what kind of evidence is needed and where it applies.

A dispute between two people would have the same form as the preceding one, which is conceived of as a self-dialogue. There is no way really to understand how this method is to work without trying it. You will find, I think, that when you try to use it, it is much easier than you might have thought.

3. Obligation versus value in act theory   We are now in a position to compare the basic units in theory of obligation with the basic units in theory of value. We shall consider only resultant theories of obligation and value.

Obligation
(F*a* & not-G*a*) → MO*a*
(not-F*a* & G*a*) → not-MO*a*

Value (noncomparative)
$(Fa \ \& \ not\text{-}Ga) \rightarrow IVa$
$(not\text{-}Fa \ \& \ Ga) \rightarrow not\text{-}IVa$

Value (comparative)
$(Fa \ \& \ not\text{-}Gb) \rightarrow (IVa > IVb)$
$(not\text{-}Fa \ \& \ Gb) \rightarrow (IVb > IVa)$

In the value area the first two pairs of conditionals represent the conditional agreement concerning the intrinsic value or the lack of intrinsic value of one thing. This is labeled the noncomparative value conditionals. The second pair of conditionals represent the comparative value judgments. In those two conditionals, we compare two different things, *a* and *b*, and find that if one set of "facts" is so, then the intrinsic value of *a* is greater than that of *b*, and if the second set is so, then the intrinsic value of *b* is greater than that of *a*.

In the consequents of the comparative pair and the noncomparative pair, the denial that any given thing has intrinsic value may be the result of the thing's having intrinsic disvalue. So, if *a* has intrinsic disvalue (IDV*a*), then it is at least true that it does not have intrinsic value (not-IV*a*). Thus you might want to claim that slavery has not just a lack of intrinsic value but some intrinsic disvalue.

4. Working with an act theory   With this last piece of theoretical explanation we might say that we have the complete theoretical apparatus of act theories before us. However, it is one thing to understand in a theoretical manner only how the method of conditional agreement is supposed to work and another to acquire some facility in using it. The comparative judgments are somewhat more difficult to work with, but they too are easy to master with practice.

Even for those of you who are able to use the method of conditional agreement, the usual kinds of questions arise. "Suppose that people do not agree with the hypotheticals?" The claim made is that for any two (or more) people, and for any dispute of value, we shall be able to discover the relevant and appropriate pair of conditional statements on which there is agreement. It is quite possible, of course, that there will never be agreement on the antecedents, that we will not be able to arrange for factual or nonvalue agreement; but that is another matter. If it should turn out that we do not find the pairs of conditional statements, this is evidence that this act theory is mistaken. The evidence presented in favor of the claim that such pairs are available is the past success in finding them. This theory of value is not thought to be immune from the evidence of our experience, it is, instead, based on what we do experience.

"Can't other theories do as good a job as the kind of act theory you defend?" The examination of rule theories reveals difficulties. This is what this chapter attempted to establish in sections C and D. Undoubtedly, however, any of the theories can explain the phenomena. That is not the primary concern of theory of value; rather it is a concern with which theory does the *best* job in explaining the phenomena. Theories that propose only one kind of thing of intrinsic value have a much more difficult time, so it has been argued, in explaining the phenomena. By this time, you have followed many arguments and have examined many theories. It should be clear that the task before us is to find the best theory, not just to find some theory or other that can do some kind of job in explaining the phenomena.

Suppose that someone wants to claim that value judgments are a disguised expression of emotion or feeling? Nothing so far said would prevent that theory from being defended. The issue represented by this question will be taken up in the next chapter, however.

It has been said that within the area of theory of value the basic operative notion is *intrinsic value,* with the notion of *value* being the basic undefined unit in that area. Within the area of theory of obligation it seems we need *obligation* and *right* as two separate notions, notions not reducible to each other. What about the relationship between *value* notions and *obligation* notions? Perhaps one of these notions is more basic than the other? This question essentially asks what the basic units and notions are within the area of morality. Again, though, this is a question that will be taken up in the next chapter. For now, we can say that we have worked out theories of value and obligation that make use of notions that may or may not turn out to be independent. If they are independent, we don't have to worry, for the theories have been worked out independently. If they are reducible one to the other, than we shall see a relationship between the two areas that we have not seen before. However, that would not really affect the normative theories worked out.

H. Taking a stand; looking ahead

In the preceding chapters we have examined the major theories of obligation and value. More important, the tools whereby one evaluates such theories have been presented. You are now in a position to select from the available theories the one best supported by the available evidence. I have, as promised, argued for one of the theories in each area. However, this fact is not astonishing. People find themselves taking stands on all manner of issues; philosophical issues are just one kind in which theories are examined. Of course, I suppose my theory is correct; after all, people do not defend a theory they suppose is incorrect. Many of you reading this book will disagree with me, but this is to be expected.

In the next chapter we shall take up the questions that have not been treated adequately thus far. We have indicated that we shall be concerned with the cognitive status of normative judgments and with basic units in the area of morality and their relation to other areas. In addition, we shall examine some problems of meaning and inquire briefly into the nature of moral predicates.

Exercises: Evaluating value theories

1. Describe a disagreement that you are aware of from your own experience. Apply the theory of value you think best to that disagreement in order to explain what was happening. Now apply what you take to be the second best theory of value. Now try to show that the theory you think is best has done a better job than its competitor.

2. Many religious traditions posit an evil being. Shall we describe such a being as one who pursues what it accepts as intrinsically disvaluable? Do your best to present a picture of what such a being would have to accept in the way of a theory of value.

3. Utilitarians have disagreed about which theory of value to adopt, some being monists and others being pluralists. Even the monists have not agreed, some being hedonists and others not. Choose one theory of value that you take to go best with your favorite form of utilitarianism, and defend your choice.

4. Perform the same task for your favorite ethical egoist position as was called for with respect to your utilitarian position in exercise 3.

5. Look at the results of your having filled out the descriptive ethics questionnaire and the values questionnaire (if you did so as you began to read this book). What theory of obligation and value best accounts for the answers you gave at that time? What changes did you have to make in your answers to achieve a consistent view? What changes would you now make in your answers to the questionnaires? What position do you now find yourself taking in theory of obligation and value?

6. The comparative form of judgments of intrinsic value was presented earlier, but no comparable kind of comparative judgment of obligation was presented in chapter 5. According to the model of the comparative judgments of intrinsic value presented on page 214, construct a model of comparative judgments of obligation. Argue that such judgments are or are not of value for normative ethics.

Recommended reading

Aristotle. *Nichomachean Ethics.* In *The Basic Works of Aristotle,* edited by Richard McKeon. Random House, New York, 1941. In books 1 and 10 you will find what is likely the first happiness theory.

Dewey, John. *Theory of Valuation.* University of Chicago Press, Chicago, 1939. An instrumentalist theory of value. Dewey is concerned with denying that anything has intrinsic value, but it is not clear that he would deny the intrinsic value of things in the sense used in this chapter.

Ellis, Albert. *Reason and Emotion in Psychotherapy.* Lyle Stuart, New York, 1962. The author presents a psychotherapeutic theory that fits in well with the views expressed in the Appendix.

Fletcher, Joseph. *Situation Ethics: The New Morality.* Westminster Press, Philadelphia, 1966. Agapism, as it is laid out in this chapter, is discussed.

Kant, Immanuel. *Groundwork of the Metaphysics of Morals,* translated by H. J. Paton. Hutchinson University Library, London, 1948. Kant seems to argue that only a good will is intrinsically valuable.

Moore, G. E. *Ethics*. Oxford University Press, London, 1965. The author presents a view of intrinsic value, primarily in chapter 7, which is quite different from the one presented in this chapter.

Nietzsche, Friedrich. *Beyond Good and Evil,* translated by Walter Kaufmann. Vintage Books, New York, 1966.

Plato. *Philebus*. In *The Dialogues of Plato,* translated by B. Jowett. Random House, New York, 1937. A rejection of hedonism from the philosopher who first stated most of the antihedonist arguments.

Potter, Karl H. *Presuppositions of India's Philosophies*. Prentice-Hall, Englewood Cliffs, N.J., 1963. The author claims that freedom, or *moksa,* is the one goal thought to be intrinsically valuable by a variety of different philosophical movements that began in India.

Appendix

Meaninglessness and futility:
An application of the tools of moral philosophy
to a traditional problem

One of the charges made against current English-language philosophy is that it does not address some important problems that trouble human beings. One of the traditional roles of philosophy is to help people solve problems that perplex them and to show ways out of personal dilemmas. There is, to say the least, not very much of that going on in current Anglo-American philosophy. However, this is not because the current philosophical methods are not able to handle such problems, but because philosophers are worried about problems that have grown distant from these concerns. In this section a problem that has traditionally been in the province of philosophy but has not recently received much attention from philosophers will be treated: the problem of "the meaning of life." I shall attempt to show how a problem such as this can be handled with the tools and techniques outlined thus far, and then I will indicate what steps individual people would have to take to solve their own problems. Some of you will be relieved to know that I will not attempt to explain the meaning of life on the "life is a fountain" model.

A. Informal statement

Sooner or later everyone asks "What is this all about?" "Why am I doing anything rather than nothing?" "After I have done all these things, what does it amount to?" "Is any of this worthwhile?" or equivalent questions. These questions begin at a relatively early age, as soon as a child or adult begins to wonder what will be done with the rest of his or her life, for then the value of alternatives must be weighed. This, in turn, gives rise to serious and often nagging doubt; if a mistake is made, one might live a life that was not worthwhile. If one answers any of the other questions incorrectly, then the rest of one's life could turn out to be pointless, based on a mistaken conception of what life is about or why anyone should do something. We don't feel we have more than one "time around," although in some cultures reincarnation is a widely held view, so we begin to attach a great deal of importance to these questions and our answers to them.

Any help we can get in answering these questions is appreciated, so it is no wonder that philosophers as well as theologians, sociologists, economists, political scientists, and football coaches have been listened to with interest and respect. The help offered here, if indeed it is help, is in the form of a do-it-yourself kit, and not a finished product. The aim is to allow each of you to have a greater understanding of the nature of the questions and the kinds of answers available so that you can arrive at an answer. It does not seem to me that there is one correct answer to any of the questions, for answers depend upon the character and talents of each person.[1] Such disclaimers are necessary, for otherwise everyone with good sense would stop paying attention right now.

B. A question of value

It is not accidental that discussion of the meaning of life inevitably involves questions of value. The usual way of answering any question about why an action is performed is to say something about the value of the action or the value of what the action achieves.

"Why did you go to that restaurant rather than another?"

"Because the food at the first is better than the food at the second."

Usually people do not use 'value' or one of its synonyms in their first or second response to questions about *why*, but the term (or one of its synonyms or species) naturally and invariably comes out. For example:

"Why do you attend this class?"

"To get a degree."

"Why do you want a degree?"

"To get a high-paying and interesting job."

"Why those things?"

"That is the kind of life I choose to live."

"Why that kind of life?"

"That is the one I think is good."

There are various kinds of stopping places to the question of why something is done. Some of them are the result of fatigue, some the result of impatience, and some the result of finding a natural stopping place. There is a way of describing the natural stopping place by means of the notion *intrinsic value*. Something is believed by a person to have intrinsic value when he or she supposes its value does not depend on leading to something else that has value. The thing may, of course, lead to something that does have value; but whether it does or not, it still has value. When we make a catalogue of all the things in a person's life that she or he believes to have intrinsic value, then we have an answer to the question "What makes my life worth living?" and "What is the meaning of my life?" If we can find the list, then we have the meaning of that person's life.[2] If the items on the list are believed by the person to be valuable

---

[1] This is especially so if act theories of obligation and value are adopted.

[2] I suppose there is a difference between what a person *believes* has intrinsic value and what *does* have intrinsic value. For the purpose of this discussion, though, this distinction need not be made; we can stick with what a person believes has intrinsic value and, accordingly, with what a person believes is the meaning of his life. This is, after all, what is important when you are talking with a person.

enough to justify his or her existence, then to that person life is worth living. Or, on the contrary, a person may say, "This is the meaning of my
life, and it doesn't come to much. These are the intrinsically valuable
things, but they do not compare favorably with the suffering or with what
I could or should have obtained."

The usual questions about goals require some answers about value. To
the question "Why should I study?" one can answer "Because it will enable
you to achieve the goal of passing the course." If one asks whether this goal
is worthwhile, one can answer by saying that it leads to getting a degree.
This, in turn, will enable one to get a certain kind of job and lead to a certain type of life. It is language such as this that one uses to answer questions about the justification of goals by saying something about the value of
the goal. A natural stopping place of such a set of questions and answers is
when something(s) of intrinsic value is (are) reached that is (are) thought to
justify all the other intermediate goals. We may say that we do everything
for pleasure, and only pleasure is pursued for its own sake. Others may say
that pleasure, even if intrinsically valuable, is not enough to justify all the
other goal-achieving (and striving); it is not sufficient to carry the weight of
all that we do.

When we list all the intrinsic goods that justify the achieving and
striving for goals—all the doings of our life—then we have rationally
explained why we live rather than die and why we live a certain way rather
than another. To find the meaning of life we must then find what things
are intrinsically valuable, and if there is more than one, place them on at
least a rough scale of relative value. It is in this way that we translate the
question concerning the meaning of life into a question about intrinsic
value.

Now we shall consider a move that is easy to see but difficult to justify in an informal way.[3] This is the assumption that unless something has
intrinsic value then nothing has value at all. Given the senses of 'value' and
'intrinsic' used, this seems to be a trivial enough truth, but there seems to
be no neat way to show that it is true.

If one wishes to find out what things are intrinsically good, a test
is of beneficial value. There is a partial test enabling one to determine whether something should be added to the list, and we call it
the *addition test*.[4] Suppose a friend of yours claims that only happiness is intrinsically good, that the only value for F is happiness when the value of M
is intrinsic value. We can show your friend that she herself does not hold
this if we can show she believes that a life (or situation) that has happiness
and freedom is of more value than one that has only happiness. If the
reasoning or the principle in the preceding is acceptable, then we must
conclude that freedom, or something that freedom leads to, has intrinsic
value in addition to happiness.

[3] See pages 185–187.
[4] See pages 194–197.

One can claim that freedom is valuable only because it leads to happiness, but then again, one can claim anything. One can claim that happiness is valuable only because it leads to freedom. The difficulty is to justify claims, not simply to make them.[5]

There are many other goals people have thought to be of intrinsic value; mentioning some of them will make things clearer: love, friendship, power, pleasure, absence of pain, freedom, peace of mind, and peace in the world, to name a few.

C. A life, human life, and sentient life

1. **Finer distinctions** The translation of these concepts into the more technical language, although a necessary first step, has not taken into account the finer distinctions we can now make.

> The life of person *a* has meaning: There is, in person *a*'s life, enough positive IV to outweigh the IDV.[6]

> Human life has meaning: There is, taking all human life together, enough positive IV to outweigh the IDV.

> Sentient life has meaning: There is, taking all sentient life together, enough positive IV to outweigh the IDV.

Obviously, there are going to be occasions and some lives where all these differ. Someone may very well live a life that contains practically nothing of value, while the lives of most other human beings contain a great surplus of intrinsic value. On the one hand, there are always those among us who live a life that is not worth very much at all. On the other hand, there are those whose lives are full of great value in the midst of an otherwise bleak period of human existence. If we shift the scale to all sentient creatures, the same kinds of distinctions can be made. Human existence may be a happy accident in the midst of an otherwise unhappy universe, or vice versa. These are often the questions we ponder without reaching any conclusion. The above distinctions do not, by themselves, of course, provide an answer, but they do provide a means of asking a clear question. Any answers will have to be provided by some means, but the means is available. Each individual is capable of determining the value and the likely value of his or her own existence, even if the determination

---

[5] These moves are covered at greater length on pages 196 and 197.
[6] As you recall, IV stands for intrinsic value and IDV for intrinsic disvalue. See pages 181–182 for fuller explanations of these terms.

requires some pain and great difficulty. Each person might want some help in doing that, help from friends, therapists, or whomever, but it can be done. Furthermore, it seems to me that this is the most important question of this type that we as human beings ask ourselves. There are some views people hold that interfere with our ability to determine the value of our life, or life in general. On this problem the philosopher can be of great help.

2. Calculus of intrinsic value   No claim is being made here that we can calculate in some precise way the intrinsic value, both positive and negative, in our life. However, it is possible to tell roughly what value there is, and in all except a very few instances, this is sufficient for our needs. The value scale talked about is a qualitative scale, but since we are all pretty much able to construct and read such scales, this is no great handicap.

3. Futility   What we as individual human beings ask is not only about whether our own life has meaning, in the sense described, but whether it has enough meaning, enough intrinsic value to make it reasonable to continue to live. We can ask that in a variety of situations. First, our future may clearly hold little of value and may clearly be filled with a surplus of intrinsic disvalue. For example, if you were told you had exactly one year to live and after one month your entire existence would be colored by intense pain, that would be a clear instance of such a case. It is tempting to say that such a life is not worth living any more. Notice, though, that this does not justify the claim that your whole life, even if you should live that last pain-filled year, would not have been worth living and would not have had a significant surplus of intrinsic value. More on this shortly.

A different kind of situation is one in which your past life seems not to contain enough intrinsic value to make it worthwhile and the future seems to hold no promise except more of the same. In both these cases it might be appropriate to say that living was futile. There are undoubtedly other kinds of cases, but not as many as you might think.

4. Journey view   One view of human life that leads some to think (mistakenly, as will be argued) that their life is meaningless and futile is the view that the value of anything is just what it spatially or, more usually, temporally leads to. Since life leads to death or to pain and misery in old age, then, according to this view, no life is worth living. As the first step in philosophical therapy we can say that the notion of *intrinsic value* or its appreciation does not include the occurrence of intrinsic value at any given time.

Some activities are clearly never done with any temporal or teleological end in view. Contrast dancing for a half hour and walking to the post office (which also takes a half hour). Each of these activities takes a half hour, but in the first there is no place to get to, no spatial or temporal end of the activity that constitutes its purpose. There is a goal, of course, but the goal is the activity, not something the activity leads to. The activity no doubt leads to all manner of things—increased heartbeat, relaxation, mild fatigue, and so on. However, these are not the goals sought in the activity, and they are not the goals that make it worthwhile. The goals are other things gained in the activity, such as a kind of communion with your partner, esthetic satisfaction, or whatever. (This is not to deny that you may have some ends that are clearly of the teleological type, such as winning a prize for dancing, making a social contact, and so on.)

Some activities lead to a goal at the end of a temporal sequence, which goal justifies the activity; other activities apparently do not require such a goal to justify them. Freedom is apparently valuable not because it leads to something else at a later time, but because of something it gives people at the present moment. It is true, usually, that freedom does lead to other things at a later time, things such as dignity, achievements that without freedom would not be possible, and so on.

A human life is apparently not to be judged worthwhile or not worthwhile on the basis of a goal achieved at the end of a temporal sequence. One clear temporal end is death, but we would all judge that death is not something of value that justifies the activity of living. It is this kind of thinking that leads some people to postulate a goal that is (temporally) beyond what we find in life. For given this kind of view about the nature of ends and values, there must be such an end or all we do now is worthless and meaningless. Such people reason that since death is not that goal, there must be something else "beyond" death that justifies the activity of living. Some ends so chosen are communion with God, another activity of living that is of a higher quality than the one carried on now, and a merging with some greater being. It may be that when death comes we really do move on to something else. The point here is not to deny that, but to try to show that this need not be assumed in order to make sense out of our lives.

All that is required for a meaningful life is that during the course of that life a certain kind and amount of intrinsic value be created. If there is such value, then this life has meaning, and perhaps enough meaning; and if not, then it doesn't. This consideration doesn't prove that your life or the life of any given person has meaning; it does show, though, that whether your life has meaning does not have anything to do with a goal to be achieved at the end of a temporal sequence.

5. Nonjourney teleological view   Some people suppose not that there is some temporal last goal toward which we are striving, but that there is some goal or set of goals that we must achieve during our lives to make living worthwhile. Furthermore, these goals have to be set by some being other than a human being. The last clause has to be added, for otherwise the view could be made perfectly compatible with what has been said here so far. A general end we are all searching after is a meaningful life; and if that is taken as the goal, then certainly the attainment of it makes life worth living and failure to attain it renders your life meaningless. However, that goal is not a specific goal, and it is likely that the people who hold this kind of view think that we must have a specific goal, such as serving God or serving God to accomplish a specific end.

D. God-given knowledge of what is intrinsically valuable

One way to interpret the introduction of God is that He is a moral expert. This is perfectly compatible with what has so far been claimed, but it is not the type of view now being considered. Suppose someone claims that unless God communicates with you, you won't *know* which goals are valuable and you won't succeed in living a meaningful life. This requires there to be some activities that will result in a meaningful life and others that won't, independently of God informing you.[7] God is all knowing with respect to all things and is thus all knowing with respect to values. Such a being is clearly the best consultant there can be. However, there seems to be a problem about communicating with such a being. So for most of us, whether there is a God or not, this is not a practical solution to the problem of coming to know which goals are valuable.

There is an additional problem that is best brought out by the numerous examples we are all aware of from the newspapers, about people carrying out what they take to be God's commands. However, if someone kills all the neighbors because, as he says, God told him to, we think the person was deluded. In a recent newspaper story it was reported that a passenger on a bus killed a fellow passenger because he thought the person was the devil and his Lord, Jesus Christ, had told him to kill the devil. Very few of us would say that Jesus Christ did indeed tell the person to murder a fellow passenger. (Suppose for a moment that Christ, in contrast with Jesus, is indeed God.) We suppose God would not tell us to do things of that sort— the sort of thing that is morally wrong. We believe this also of things of value; God would not have us pursue something if it was not, finally, of some intrinsic value. If someone whispers in your ear, or speaks through a burning bush, or communicates in some way that the sole intrinsically valuable end is counting the number of hairs on your body, then you take this to be very good evidence that it isn't God who is speaking.

Human beings, especially those who are most religious, use a value test for whether information given is from God or not. If the information is *not* in accord with what we know, independently, to be acceptable moral advice, then it is not from God. If this is so, and it does seem so from just

[7] The activities and goals are not ones that God *makes* valuable; they are ones He *knows* about and tells you about so that you too will know.

a simple inspection of the kind of case mentioned above, then we cannot rely on God to tell us everything, or even all the important things with respect to value. We have to know such things already in order to make use of God as a moral expert.

Whether God exists or not, and whether He gives moral advice or not, it is not prudent to depend on hearing from Him. Life continues, and if God can know, there is some chance that you can know, however imperfectly, what He would have told you. Others seem to have discovered activities that are worthwhile, and that is some evidence, again, that you can too.

E.   God and what *is* of intrinsic value

A stronger claim can be made that requires God's existence for anything to *have* value, not just for knowledge about it. In response, we can point out that nothing about the nature of intrinsic value and its application to goals seems to require that they be set by some external being. The claim that such a being must set the goals for them to be valuable requires some support for our acceptance; and failing such support, there is no reason to accept the claim. Since there is some reason to suppose we understand the nature of goals, and that they have value without the aid of such a being setting them, we would be justified in rejecting such a view. Finally, if it is a general truth that in order for a goal or an activity to have worth there must be some being external to the being reaching the goal or carrying on the activity who sets it, then this requirement also applies to God. He has, so it is supposed, the goal of setting goals for human beings. This, plus the general principle just stated, would require a being that sets the goals for God, otherwise His goals, and thus, I assume, our goals, would have no meaning. And so on, *ad infinitum.* Thus the postulating of a being would not solve the problem, but only replace it with one that we know can't be solved—namely, escaping a vicious infinite regress.

Suppose, as the last view of this type to be considered, someone claims that it is God's existence or His activities alone that have intrinsic value, everything else has only beneficial value insofar as they lead to those. First, it is not God's existence alone that could render some meaning to our lives, for nothing we can do or fail to do can have any effect on God's existence. It does not seem that the mere existence of anything has value, it is either something that the existent thing does, or some character trait the thing has. Character traits, though as we understand them, are explained in large part by the actions that follow from them. For example, we understand the character trait of honesty in terms of the kinds of actions an honest person performs.[8] If God has character traits of this type, then, once

[8] See pages 184 and 185 for a fuller discussion of this point.

again, our understanding of His nature requires some kind of action. There may be some other kind of character trait, or God may have no character traits, but then either the person making the claim about the necessity of God's existence for value is speaking without knowledge or understanding, or we are told that a being with no character traits has value. In either case we are being told something that is very difficult to understand or make sense of.

Let us consider the second possibility, that God's activities (and the goals reached through them) alone have intrinsic value, and that without these, our activities would not have any value. Those who hold this view suppose that God brings us into existence in some way or other. (This need not be supposed, of course, but let us consider the view held by people and not consider every possible view that could have been held.) The crux of the counter-argument is that God's action of creating human beings is sufficient evidence that the activities of human beings and at least some of the goals reached through them do have intrinsic value independent of God's activity, except, trivially, the action of creation.[9]

We must admit, first, that God does not do anything that is purposeless; He is not a capricious God. The addition test shows us that a universe with human beings must have more value than a universe without human beings, for otherwise God would not have created a universe in which there are human beings.[10] No being who is all good, all knowing, and all powerful will create a universe that is less valuable than another possible one. (Is this really the best of all possible worlds?) Thus it must be that human beings, either in their activities or what they bring about through their activities, increase the intrinsic value in the universe. This can only be done if those activities or ends do have some positive intrinsic value. So if God exists, then, contrary to the claim, the actions of human beings have intrinsic value independent of the value of the actions of God. If God does not exist, then of course the argument that begins with the assumption of His existence does not get started.

The above argument notwithstanding, you may be uncertain about the amount of intrinsic value in your life, but that is another matter. All the argument is intended to show is that the intrinsic value of God's goals and actions plus the intrinsic value of the actions and goals of human beings is greater than the intrinsic value of God's actions and goals alone. This, as a simple application of the addition test, shows at least some actions and goals of human beings have intrinsic value. The value of the goals we now have and the actions we carry out do not depend on the value of the goals that God has and the actions that He carries out.

[9] However, your parents are the cause of your existence, but the value of what you produce is not dependent upon the value of the creation, birth, conception, or anything of that sort.

[10] Remember, this is a particular God being discussed, and so do not, in answering this argument, talk about another God. If you seriously hold that another kind of God works in the universe, then such a position will have to be worked out separately; for each position deserves and requires separate attention.

F.   Additional topics

Here now, in brief form, are some other topics that at another time we may want to discuss at greater length.

1. Intrinsic value and transience   From the fact that something passes away, say, a certain state, it does not follow that it did not, during the time it did exist, have value. Human life and especially individual humans come into existence and go out of existence, but this does not show that a human life did not have value and, indeed, a great deal of value. Sometimes, the value of something depends on its passing out of existence. This is clearly true of food; perhaps youth is another instance—although it is certainly more controversial.

2. Intrinsic value and regret   It might be regretted that something passes away, say your own life, but it is one thing to regret the passing away of something and another to claim that because it passes away it does not have value now. The fact that it will not exist at some future time does not show it to be valueless now.

3. Intrinsic value and finiteness   Some people claim that finite beings do not know enough to set their own goals and only an infinite being can know what is valuable. We have talked about many goals and activities that appear to have intrinsic value, as well as lives that appear worth living, so there seems no reason to accept this claim.[11]

4. Intrinsic value and pessimism   Skepticism is very debilitating, and occurs frequently. Individuals may very well accept all that is said here and yet be pessimistic with respect to their own life. This pessimism often takes the form of great despair as a result of what seems to be the futility of doing anything. I suggest that this sense of futility results primarily from a lack of knowledge about what is available, or a mistaken theory about what is valuable or what value is. There are steps that can be taken even for such a person.

G.   Philosophical therapy and futility

According to the view presented here, even though you may receive comfort from others, including God, the meaning of your own life is determined by what you do. The meaning of your life is determined by factors primarily internal to you, not external. However, as indicated, a chance

---

[11] Furthermore, the preceding examination of theories of value does not justify this pessimism.

exists that any given person will have lived a life with little meaning or significance. All of us suspect, on some occasions, that our own life is one of those. There are various things that one can do to overcome this suspicion and the feeling of futility that often accompanies it:

1. Talk with others who have had the same kinds of problems and who share the same kind of outlook as you do.

2. Calculate, from the opportunities available, what you can do with the rest of your life. It is the rare person who cannot, living within his or her abilities, live a life worth living, one with enough intrinsic value to make it worthwhile. There is the friendship of many, the love of a few, the satisfaction of a job well done, the experiences of the senses, and many other things.

3. Consider the philosophical positions you may have adopted that have led you to consider that life is futile and meaningless. Presented here are some tools that can be used to combat positions leading to conclusions that make futility a perfectly understandable and justifiable position. If you can show yourself that the philosophical positions that support the claims of meaninglessness are not justified, then you can often dispel the feeling of futility. This kind of activity can, without obscurity, be called philosophical therapy.

4. There are those, however, who know all the philosophical "moves" and yet find that they cannot apportion their emotional responses to fit what their reason tells them. This is not a philosophical problem, but a psychotherapeutic problem. Since the whole tone of this book has been rationalistic, I should point out that this is no cause for despair, for there are methods of psychotherapy that do not depart from this rationalistic mode.

Seven

Chapter seven

Meta-ethics

In the first six chapters various normative ethical theories were examined. Such theories aim at providing us with singular moral judgments, whether of obligation or value and whether the mechanism for arriving at such judgments essentially involves a rule or not. The rules may be direct, ones that allow the direct derivation of singular moral judgments, or indirect, those that pick out the direct rules. I have opted for a special theory of obligation and value. Your obligation (intellectual) has been to enter into the activity of evaluating competing theories, not to follow me in my views.

The activity of choosing from among the competing normative ethical theories required the discussion of many problems that were not at first sight closely related to this primary task. The discussion of a psychological theory of motivation in chapter 2 and the discussion of basic units in chapter 5 are examples. There are, though, a number of problems in moral philosophy that are, as it were, left over. These are problems that have yet to be discussed or, at least, yet to be discussed fully. In this chapter we shall briefly discuss a number of problems and indicate, for most, the kind of solution that seems best. In the following list of topics to be covered, B, C, and D seem to be related in a more important way than any of the others—either to each other or to the three mentioned.

A. The nature of normative ethics: a review
B. Basicness
C. M
D. The moral connection
E. Human nature and moral philosophy
F. Free will
G. Related normative concerns
H. Paradigms
I. A final word

A. The nature of normative ethics: A review

A specific view of the nature of normative ethics has been presented in this book—namely, that normative ethical theories are directed primarily to the task of arriving at justified singular moral judgments. Human beings find this task of importance, so it was suggested, because they choose actions in part on the basis of their judgments of value and obligation. Thus the activity of arriving at such judgments has, as we might say, practical importance. The theories we choose to enable us to arrive at singular moral judgments are not of theoretical importance alone. This is not to say that all or even most people consciously use these theories. Perhaps the world would be a worse place if they did, but it might be a better place if they did. This kind of concern is important, but should be handled by the social scientist and not the philosopher.

A minimal number of assumptions were made in the examination of various normative ethical theories. It was assumed that moral phenomena exist, but they are those items we accept at the beginning of our investigation and not the ones that represent facts or undeniable conclusions. We assumed, also, that we could distinguish the better from the worse in theory evaluation. The criteria of acceptability, though, were not thought to be peculiar to moral philosophy, but are the kind of tests used in every area. Armed with the criteria and making use of the phenomena as the ammunition, we evaluated the main kinds of theories of obligation and value. The primary value for you was the acquisition of the skills to do a bit of philosophical hunting. I suppose I have, to continue the metaphor for a moment, hit the target, but you are asked to determine that for yourself.

There are other conceptions of what normative ethics should be that follow from certain other positions philosophers have taken. In what follows, some of these alternative conceptions will be mentioned and briefly discussed. None of them will show that if we had accepted them, we would have been wasting our time doing the kind of thing done in the past six chapters.

B. Basicness

In chapter 5 the notion of what is basic arose for the first time in a substantive way. Now, after our survey of normative ethics is complete, we can restate that concern with basics in a more general way. In what follows, three separate concerns about what is basic will be examined: which *notions* are basic within the area of ethics, which "units" of justified judgment are basic within the area of ethics, and whether the notions and units that are basic to ethics are basic to all areas. The task of explaining these questions and describing some of the important alternatives starts, once again, with our familiar general scheme:

Rule theories
(x) (Fx→Mx)

Act theories
Fa→Ma

The rule theorist directs us to find the appropriate covering rule if we wish to justify a singular moral judgment, that is, something of the form shown above. Once we have found that, it is a straightforward matter to determine the "facts," that is, Fa, and thus to arrive at Ma as the justified singular moral judgment. The act theorist, in contrast, attempts to find the appropriate covering unquantified conditional (we might call it a singular conditional statement). That found, the justification would proceed in the same manner as the rule theorist suggests. When we have arrived at Ma, we suppose we have a justified judgment; but given all that has been said, for almost all the theories examined, that justified judgment is justified only because it stands in a certain relation to another judgment that contains at least one moral notion—namely, the first statement of the general scheme. Without attempting to be very precise about it, although one could be, we can say that since the singular moral judgment, Ma, requires the conditional moral judgment (either as a rule or as a singular conditional) for its justification, that singular moral judgment is not a basic justified unit within the area of morality. When we have reached the unit within an area that is required by some other unit within that area for justification but that itself does not require justification within that area,[1] then we have reached a basic justified unit within that area.

To claim that a unit is a basic justified unit within an area is not to claim that it is necessarily true, that it is undeniable, or that we have arrived at it by some particular faculty. It is a very minimal claim to point out that within every area there are some statements or judgments that are accepted or acceptable without further justification in that area. Of course, different areas have different characteristics, so the characteristics of a formal axiom system are quite different from those of common sense. It is not necessary to enter into the discussion of whether the axioms of a formal system are "arbitrary" or descriptive of necessary truths of the world we live in to say what has been said so far.

To make what has so far been said clear, we need some examples. Most people learn plane geometry axiomatically; they study some variation of Euclid's system devised more than 2000 years ago. One of those axioms says, roughly, that when equals are added to equals, the results are equal.

---

[1] It may also be that it is not possible for us to find justification for the unit within the area, but this is a much stronger claim, one that we do not have to make now.

On the basis of this claim, and some others, as well as the various rules of inference, we can deduce the theorems of plane geometry.

When one practices the science or art of sociology, it is assumed one can know when a person is alive and when that person is dead, that person a is the father of person b, that person a learns from person b, and so on. The claim that person a is the father of person b or that person a is of culture C is determined to be correct by the tools or techniques of other areas. For example, we accept a certain view about parenthood as part of a view about biology. If, in the course of a sociological study, we need to claim that person a is the father of person b, we make this claim without the need for any sociological evidence. If someone challenges the claim, we would provide evidence, but it would not be evidence that we call sociological evidence.

The claim that someone's aortic valve is defective and requires replacement is a medical judgment that needs to be justified. The justification consists of presenting the evidence of certain tests, x-rays of the heart, internal measurements of the flow of blood through the aortic valve, and other evidence of that sort. This evidence supports the claim that the valve is deficient and has to be replaced if death is not to occur in a short time. This situation shows that the claim that the valve is defective is not basic within the area of medicine, for other support is required for it within the area of medicine.

Some of the claims that support the claim about the valve are further justifiable and sometimes require justification, even though some of them cannot be justified within the area of medicine. The reliability of x-rays is supported by evidence provided by physicists or gathered at autopsies or from open-heart surgery. Suppose, for example, the diagnosis is that the aortic valve is deficient because calcium deposits have built up around a congenitally defective valve. When the chest is opened, the surgeon observes that calcium is deposited and the valve is defective in the ways predicted. This confirms the claims made on the basis of the x-rays and shows that such claims can be relied on in the future. Of course, there is more support from knowing the nature of x-rays as a result of studies in physics. These two methods of providing evidence for the claim that x-rays show how the heart is working are methods from other areas; one is from physics and the other, as we might say, is from common sense. What, though, is common sense in this context?

The surgeon has all manner of medical knowledge that enables her or him to recognize calcium deposits and defective valves in the exposed heart. There is no denying that. However, the method used to establish the claim that there is calcium and that the valve is defective is *looking*. [2] This is a

---

[2] It is not part of the view being expressed that one sees calcium without knowing what calcium is. To know this requires sophisticated theoretical knowledge, just as, in my view, to see anything in a way that results in knowledge requires some theory that you have and use. We are here interested in the method of gaining knowledge and not what additional knowledge we would need to make the method work.

method that is not part of the area of medicine, although those who practice medicine use it all the time. It is a method used by those who practice
physics also; philosophers use this method, as does almost everyone else
who does anything. We all adhere to some form of "seeing is believing."
This is not to say that we cannot distinguish between trustworthy and un-
trustworthy perceptions. However, even though no analysis of the fact has
been given, we do use visual perception as a means of gathering reliable information and base many of the claims we make about the world on such
information.

  Within the area of medicine are some claims that are supported by
other claims within the area of medicine (for example, that the heart valve
is defective) and others that are not (for example, that this substance around
the valve is calcium). Claims that require support from other claims in an
area are not basic but are, in contrast, derived. If the surgeon has doubts
about the nature of the substance in the valve, he will send it to a chemist
who will, exercising expertise as a chemist, determine that it is calcium. In
this instance, the claim that x is calcium is supported not within the area of
medicine but within the area of chemistry. So the claim may be said to be
basic within the area of medicine [3] but derived within the area of chemistry. A claim that is basic in an area and sometimes requires support from
another area is one that is basic within the first but not basic among all
areas. A claim is basic among all areas when it is justified but there is no
area in which there is evidence that supports it *and* that is required to support it.

  This may be what is required for a claim to be basic among all areas,
but are there any claims that fit this description? If there are any, they are
likely to be of the sort called common-sense claims. [4] The claim that an object is red or square is often justified but does not require some area in
which it is justified. Suppose you look at any object and make the claim
that it is red. Isn't there a great deal you can do to support this claim? Yes,
of course there is. You can ask someone else what the color is, or you can
determine which wavelengths of light the object reflects and check on
a chart to see which color that is correlated with. You can look again, you
can take a picture, and so on. All this would supply additional evidence for
the redness of the object. Similar moves would be made with the claim an
object is square. You can measure the sides and angles to determine if they
approximate the relations that hold when something is a square. You can
ask others, look again, and so on.

  When we check a chart after getting a reading from a machine, we
require a number of prior justified judgments that some objects are red.

  [3] There are some claims that are basic within an area that occur in other areas,
and others that do not. The claim 'x is red' does not occur within the area of arithmetic.
  [4] Recall, though, that these will not turn out to be undeniable claims.
Common-sense claims are, in some sense, based on phenomena as well as is any
other kind. They are consequently correctable, just as any claim based upon the
phenomena is correctable.

Whoever made the first correlations had to do so without the aid of such a chart; that is, the person knew that things were red without using a chart. If there were not such a person, then no chart would have been constructed. So for at least some ways of supporting a claim, those ways presuppose some method of supporting the claim other than the ones used. In addition, even when there are further ways of supporting a claim that is, as we want to say, basic among all areas, none of them is *required* to support the claim. We can tell the color and shape of an object, as we say informally, without using such methods.

The above kinds of claims are apparently justified, and there is no requirement of support for these claims (from another area). We might call these the five (or seven) senses claims. There may be additional claims of this sort, for there is no reason to limit the kinds of claims to one type. More specifically, some have claimed that whatever the basic units within the area of ethics are, those units are basic among all areas. This kind of claim does not depend on the kind of normative ethical theory one holds, for rule theorists and act theorists might agree that the basic unit within the area of morality is basic among all areas and yet disagree about which unit is basic within the area of ethics. The rule theorist holds, as you have seen, that one or more rules are the basic unit within the area of morality, whereas the act theorist (of the type defended) holds that a singular conditional statement of the form Fa → Ma is the basic unit.

We have examined at least one kind of normative ethical theory that appears to be committed to the view that the unit that is basic within the area of ethics is not basic among all areas—namely, relativism. One way of understanding such theories is to see that they claim that moral rules, whether direct or indirect, are justified by their being in a certain relation to the mores of a society. In this instance, the moral rules can be said to be the same thing as the mores, or, to add the proper flavor to the claim, moral rules are nothing but mores. Mores, as an object of study, are completely within the area of sociology-anthropology, or sociobiology, according to some social scientists. Thus, according to this interpretation, mores are more basic than moral rules within the area of sociology.[5] Is this true? Well, in part we can determine the acceptability of this particular claim by determining the acceptability of ethical relativism. This task has been attempted, at least, in chapter 4 (page 145) and chapter 6 (page 204).

One can claim that moral rules require further evidence for their support in the form, say, of the mores of a society. This claim, as we saw, is difficult to support, but it is a clear kind of claim. One way in which a claim of nonbasicness can be supported, then, is via one's normative ethical

[5] Suppose that two people each claim that *their* area is more basic than the other and that the basic unit within the other area is reducible to something in theirs. In other words, each claims the basic unit within the other area requires support from their area. Given what has been said, they are not both correct, even though they both suppose they are correct. The way we would determine which of them was correct is the way we determine the correctness of any theory of that type. More will be said about this shortly.

theory. The fact that the only instance we saw of this appears to be a failure does not detract from this view—nor would the failure of all such attempts, for we are interested in ways in which such claims might be supported, not just in the ways that succeed. Let us first review what we have said so far and then ask again about how one shows that a unit is basic among all areas.

An attempt has been made to make clear the notion of a basic unit within an area and to contrast that with being basic among all areas. If we ask the question "Which units are basic within the area of ethics?" the answer supplied by the rule theorist will be different from the one supplied by the act theorist. The former will say one or more moral rules, and the latter will tell us that singular conditionals are the basic units within the area of ethics. The rule theorists will continue the discussion among themselves as to whether the rule is one or many and whether it is a direct moral rule or an indirect moral rule. Having answered the question of which unit is basic within the area of ethics, though, we may go on and ask if it is basic among all areas. This question, however important, is different from the first.

Another question concerns not the basic unit of justified judgment, but the basic notions or terms within the area of ethics. We say, for example, in chapter 2, that we can interdefine *right to* and *obligation,* but that neither of these notions could be used to define *right.* Given the theory of definitions presented in chapter 1, when we offer a definition we are not simply proposing a verbal equivalence but are offering at least part of a theory. If we accept the definition, we are no doubt accepting a lot more than a formula of the form p =df q. One way to find the basic notions within an area is to find the basic units of justified judgment in that area and then see which notions in that area occur in them. For example, if utilitarianism (direct) is correct, then the base unit within the area of obligation is something to the effect that "If any action maximizes good for the greatest number, then that action is right." We might also find a rule concerning *obligation* that is separate from and not reducible to the rule concerning right (see chapter 3, page 86, for the discussion on this). We also know, given this normative ethical theory, that some value notion such as *good* is more basic within the area of ethics than notions in theory of obligation, for obligations and right actions are a function of value brought into existence. In this way we would have made a choice as to which notion in the area of ethics is most basic, and we would have determined this by finding out which unit of justified judgment is most basic within that area. If this approach is used, though, we have to finish, as it were, our normative ethical theory in order to determine which notion or notions are the ones basic within the area of ethics. If one holds to the kind of act theory outlined in chapters 5 and 6, one may then suppose that there are at least two kinds of notions in ethics, value notions and obligation notions. In addition, there may be at least two kinds of obligation notions that are equally basic within theory of obligation. In general, the suggestion is that to find which notion is basic, or which notions are basic, find the basic units. To do the latter task, though, you must do normative ethics. Since we have done that, though, this is not a setback in our investigation.

At the end of this section you will find some representative statements of various positions. You can examine those and see how philosophers have stated actual views of the different sorts mentioned earlier. In addition to the normative theories, which sometimes commit one to a view that *good,* say, is the basic notion within the area of ethics, there are theories that appear to have other considerations.

> What we ought to do, in fact, is limited by our powers and opportunities, whereas the good is subject to no such limitation. And our knowledge of goods is confined to the things we have experienced or can imagine; but presumably there are many goods of which we human beings have absolutely no knowledge, because they do not come within the very restricted range of our thoughts and feelings. Such goods are still goods, although human conduct can have no reference to them. Thus the notion of good is wider and more fundamental than any notion concerned with conduct; we use the notion of good in explaining what right conduct is, but we do not understand the notion of right conduct in explaining what good is.[6]

These are the words of Bertrand Russell, who was at the time following Moore. This kind of view is in sharp contrast with the claims of Ewing in the following passage.

> We might define "intrinsically good" as "worth choosing or producing for its own sake." However, even though this definition will mostly serve, there may be cases where it cannot well be applied, and it is difficult to find a single form of words which is always applicable. But we might adopt a technical term and define "good" as what ought to be the object of a pro attitude (to use Ross's word). "Pro attitude" is intended to cover any favourable attitude to something. It covers, for instance, choice, desire, liking, pursuit, approval, admiration. . . . When something is intrinsically good, it is (other things being equal) something that on its own account we ought to welcome, rejoice in if it exists, seek to produce if it does not exist. We ought to approve its attainment, count its loss a deprivation, hope for and not dread its coming if this is likely, avoid what hinders its production, etc.[7]

[6] Bertrand Russell, "The Elements of Ethics," in *Philosophical Essays,* Simon and Schuster, New York; reprinted in *Readings in Ethical Theory,* eds. W. Sellars and J. Hospers, Appleton-Century-Crofts, New York, 1970, p. 5.
[7] A. C. Ewing, *The Definition of Good,* Routledge, London, 1948, pp. 148–149.

These are but two authors who disagree; there are many who line up on one side and many on the other. Given the difficulty of the task and the necessity of a long discussion, in this instance I shall not take a stand on the issue. An act theory could maintain either that *good* is the basic notion or that *obligation* is, or that they are equally basic. Since this is so, I shall not try to decide the issue.

There is a distinction, then, among the claim that a notion is basic within an area, the claim that a unit of judgment is basic within an area, and the claim that the notion or unit that is basic within an area is (or is not) basic among all areas. These are issues philosophers have been concerned with and continue to be concerned with, as the citations included will show. However, it is likely that enough has been done here to make you aware of the kind of problem.

C. M

In the general scheme we used the letter 'M' as the replacement for the most general moral notion, as in $\{(x) (Fx \rightarrow Mx)\}$. Let M stand for whatever moral predicate or moral predicates you suppose are or represent the basic notion(s) within the area of ethics. There are a variety of questions we have to ask about this predicate:

1. How many places does the predicate have?
2. To what kind of "thing" does M answer? (Is it a property, like 'square'; a relation, as is 'to the left of'; or what?)
3. What is the meaning of 'moral predicates'? (This may be the same as question 2, depending on what your answer is there.)

1. **How many places does the predicate have?**   The answer to this question will depend on whether you are concerned with value predicates or with obligation predicates. You may recall that obligation predicates usually have at least three terms and perhaps five or more. For example, suppose we translate the following judgment into an entirely unambiguous set of symbols: "Peter is obligated to pay Paul 10 dollars for the chair he bought at Paul's garage sale"; p = Peter, l = Paul, $ = 10 dollars, c = chair, and C = circumstances in which Peter brought a chair from Paul at this garage sale. With these symbols we can offer up a complicated obligation statement (O = obligation): Opl$cC. This obligation statement has five terms; five different symbols follow O, all of which are required for the translation. In this text most examples were simplified for discussion, so we often translated such judgments as Ox. However, when we are concerned with being more precise, we must perform some translation such as this.

Value predicates are more difficult to capture, because of the different uses to which such predicates are put in contrast with obligation predicates. We used the letters 'IV' to stand for 'intrinsic value' and then translated statements such as "Pleasure is intrinsically valuable" as 'IVp'. We did not include any person variable in the statement, but it is obvious that pleasure is always an experience of a person or other sentient creature. So a more precise statement would include reference to at least one person—perhaps to any people or all people. We might then translate the hedonist's claim that pleasure is the only intrinsically valuable thing as "For any person, the only thing of IV is pleasure." When we discuss such proposed intrinsically valuable things as freedom and love, the situation becomes more complex. Freedom, taken for a moment in contrast with slavery, involves a reference to at least two people. We have to say that person *a* loves person *b*, and that person *a* is free within a given political system or government (which is a legal person). So when we translate a claim about love, we have IV*ab*, which may be the claim that the love between person *a* and person *b* is intrinsically valuable. Just as we did for obligation, though, we may want to add some information about the context. When such things have been pointed out, then we are more fully aware of the nature of the predicate M. This will help avoid certain mistakes that result from an oversimplification of moral predicates.

2. To what kind of "thing" does M answer?   In all the discussions so far no claims have been made about the kind of predicate M is—no specific theory of moral properties or predicate has been presented. The term 'predicate' has been used deliberately as a neutral term with respect to the kind of predicate moral predicates are. We could have used the term 'property', but some philosophers suppose that if you use that term you commit yourself to the view that moral properties are like the property of squareness or redness. Let us look at a few models of the notion of *predicate* (or *property*).

There is a view that predicates refer to something that is very much like an entity. A view often attributed to Plato is that predicates such as 'red' and 'square' refer to entities in very much the same way a proper name such as 'Socrates' does. When we predicate 'square' of two different objects, they have in common a thing that is squareness. Since, as the Platonic version goes, what they have in common is not something that is just at one place, then there is something that is at both places (or perhaps in a different third place) that is what they have in common. G. E. Moore seems to have a version of this view, and it is no doubt Moore that philosophers have in mind when they react so strongly against this kind of position.

When we adopt the Platonic model, one property of predicates such as 'red' and 'square' is that they do not depend on any other predicate of the same type. Two shapes can differ only in their color, and two color patches can differ only in their shape. If we consider such a type of property or predicate as visual discrimination or perhaps the five (or seven) senses, then this claim is easier to accept. If moral predicates were of this type, then their relation in our knowledge of moral matters would be more difficult to understand.

Suppose that we are agreed that moral predicates are not to be understood as being Platonic. We are left, then, with the original question of the kind of predicate we are dealing with. Some people have suggested that we should compare moral predicates with other predicates, but we must be careful to choose the proper predicates for our comparison. Some have said that moral predicates are more like 'to commend' than like 'square'. It is people who commend, and when we say that person *a* commends x, we are not thereby attributing a predicate such as square to what we are talking about. When people commend something, though, they do so on the basis of some other properties of the "object."

In general we can make a distinction between those who claim that moral predicates are justifiably applied only when some other predicate applies and those who think that moral predicates are justifiably applied independent of any other predicates. You may recall that in chapter 5 two different act theories were distinguished on the basis of supposing that the basic moral unit was Ma or, in contrast, Fa→ Ma. The former view supposes that Ma is not a resultant from Fa, but is nonresultant. This can be put as a theory about *justification,* or about the *predicate* whose application is justified or not. A resultant theory of justification holds, then, that the basic moral unit, whether a rule or a singular conditional, always has the moral notion resulting from a nonmoral notion of that type. A resultant theory of the nature of moral predicates states that the moral predicate applies or not and is true of the action or thing or not, depending on whether some other nonmoral predicate is true of the action or thing. The nonresultant view is that the basic unit of justified moral judgment has no nonmoral notion in it—it is of the form Ma. Similarly, when we talk just about the predicates, we can say that the moral predicate is not dependent upon any other kind of predicate. For short, let us call the two views outlined a resultant and a nonresultant view.

When you hold a resultant view you have not thereby explained the nature of the connection between the nonmoral and the moral predicates. It is to that issue we next turn, aware that we have said a small amount about the nature of M but hopefully enough to turn to the next topic.

D. The moral connection

The nonresultant views would not, of course, have a problem about the nature of the connection between nonmoral and moral predicates, for those views suppose, at most, only an accidental connection. If you suppose only an accidental connection between a tennis ball and its color, you suppose that a tennis ball can be any color and that any relation between a tennis ball and its color is accidental and could easily be otherwise. It might be true at some time that all tennis balls were orange; then we could claim that all tennis balls *were* orange. However, we know that any color could be used for tennis balls. If we ask what is the connection between the predicates 'x is a tennis ball' and 'x is orange', we can say there is really no law-like connection, no causal connection, no "metaphysical" connection, but only an accidental connection. According to this model, the connection between any nonmoral property and any moral property is merely accidental.

Since the nonresultant theories have no concern with a connection between nonmoral and moral predicates, we shall not be concerned any further with such views. This leaves us, though, with the vast majority of ethical theories, for they do suppose moral predicates are resultant. What are some of the options before us?

1. Logical connection
2. Nonlogical necessary connection
3. Causal connection
4. Noncognitive connection
5. Moral connection

1. Logical connection Logical relations are clear instances of a connection between one set of predicates and another. This is seen most clearly in argument forms such as affirming-the-antecedent. If we establish that 'if p then q' and 'p' then 'q' follows. The connection between the first two claims and the third is logical. We can say that the first two are logically sufficient for the third, or that the nature of the connection is logical. When we have a logical connection, the denial of the part that is said to follow from the first in conjunction with the first results in a contradiction. If we assert 'If p, then q and p', and then deny 'q' by asserting 'not-q', we can derive the contradiction 'q and not-q'. We can do this by the use of truth tables or various other techniques that rely on rules of inference and axioms.

Does the nonmoral claim provide a logical support for the moral part of the resultant theorist's basic unit? We are asking this of the act theorist and the rule theorist, whether the basic unit is Fa$\rightarrow$ Ma or (x) (Fx$\rightarrow$ Mx), and whether the rule is direct or indirect. It would seem that no matter what the unit, we cannot derive a contradiction from the assertion of the nonmoral part and the denial of the moral part. To see what the problem is, let us choose some theory, such as utilitarianism. A simple direct rule theory version of utilitarianism would maintain the rule "If any action maximizes the greatest good for the greatest number, then that action is obligatory." The F is the antecedent part, which is about maximizing the greatest good for the greatest number, and the M part concerns *obligation*. If we consider the negation of this rule, an instance in which the antecedent is true and the consequent false, the resulting statement "Some actions maximize the greatest good for the greatest number and they are not obligatory" does not seem to be self-contradictory. It is inconsistent with the original rule of which it is the contradiction. This constitutes evidence, concerning this one rule, that the relation is not one of logical sufficiency. Of course, it also would appear the same way if we were to consider any other rule and its negation, and any particular Fa$\rightarrow$ Ma. If this latter were to be so, then we would have a good deal of evidence that the relation, no matter what ethical theory should turn out to be correct, is not one of logical sufficiency.

At this point we must guard against a tempting move. One might think that this argument against the moral connection's being logical sufficiency works only against discredited theories and, if we chose a correct theory, the argument would not work. This response, though, confuses a self-contradiction with an inconsistency between two statements. Choose any claim whatsoever, for example, "The earth is a sphere," and this statement and its negation when conjoined result in a contradiction. This does not show that the original statement is logically necessary. In a similar manner, choose any true "if . . . , then . . ." statement, for example, "If you eat ten hot dogs at one sitting, then you will have a stomachache," and if you conjoin it with its negation, you will have an inconsistency, and a contradiction will be easy to come by. This does not, of course, show that eating ten hot dogs is logically sufficient for a stomachache, for it clearly is not.

2. Nonlogical necessary connection   There are kinds of sufficiency short of logical sufficiency that we must look at. One such purported relation involves some kind of necessary connection between properties or predicates, but not a logical one. Such claims as "If something is red, then it is colored" and "If anything is an event in the physical world, then it has a cause" are examples of such statements. It has turned out, most would agree, not to be possible to derive a contradiction from the negation of such claims, but they are somehow necessarily true. Perhaps, the claim would now go, the basic moral units are necessarily true, and the connection between the F's and the M's would be a necessary connection. This is an appealing view to people who hold a kantian position, for they are inclined to think that the categorical imperative, here interpreted as an indirect moral rule, is in this sense necessarily true. Kant indicates this position in the following passage.

> If then there is to be a supreme practical principle and—so far as the human will is concerned—a categorical imperative, it must be such that from the idea of something which is necessarily an end for every one because it is an *end in itself* it forms an *objective* principle of the will and consequently can serve as a practical law. The ground of this principle is: *Rational nature exists as an end in itself.* This is the way in which a man necessarily conceives his own existence. . . .[8]

One does not have to be a kantian in normative ethics to hold to this kind of view. It would be more difficult to adapt this kind of view to the basic unit of the act theorist, but there is no reason not to apply it to any

[8] *The Moral Law: Kant's Groundwork of the Metaphysics of Morals,* translated and analyzed by H. J. Paton, Hutchinson University Library, London, 1948, p. 96.

theory—supposing it is the best account of the connection between non-moral and moral predicates.

A view often associated with the "necessary connection" view is the corresponding account of our knowledge of the basic unit. A clear statement of this kind of view is found in the following passages from Sidgwick and Ross, respectively:

> The supreme rule of aiming at the general happiness, as I had come to see, must rest on a fundamental moral intuition, if I was to recognise it as binding at all.
>
> The Utilitarianism of Mill and Bentham seemed to me to want a basis: that basis could only be supplied by a fundamental intuition. . . .[9]

> That an act, *qua* fulfilling a promise, or *qua* effecting a just distribution of good, or *qua* returning services rendered, or *qua* promoting the good of others . . . is prima facie right, is self-evident. . . . It is self-evident just as a mathematical axiom, or the validity of a form of inference is evident. The moral order expressed in these propositions is just as much part of the fundamental nature of the universe . . . as is the spatial or numerical structure expressed in the axioms of geometry or arithmetic.[10]

To show you that this view has been held by some who are act theorists, and apparently resultant act theorists, consider this passage from H. A. Prichard:

> The sense of obligation to do, or of the rightness of an action of a particular kind is absolutely underivative or immediate. The rightness of an action consists in its being the origination of something of a certain kind A in a situation of a certain kind, a situation consisting in a certain relation B of the agent to others or to his own nature. . . . But, given that by a process which is, of course, merely a process of general and not of moral thinking we come to recognize that the proposed act is one by which we shall originate A in relation to B, then we appreciate the obligation immediately or directly. . . .
>
> This apprehension is immediate, in precisely the sense in which a mathematical apprehension is immediate, e.g., the apprehension that this three-sided figure, in virtue of its being three-sided, must have three angles. Both apprehensions are immediate in the sense that in both insight into the nature of the subject directly leads us to recognize its possession of the predicate; and it is only stating this fact

[9] Henry Sidgwick, *The Methods of Ethics,* Macmillan, London, 1962, pp. xxix–xxi.
[10] W. D. Ross, *The Right and the Good,* Claredon Press, Oxford, 1930, pp. 29–30. Reprinted by permission of the Oxford University Press.

from the other side to say that in both cases the fact apprehended is self-evident.[11]

It is interesting to note that all three of the authors cited supposed that mathematical truths were not what has been called a logical truth in the previous section. The view held was that mathematical and logical claims were descriptive of the world and were necessary but not in the manner now thought to be true of axiom systems. If we give up this view of such logical knowledge, it would be more difficult to continue to hold this view concerning moral knowledge.

3. Causal connection   There are a variety of causal connections that people have proposed to explain the relation between F's and M's, but usually the causal connections are concerned with an explanation of why people accept something as being right or valuable. For example, cultural relativism is the view that the cause of our accepting any given moral rule is societal pressure, or training, or some such. This does not, of course, establish any normative theory as being correct, as we saw in chapter 4. The same observation holds when we consider psychological egoism as a causal explanation of a person's holding a given moral judgment to be correct.

Some philosophers have argued that there are no evidential relations between nonmoral and moral predicates at all, there are only causal ones. If one were able to make this view understandable and plausible, then perhaps one could rehabilitate some form of egoism or relativism, but that remains to be seen.

4. Noncognitive connection   Some philosophers don't worry about any connection between the *predicates* in the basic moral unit, as such, for they emphasize the decision-making aspect of the *people* adopting some basic moral unit.

> To make a value-judgment is to make a decision of principle. To ask whether I ought to do A in these circumstances is . . . to ask whether or not I will that doing A in such circumstances should become a universal law.
>   . . . If pressed to justify a decision completely, we have to give a complete specification of the way of life of which it was a part. . . . In the end everything rests upon such a decision of principle. [A person] has to decide whether to accept that way of life or not; if he accepts it, then we can proceed to justify the decisions that are based upon it; if he does not accept it, then let him accept some other, and try to live by it.[12]

---

[11] H. A. Prichard, "Does Moral Philosophy Rest on a Mistake?" in *Moral Obligation*, Oxford University Press, London, 1957, pp. 7–8.
[12] R. M. Hare, *The Language of Morals*, Clarendon Press, Oxford, 1952, pp. 69–70. Reprinted by permission of the Oxford University Press.

This is a view put forward most strikingly by the existentialists, who stress the fact that each of us *must* make such decisions, for no one else can make them for us. Even if we choose someone to adopt principles for us, we are responsible for choosing that person, and usually know which principles that kind of person will choose anyway.

When we ask of such a view what is the connection between non-moral and moral predicates, the answer will be that there is the connection made by our choosing *that* as a principle or *that* as the action in the set of circumstances we will perform. In this sense, there is no connection between the predicates except the connection made by some person making a decision. The decision is not based on anything else within the area of morality, and for the people cited, it is not based on anything in some other area. It is not our "practical reason" that discovers a connection, or even forges it, it is something else. Exactly what this something else is, though, we shall have to leave for those who hold the position to explain.

There are a number of views that hold the connection between the F's and the M's is made not by your choosing or my choosing but by some more ideal person or persons choosing.

Now since laws determine ends as regards their universal validity, we shall be able—if we abstract from the personal differences between rational beings, and also from all the content of their private ends—to conceive a whole of all ends in systematic conjunction (a whole both of rational beings as ends in themselves and also of the personal ends which each may set before himself); that is, we shall be able to conceive a kingdom of ends which is possible in accordance with the above principles.

For rational beings all stand under the *law* that each of them should treat himself and all others, *never merely as a means,* but always *at the same time as an end in himself.* . . .

. . . This making of laws must be found in every rational being himself and must be able to spring from his will. The principle of his will is therefore never to perform an action except on a maxim such as can also be a universal law, and consequently such that the will can regard itself as at the same time making universal law by means of its maxim.[13]

Here Kant is apparently following up earlier suggestions of Rousseau:

Each of us places in common his person and all his power under the supreme direction of the general will; and as one body we all receive each member an indivisible part of the whole.

From that moment, instead of as many separate persons as there

[13]*The Moral Law: Kant's Groundwork of the Metaphysics of Morals,* p. 101.

are contracting parties, this act of association produces a moral and collective body. . . .[14]

The view that somehow human beings become ideal observers or judges when the particular characteristics and concerns are not counted is widespread in the history of philosophy. Sometimes a single being is posited, but usually we are to think of each of us as an ideal judge. This view is still common today.

In justice as fairness the original position of equality corresponds to the state of nature in the traditional theory of the social contract. This original position is not, of course, thought of as an actual historical state of affairs, much less as a primitive condition of culture. It is understood as a purely hypothetical situation characterized so as to lead to a certain conception of justice. Among the essential features of this situation is that no one knows his place in society, his class position or social status, nor does any one know his fortune in the distribution of natural assets and abilities, his intelligence, strength, and the like.[15]

Rawls sets up the original position and then posits principles of justice that people in that state would legislate. It does not matter what principles are legislated, or what moral rules—direct or indirect—come out. What is of concern here is that when we ask what connection there is between the nonmoral characteristic and the moral characteristics, we are given what looks like an epistemological answer based upon the nature of human beings. Human beings assert or judge these principles when they will as members of the kingdom of ends, or insofar as they are part of the general will, or in the original position. It is in this state or position that the reason of humans properly discovers moral principles. (One could hold an act theory coupled with this view, but it would be slightly different. It would maintain that any given singular conditional is one that would be willed by a person in such a position.)

Sometimes a single being is thought to have certain characteristics that ensure the proper moral judgment, but for our purposes we shall not sharply distinguish this view from the others.

5. Moral connection   What about the view that the connection between moral and nonmoral predicates is a *moral* connection? This is an answer that has to be put into a context before it can be understood as making any kind of claim at all. When we characterize any connection, we can use terms borrowed from outside the area in which this connection is used. For example,

[14] Jean Jacques Rousseau, *The Social Contract,* Hafner, New York, 1964, p. 15.
[15] John Rawls, *A Theory of Justice,* Harvard University Press, Cambridge, Ma., 1971, p. 12.

when we explain causal or physical connections, we can talk about similarities and differences between them and logical connections. We can say that when we assert "If any person is cut into pieces, burned to ashes and the ashes scattered in the ocean, then that person is dead," we can say that the antecedent is physically sufficient and not logically sufficient for the consequent. We can say that we are invoking a physical and not a logical law, that it would be physically impossible for the person to be alive but not logically impossible. (It would not be a contradiction to claim that the person was alive, although given what occurred, some physical laws we now think acceptable would turn out not to be acceptable.) We might try to avoid using the term 'physical' or 'logical' by talking about *sufficiency,* as in "The event mentioned in the antecedent is sufficient for the event mentioned in the consequent." However, the *kind* of sufficiency is what we are interested in, and that seems to require some such additional word as 'physical'.

Generally we can talk about sufficiency in an area and say that it is explained by whatever turn out to be the correct theories in that area. If this is the model of explanation, we can do the same thing in ethics. We can say that a given antecedent is sufficient for a given consequent, given that indirect utilitarianism or some other theory is correct. We could then use the kind of language Mill and Kant use when they talk about the laws of morality. The principle of utility, for example, being the ultimate law of morality, would enable us to claim that it is impossible for a rule to be one that we act from, one that maximizes the greatest good for the greatest number, and yet not be a direct moral rule. The term 'impossible' requires its explanation in terms of the theory, say, indirect utilitarianism, that is assumed to be correct. This is directly modeled on the claim, for example, that is is impossible for an unsupported body not to fall and it is impossible for something to be red and not red at the same time in the same respect. We refer, in those instances, to what we take to be a correct theory of physics and a correct theory of logic. What kind of sufficiency are we talking about then, in terms of this view? Moral sufficiency. This may strike you as unenlightening, but it is as enlightening as other answers from other areas. In addition, it allows us to explain the moral connection via the work done in normative ethics. From the point of view taken in this book, that is all right, for we know how to find the correct normative ethical theory.

6. **Other views of the connection** Let us now simply list other views about the connection between the moral and nonmoral predicates very briefly, keeping in mind that a full treatment of any view is not here possible. The marxists, or some varieties of that view, hold that the connection between the F's and the M's is explained in terms of the function of a normative theory. Ethical theories are designed, consciously or not, to reflect the view of the ruling class—specifically to reflect what things they want to maintain. So, the capitalists will adopt moral rules that will tend to keep them in power as a class. Moral basic units are just the devices used by the ruling class in a given society to maintain its position. This is also true of

the proletariat, although most marxists "prefer" the rules of the proletariat to those of the bourgeoisie.[16]

One might want to talk about a number of views that hold, in some sense, that it is an "illusion" to apply any moral predicate. Some people say that moral predicates are actually some other kind of predicate. Whenever we say that something is good, for example, we could say the same thing by saying that we like the thing or desire it. People holding this view and others related to it have gone under the names "subjectivist" and "emotivist." One might think a normative ethical theory, according to this view, would be a very simple matter of finding out what you like—this would be a version of egoism as a normative ethical theory. People who hold such views, though, deny that there are such things as normative ethical theories at all.

So, what is the nature of the connection between nonmoral and moral predicates? A variety of answers have been proposed, many of them have been reviewed here, but no attempt at selecting one of them has been made. Given your choice of a normative theory and your commitment to other philosophical positions, one of the views is likely to interest you more than others. For now we can say that we see the place of the question's answer in relation to the main task of our work—namely, discovering the best normative ethical theory.

E.   Human nature and moral philosophy

In a course of choosing a normative ethical theory, we had to make a number of decisions about human nature. When we rejected psychological egoism and psychological altruism, we denied that humans are entirely self-regarding or that they are entirely other-regarding—at least not by nature.

---

[16] This is, of course, not an adequate treatment of marxist ethics. There is an immense amount of work being done in the field of ethics by marxists. Please see some of the entries in the bibliography. There is, though, the additional problem of trying to say what a marxist ethics is. "Marxists, in fact, have failed to develop an original or comparatively coherent view of ethics that can be ranked as a 'type of ethical theory' finding its natural place beside utilitarian ethics . . ." (Eugene Kamenka, *Marxism and Ethics,* St. Martins, New York, 1969, p. 1).

Engels says briefly what a good number of marxists have continued to say since. "The Feuerbachian theory of morals fares like all its predecessors. It is designed to suit all periods, all peoples and all conditions, and precisely for that reason it is never and nowhere applicable. It remains, as regards the real world, as powerless as Kant's categorical imperative. In reality every class, even every profession, has its own morality, and even this it violates whenever it can do so with impunity" (Frederick Engels, "Feuerbach and the End of Classical German Philosophy," in *Karl Marx and Frederick Engels: Selected Works,* Progress Publishers, Moscow, 1970, p. 607).

A psychological theory of motivation that proposed only one source of motivation, either to benefit oneself or to benefit others, would not be acceptable. However, this is not to say that someone could not posit a goal to act
in either way. It might be that we reserve the term 'selfish' for those who
choose to act only for self-benefit and the term 'saint' for those who choose
to act only for the benefit of others. Are either of these ways better? That,
of course, depends on what has value. The theory of value investigation did
not reveal that only one character trait, say, selfishness, had value. If we
hold to a multiplicity of things of intrinsic value, then neither of these
views of the character trait to be cultivated is acceptable.

When we rejected psychological hedonism, we thereby denied that
only one goal is sought by human beings. If we had affirmed this view, it
would have told us a great deal about human nature, and it would have
provided us with a simple model of what human nature is. When we deny
any view that suggests that we pursue only one goal, we thereby complicate
the model we have of human nature. So from the discussions in theory of
value and theory of obligation we find that we have adopted a view of
human nature that takes human beings to be complicated, subject to a variety of motives, pursuing a variety of goals, and difficult to describe in any
one way.

The topic of human nature is eternally new, and new theories or new
variations on old theories are always being discussed. The latest such view
is included in the view called *sociobiology*. W. D. Hamilton's discussion of
inclusive fitness has given rise to a variety of views involving that and
related notions. The following passages from Irven DeVore will give you a
flavor of what is being discussed.

> . . . We're learning about many other kinds of behavior that could
> not be explained without an understanding of adaptation, including a
> genetic theory of inclusive fitness which Darwin couldn't have known
> about: essentially, any behavior that leads an individual to leave fewer
> offspring. Why are there sterile castes of bees and ants, for example?
> Why would any animal risk its life to help another? Why, when a
> predator approaches, would an animal give a warning cry to other
> animals, attracting the predator's attention to itself, rather than just
> fleeing quietly? . . .
>
> The answers began to come out of a theoretical approach to be-
> havior that was emerging. . . . First developed by W. D. Hamilton
> in 1965 and quickly picked up by other biological theorists like John
> Maynard Smith, G. C. Williams, Robert Trivers, E. O. Wilson, and
> Richard Alexander, it pointed out what Darwin could never have
> seen; namely, that is is misleading to focus a theory of evolution on
> individuals or even clusters of individuals. What you are really inter-
> ested in is the *genes*, because it is only the genes that are passed on to
> future generations.
>
> . . . We are ultimately concerned not with individuals, but

with individual genes and their replicas in other members of the species—what we call an individual's inclusive fitness.[17]

There is not time to explore the implications of such views, but the usual concerns will arise. Shall we take this to be an added feature to a theory of motivation? Shall we attempt directly to draw any normative conclusions from such theories? One would have a difficult time defending the view that an individual's only motive is to replicate his or her genes in other members of the species. Perhaps the motive is not a conscious motive having to do with voluntary actions at all? These are the kinds of concerns we would have to pursue were we seriously to take up this view.

Sometimes we ask if human beings are by nature good or by nature evil. If this is the question of whether human beings, in fact, pursue only what they perceive as good, the answer is apparently no. It frequently happens that we decide, as best we can, what is good (what has the most intrinsic value) in a given set of circumstances and then find that we do not pursue it. This happens, as we say, even when we are free to do so. We think, for example, that it is to our interest not to eat foods high in saturated fats, to cut down on the amount of food eaten, and to get plenty of rest. Yet we find ourselves eating potato chips, pastry, and all manner of other such foods in great quantities far into the night. This is sometimes described as the problem of weakness of will; we fail to act in ways that we apparently know are right and fail to pursue goals that we apparently know are the best in a given set of circumstances.

Many philosophers have claimed there is really no such phenomenon; for if we really accepted the action as right and the goal as the best one, then we would act in the appropriate manner. It is difficult, when we concentrate on our own experiences, though, to accept this view. Unless someone were to provide a theory of human nature that would show such a connection, it would be difficult to accept the theory as stated.

F.   Free will

A problem related to weakness of will is the problem of free will. This question is a very difficult one to get a clear understanding of and a difficult one to discuss briefly, but nevertheless here is a try. We would all agree that part of the phenomena is the apparent fact that unless people are responsible for an action, they cannot be said to be doing what is right or wrong; that unless they can do and avoid an action, they have no obligation concerning that action. Sometimes this set of claims is stated in a shorthand way as "ought implies can." We can say that unless people

[17] Irven DeVore, "The New Science of Genetic Self-Interest," *Psychology Today,* February 10, 1977, 44–45.

are responsible, then no judgments of obligation, including right and wrong, are justified. More schematically, with M standing for any term of obligation, we have:

If any person *a* is justifiably judged to have performed an M action, then person *a* is responsible for that action.

Furthermore, if a person is responsible for an action, then the person is free, in some way, both to perform the action and to abstain from performing it. These are both, as we say, options open to the person before the action is done.

If any person *a* is responsible for performing an action, then person *a* is free to perform that action and free to abstain from performing the action.

When we assert these two "if . . . , then . . ." claims we do not thereby assert either of the antecedents or deny either of the consequents. Furthermore, and more seriously, we have not specified the way in which people have to be free for even the "if . . . , then . . ." statements to be true. Some people suppose that in order for someone to be free, the causal order must be "suspended," the person must perform some contracausal action. If this were not so, such people reason, then we would have to suppose that people are caused to do what they do by education, social pressure, character, and the like. Such causal influences are beyond the power of people to alter, so it is said, and thus no one is free to perform an action or to abstain from doing it if the causal conditions for doing one or the other are present. Others, however, claim that no such contracausal freedom is needed; all that is required is the absence of coercion or force. There is a difference between having a device attached to your hand that exerts a force beyond your physical strength to resist and causes your finger to tighten on a trigger thus causing someone to be shot and your doing this without such coercive influences. It is the lack of force and coercion that is the test of freedom, and not some contracausal activity.

We shall not attempt to settle this issue here, for it is complicated. However, you are directed to the readings on page 260, which will lead you to fuller discussions that might enable you to make up your mind about what *freedom* is. It should be noticed that if any ethical theory is correct, and we go about determining whether a given action is right, say, or not, then any decision we reach would be an instance of affirming the antecedent of the first of the two "if . . . , then . . ." statements. This would entitle us to conclude that some people are responsible for some actions, and *this* would, in conjunction with the second "if . . . , then . . ." statement, allow us to conclude that such people are free to perform those actions or to abstain from them. This would lead us to say that it is a moral phenomenon that people are free, although it would not tell us what it is for people to be free. It is at this point that we shall leave the issue.

G. Related normative concerns

There are a number of concerns related to our main normative concerns but which we have not directly discussed, or discussed only in passing. In this section these will be identified and, where possible, related to tasks already performed.

    1. Skepticism, amoralism, and nihilism
    2. Social and political theory
    3. Religion
    4. Various philosophical movements

1. **Skepticism, amoralism, nihilism**   At the beginning of the book general skepticism was discussed, and there was found to be no reason to adopt the view that we know nothing or that we are not justified in asserting anything. The main reasons for holding to skepticism seemed to be the "possibility" argument and the view that items known must be incapable of being false. However, there are good reasons not to adopt the first position, and no reason to adopt the second. Since we make use of what appear to be justified judgments (for example, we plot the course of spacecraft to Mars and land the craft on that planet successfully), there is reason to suppose that some of our judgments are justified. The explanation of a judgment being justified was given in terms of a theory explaining a set of phenomena. This explanation applies, apparently, to moral phenomena as well as to any other kind of phenomena. Someone could claim that there is a difference in the relation, but then we would have to see the difference that is supposed to make a difference in terms of justification. Of course, someone may have a special account of how the basic units within the area of morality are to be explained, but, as was seen in section D that is apparently compatible with any normative theory adopted. We are imagining not that kind of view, but rather the position that we cannot justifiably claim that one normative ethical theory is better than any other, or put negatively, that each fails to be justified. This moral skepticism would follow from a general skepticism, but there is apparently no way to establish that view.

    People sometimes distinguish moral skepticism from amoralism and nihilism. *Amoralism* is the view that moral terms have no peculiar sense, and that all that one wishes to claim by use of moral predicates and terms can be claimed by using other terms. According to this view, morality is in some sense an illusion.

    We cannot discuss all the views that hold that in some sense morality is an illusion, so I shall try to address a kind of amalgam position. According to this view:

> In the world everything is as it is and happens as it does happen. *In* it there is no value—and if there were, it would be of no value.[18]

> There are no moral phenomena at all, but only a moral interpretation of phenomena.[19]

In the terms used in this book so far, the amoralist is of the view that normative theories are all mistaken. It is true, they would be wise to concede, that there is something to explain. We have to explain choices; we have to explain a feeling of what is called "obligation"; and we have to explain a good deal more phenomena of this type. However, all the theories that propose the application of obligation and value predicates are mistaken—there is another theory that does a better job than any of those, and it does not make use of any of the moral notions.

Let us choose one such theory, look briefly at the reasons given, and then respond on behalf of those who suppose that some normative theory does a better job than the nonnormative (amoralist) theory. The theory of amoralism, then, claims:

1. No judgments containing normative predicates (such as *right* and *good*) are justified.
2. Normative utterances have a function—namely, to make society secure and ensure its continuance.
3. All the phenomena normative ethical theories attempt to explain can be explained by the function of moral utterances and perhaps by some theory about the psychological or sociobiological state of human beings.

The claim that all singular moral judgments are not justified is not the claim that they are all deficient but some others might be discovered someday that are not deficient. Such judgments fail to be unjustified for the same reason they fail to be justified. It is part of many Buddhist positions that both the affirmative and the negative judgments are to be rejected as illusions. Some Buddhists apply this view not only to morality but to judgments and all areas. However, let us here understand the view as claiming that there is no justification for this (moral) kind of judgment.

A reference to another area would be helpful in understanding this claim. Suppose, as seems to be true, that we no longer believe that such a

---

[18] Ludwig Wittgenstein, *Tractatus Logico-Philosophicus,* Routledge, London, 1955, p. 183 (6.51).
[19] Friedrich Nietzsche, *Beyond Good and Evil,* trans. Walter Kaufmann, Vintage Books, New York, 1966, p. 85.

thing as caloric fluid exists. We suppose that the phenomena concerning fire are explainable without the positing of such a fluid. All judgments that have caloric fluid notions in them fail to be justified, except those that claim there is no such thing as that fluid. The judgments internal to the theory are, of course, consistent. We can have a systematic presentation of that theory, but the theory has, as we say, no counterpart in reality. The ancient Greeks posited a number of gods to account for such phenomena as rain and the growth of plants. They then set forth a description of the relation of the gods to each other. We do not precisely or correctly describe our view if we say that Zeus doesn't rain, unless we add that rain has nothing to do with Zeus. Did god x marry goddess y? Was the plot to revenge the death of god x by god y of this type or that? What is true, as we suppose, is that the phenomenon of rain does not require reference to gods at all. So all the judgments about what happens in the internal affairs of the gods is empty talk—it is about nothing. This is the way moral language is viewed. Somehow we have gotten off the right track and have constructed vast theories about the workings of something called "morality," but there is really no such thing.

The second claim—that the function of moral language is to serve the interests of society—is easier to understand. There is the phenomenon of the use of moral language, and this has to be explained. We also have to understand why people feel guilty if they do not do what they suppose is morally obligatory, and other action-related phenomena. One way to account for these phenomena is to point to the social function of morality, particularly moral language. When people suppose that they have moral obligations, it is easier to make societies work, for people can be relied on; they are more inclined to work hard, to pay debts, to feed their children; and such. This phenomenon, that of people believing themselves to have moral obligations, is accounted for by the supposition of training by members of society because these beliefs are useful. Again, let us make reference to another area to make this clear. Chemists draw pictures to talk about their subject matter; they draw lines and talk about bonds in order to arrive at conclusions. Do chemists believe there are things like lines that bond? People postulate Santa Claus so that their children will behave, but they do not suppose there is such a being. (Even if they do suppose such a being exists, they are mistaken.) We might all find it useful to postulate the existence of Santa Claus if we could find that it prevented a world war or could bring something good (as we say) into existence. If we did that we would be doing something of the sort the amoralist claims about morality.

The third claim—that we can explain all the phenomena normative theories handle without the use of normative notions—would really require an extensive investigation of some amoralist theory. However, we have seen something of the kind of explanation suggested in the treatment of moral language and behavior. In addition, we would want to see what kind of theory of motivation is proposed. For the rest of this third part, we can see what would have to be done by offering a critical analysis of the theory as outlined.

The first claim is one that requires comparison with the best normative ethical theory to arrive at a decision. This is the claim of the amoralist,
but is it a justified claim? This has to be determined in the same way we
justify any claim that a theory does a better job than its rivals in explaining
a range of phenomena.

The second claim can be handled more directly; for as it is stated, it
does not apparently do the job that the amoralist wants. To see this, consider similiar claims made about other areas of human concern and a different range of phenomena. Instead of talking about normative utterances,
let's talk about human contrivances, the fruits of technology. Such devices
have historically made society more secure and have usually ensured its continuance. The use of weapons against animals certainly made society more
secure, and the use of dams and other devices to ensure a supply of water
for crops was extremely useful. Shall we say of technology and all the
machines we have built, that since they have this social function, they have
no reality, and that there is no fact of the matter other than the desire of
society to be safe and to ensure its continuance? This appears to be a clear
instance in which this inference is not justified. However, if it is not justified here, then it would seem that we need some reason why it is justified
in the morality instance.

It is not open to the amoralist to claim, at this point, that there is a
difference between technology and morality in that there is some fact of the
matter about technology but none concerning morality. At this point, this
decision depends on whether amoralism or one of the normative theories is
correct. Since this is so, the claim cannot be simply asserted without some
kind of evidence.

It is interesting to note that to those who are inclined to take an extreme Buddhist view claiming the inapplicability of any concepts and any
theories to anything, the above move of the amoralist is not open. We shall
return to this kind of extreme view shortly.

What the amoralist is apparently committed to claiming is not just
that normative judgments and actions have a social function, but that the
social function is the total explanation of such judgments and actions.
Otherwise we could agree that the social function exists but still maintain
any one of the normative ethical theories examined in this book. But why
should we believe that there is only the social function and none of the
other functions described by the normative theories so far discussed? Why
should we not think that there is a moral fact of the matter along with facts
of the matter? The final answer, again, would have to be in the way of
comparison of the best amoralist view with what we take to be the best
normative ethical theory. We can, though, forestall some bad moves that
are not open to any amoralist.

No one can claim, without inconsistency, that the reason we decide to
abstain from using moral language is that it is bad for individuals and society. This use of a value notion *bad* is inconsistent with the claims of the
theory. This is also true of any claim to the effect that we *ought* not to use
moral language. Someone might say, though, that the use of 'ought' in this

context means that we are making a mistake, because amoralism is the best theory in the area. Yes, we might say, when amoralism is established, then you will be justified in making that claim. However, the notion of *prudence* might be used to explicate the 'ought'. It might be that the amoralist is saying that the prudential course is not to use such language as 'right' and 'good'. However, this will not do, for prudence appears to have as part of its explanation an aim at good and an avoidance of evil. It is not prudential to walk across the river when it is iced over because the ice is likely to break. If the ice breaks, we shall fall in and drown or, at best, receive an extremely chilling experience. These are things that we suppose have negative value, they are either maleficently or intrinsically disvaluable.

Finally, the amoralists may be confused about the position and really be aiming to defend some kind of noncognitivism. They may wish to claim that our choice of a normative ethical theory is a function of our affective life and not of any rational process. This, though, is a different claim and is discussed elsewhere.

So, the tentative decision is to reject amoralism pending a reply on the part of some irate amoralist who will accuse us of failing to understand the view properly, or some amoralist who compares his or her view, fully worked out, with some range of the normative theories thus far considered. Perhaps some feel that such views have been presented by the stoics or the Buddhists. We shall see.

Nihilism is usually very much the same view as amoralism, but insofar as it is different, it is the view that nothing has value at all. It is a kind of moral despair rather than a kind of moral skepticism or a replacement theory, as is amoralism. However, once again, whether this is true or not depends on whether any of the theories of value is acceptable, and whether they apply. If they do, as has been argued in chapter 6, then nihilism is not justified.

The strategy of discussing these kinds of views is to engage them into the mechanism of normative ethics. Once that is done, all the results of that area are applicable, and we can use the tried-and-true (hopefully) strategies developed there.

2. Social and political theory

There are a number of concerns that are normative; ethics is one, but so are aesthetics, philosophy of religion, and social and political philosophy. In the latter areas, we are concerned with the kind of political system we ought to adopt, and what kind of society we should strive to establish. If we use value notions, we would ask which of many societies we could strive to establish was best, and which political system was best. However we state the normative concern in those areas, it is obvious that we will make use of whatever normative ethical theory we have worked out to answer these questions. This is not to say that ethics is "first" or more important, for that is not the view being put forward. Whatever normative ethical theory we adopt will have to be serviceable for social and political concerns, and whatever social and political theory we choose will have to be consistent with our ethical theory.

Some political theories seem to go naturally with some ethical theories. J. S. Mill thought that utilitarianism and representative democracy went together quite well, for example. Thomas Hobbes seemed to suppose that a version of ethical egoism and monarchism went together in a natural way. If one were to continue this work into the area of social and political philosophy, one would want to list the phenomena (as we did for ethics), state the main theories, evaluate them, and finally indicate which of the ones before us appeared to do the best job in explaining the phenomena. In the course of doing this we would have to say, for every such theory, how it related to various ethical theories. This is a task that will not, as you no doubt have guessed, be carried out here.

3. Religion   Religion is another normative area we have said almost nothing about, but which is related very closely in many people's minds with normative ethics. When we examined the Ten Commandments theory and especially in the appendix to chapter 6, the area of religion was discussed. It was suggested, negatively, that we cannot suppose that what it *is* for an action to be right, say, is for God to approve or command it. This does not preclude people supposing that God provides guidance in our daily lives or that moral revolutions are divinely inspired. Many moral reformers, such as the antislave people in the United States, supposed themselves to be carrying out a divine mission. The only stake normative ethical theory has here is to point out the independence of the rightness of the cause from God calling upon people to carry it out. To borrow from Plato, God calls upon people to perform actions because they are right, they are not right because He calls upon them to carry them out. This is a claim that anyone, theist or atheist, can suppose is true.

One of the roles religions play is to provide models or paradigms of action for people. This is an important feature of our moral lives, and yet almost nothing has been said about it. Philosophers often talk about emulating the life of Socrates, but Christians much more frequently choose the life of Jesus, and Buddhists the life of Gautama. This is a strategy to follow: select the life of a good person and emulate it so far as you can if you seek to be a good person. This advice, though, requires that we know what a good life is independently, for otherwise we could not rationally choose this life rather than that to emulate. In addition, we must frequently make judgments about how far to depart from the life we emulate. For example, would you choose to wander about the streets, as did Socrates, or would you attempt to get a job and talk with others interested in philosophy in enclosed places, such as bars? In terms of this view of the role of religion in our moral lives, it is an aid and offers a guide, but it is no substitute for the tasks of normative ethics—especially the task of choosing the best normative theory.

4. Other ideologies   The kinds of comments made about religion apply also to various ideological movements. Marxism, existentialism, and liberalism are movements that frequently have an attendant normative ethical theory, although it would seem that almost any normative theory is compatible with most ideological positions. If you adopt an ideology, you adopt a theory with a very broad scope, one that purports to explain the place of human beings in society, the nature of the relations of people to each other, and frequently many nonhuman phenomena also. Insofar as this is so, these ideologies can play the same role as a religious view in providing a general explanation or theory about how all the phenomena fit together within one coherent theoretical system. You can find your moral paradigm, for example, Lenin, within the ideology, just as one can from religions. If you are an existentialist, of course, you will emphasize the necessity of each person choosing his or her own paradigm.

There are some normative ethical theories that go well with some of the ideologies and some that don't fit very well at all. If you are a marxist, for example, you are not likely to suppose that only pleasure has value, for the value placed on freedom is very high. Similarly, though, many marxists in the past have adopted some form of ethical relativism. This is not so common now as marxists have continued their research into normative ethics.

Pragmatism as a philosophical movement has had more influence on contemporary American philosophy than any other. I consider myself to be a descendant of Peirce, James, Dewey, Lewis, and others who have worked out the views known as pragmatism. These views have become so much a part of the philosophical landscape, however, that it is difficult to pick out any one aspect that is unique. In normative ethics I hope to have satisfied Dewey's concern about the interconnected nature of means and ends by defining intrinsic value in such a way that something of intrinsic value can always be something of beneficial value also. By choosing an act theory I hope to have realized the claim of Peirce about the changing nature of problems and the flexibility that must be built into any method. Is there such a thing as a pragmatic ethics? If there is an ideology that is pragmatic, then what I say about other ideologies applies here. However, there are certainly ethical theories that have been developed by pragmatists. Such theories range from a sketchy ideal-observer-type theory of Peirce, to a naturalistic theory of Dewey, to the complicated epistemological account of C. I. Lewis. My hope is that the act theory views presented here provide another kind of normative ethical theory that is consistent with the basic positions in epistemology and metaphysics taken by those who are most clearly pragmatists.

H. Paradigms

All the talk about moral paradigms in the last section leads me to say something about a theory that will no doubt be seriously put forward soon, although it has not yet appeared in a clear form. This would be the view that every society adopts a moral code, describable by an ethical theory, that is suitable for solving certain problems in the society. The code is adopted because some kind of crisis develops in the use of a different code. For example, the Hebrews made use of the rules of Abraham and their other forefathers right through their stay in Egypt. However, the exodus from Egypt brought on a crisis, due no doubt to the destruction of the structure of their society as it had existed in Egypt. A moral genius, Moses, devised a new moral code, the Ten Commandments, which was able to solve the problems associated with the crisis. This code became the standard and offered a standard way of solving moral problems. Solutions to moral problems were derived from making the appropriate use of this new paradigm.

According to this view, the moral history of humanity is just the history of the replacement of old moralities with new moralities, of old paradigms with new paradigms. We can see, if we accept this view, Christianity replacing Judaism, Islam replacing Christianity, and so on. Of course, the 'and so on' is difficult to make out, for there are a number of phenomena that will be very difficult to account for. However, the exact details of this view will be left to those who are fated to develop it.

The question that interests us here is the relation of this kind of view to the main enterprise of developing a strategy for evaluating normative ethical theories. Insofar as the paradigm view suggests that the only test for the acceptability of any singular moral judgment is a standard accepted by a society, then that view is the same as the indirect relativism view discussed in chapter 4. The only additional point of interest is the use of the notion of *paradigm* and its application from philosophy of science. However, it does not seem that this notion makes any difference in the acceptability of a normative theory.

It may be that the theory of paradigms makes sense of the change of rules, but notice that this is a view that fits in well with an act theory. The changing of sets of summary rules may well be described by the paradigm shifts that philosophers are wont to talk about, but this kind of explanation would not itself constitute a normative ethical theory, but rather a sociological theory offering an explanation of why moral rules are changed. This would not, by itself, tell us anything about the nature of the rules that are given up or adopted. One would have to determine this within the context of normative ethics—and hopefully the strategies that are usefully within this context have been made clear.

I.   A final word

The title of this book, *Strategies of Ethics,* describes what is contained in it. It does not tell us, though, how the concerns of normative ethics are connected with other philosophical matters, let alone how philosophical matters are connected with concerns in other areas. The development of a more complete philosophical context, a more complete account of all justified judgments and not just justified normative judgments, and a fuller treatment of the many metaphysical issues would help to illuminate the conclusions drawn here. Such an enterprise would not begin with an examination of rival normative ethical theories using a strategy developed for such a purpose but with the exposition of what is taken to be a correct ethical theory and what is required for it. We would need to find out what kind of epistemology and metaphysics is required and what view of science must be supposed. This task is not required for the work in this book to stand, for the two tasks would be mutually supportive.

The final advice for those who have worked their way through this book and have made it to this last paragraph is to be as critical as they can. Don't accept one word without thinking about why you should. If there are lessons to be learned, they are lessons of methods and not of truths.

Recommended reading

Ayer, A. J. *Language Truth and Logic.* Dover, New York, 1946. The author claims that moral judgments are not true or false but only express or evince emotions.

Barnes, Hazel E. *An Existentialist Ethics.* Vintage Books, New York, 1967.

Firth, Roderick. "Ethical Absolutism and the Ideal Observer." *Philosophy and Phenomenological Research,* XII (1952), 317–345. This is also to be found in *Readings in Ethical Theory* (see below).

Prichard, H. A. *Moral Obligation.* Clarendon Press, Oxford, 1949.

Sellars, W., and John Hospers, eds. *Readings in Ethical Theory.* Appleton-Century-Crofts, New York, 1970. This anthology contains a number of very good articles that would give you a "flavor" of contemporary meta-ethics.

Stevenson, C. L. *Ethics and Language.* Yale University Press, New Haven, 1944. This work is one of the most completely worked out noncognitivist theories available.

Wellman, Carl. *The Language of Ethics.* Harvard University Press, Cambridge, Ma., 1961.

Index

D

E

R

Value (*cont.*)
  phenomena for   184–185
  underwhelming   194
  see also Benefit, Intrinsic disvalue, Intrinsic value
Value relativism   201–205
Value, theories of
  act   208–215
  basic notions in, contrasted with theories of obligation   185, 187,
      15(fig.)
  categorical rule   188–208
  concern of   14, 15, 180
  contrasted with theories of obligation   185, 187
  happiness   190, 197–199
  hedonism   189–197
  instances of F, M, and X in   15(fig.)
  monistic   188–200
  pleasure   189–197
  pluralistic   188, 206–208
  prima facie rule   206–208
  relativism   201–205
  teleological   177, 180
Vicious infinite regress   131, 225
Voluntarism, theological   9, 118–120, 225–226
Voluntary action   43, 44

W

Warnock, G. J.   176
Weakness of will   250
Weiss, R. F.   57
Williams, G. C.   249
Willing and wanting   44
Wilson, E. O.   249
Wittgenstein, L.   253